TIME
IS
TIGHT

TIME
IS
TIGHT

My Life, Note by Note

BOOKER T. JONES

Little, Brown and Company
New York Boston London

Little, Brown and Company
Hachette Book Group
1290 Avenue of the Americas, New York, NY 10104
littlebrown.com

First Edition: October 2019

Little, Brown and Company is a division of Hachette Book Group, Inc. The Little, Brown name and logo are trademarks of Hachette Book Group, Inc.

The publisher is not responsible for websites (or their content) that are not owned by the publisher.

The Hachette Speakers Bureau provides a wide range of authors for speaking events. To find out more, go to hachettespeakersbureau.com or call (866) 376-6591.

Lyrics from "Ole Man Trouble" reprinted with permission of Downtown Music Publishing

ISBN 978-0-316-48560-9
LCCN 2019946168

10 9 8 7 6 5 4 3 2 1

LSC-C

Printed in the United States of America

To Nan Jones, my California girl

CONTENTS

AUTHOR'S NOTE

Time doesn't always move straight forward. I followed my thematic impulses to guide me to connect events from different periods of my life. I wanted you, the reader, to sense the flow of time—not only from the early beginnings to now but jumping forward and circling back when moments were joined more by truth than minutes.

It's a song that returns again and again to choruses that are different and somehow the same. I encourage you to let your mind open and free yourself of constraints. Time is open, and yet time is tight.

I have recalled the events depicted in this book to the best of my recollection. While all the stories are true, some names and identifying details have been changed to protect the privacy of the people involved.

Throughout the text, just after the subheadings, are eighth notes followed by numbers that refer to various musical phrases I have composed for this book. Each phrase is a musical representation of a feeling or temperament that matches or resembles the scene that follows, note by note.

TIME
IS
TIGHT

PROLOGUE

Acapulco Gold—like dinner at a fine restaurant some have described it.

On the morning of February 9, 1971, I had a saddlebag full of it, which tumbled down when I pulled the saddle off my horse. On the trail riding Skeeter, my polo pony, I shared the weed with my riding friend, Glyn Turman, who was never without a generous flask of expensive southern whiskey in his saddlebag. Glyn waved goodbye at my gate and trotted off to his ranch, just north of mine in the Malibu Hills.

I put my horse away and hung the saddle and gear in the tack house. Then I laid a blanket on the ground a few yards away to rest and enjoy the beautiful morning on my Acapulco high. The sky was clear, and the crisp morning air felt good to my lungs as I stretched out and recognized an acute sharpness in my perception that I had not experienced before. I felt I could see, hear, taste, smell, and think better.

My mind eased into reflection as I lay on the ground and appreciated how the mountains and surf gave me a sense of peacefulness and safety. My adventurous, curious nature had led me from Memphis to this exotic locale just steps from the Pacific, where I fell into loving the smell of sweaty horses and musty hay. I met new people who stimulated my musical sensitivities—Ramblin' Jack Elliott, Bob Dylan, Stephen Stills, Bill Withers. These Malibu natives were my new family. Life was different here, and I felt deep appreciation for the steady, loving, unwavering support from my parents, teachers, and neighbors in Memphis. I felt secure and stable enough to wander. I loved my new home.

Then the horses started whinnying in the barn. The dogs began barking at the sky.

I became aware of a faint reverberation, way down deep on the other side of the earth. Paranoia set in. *I'm not sure this is the best time to experience my first earthquake.*

The rumble quickly became a bass drum roll, then expanded and condensed into a violent jolt that shook the ground. The whole ranch seemed to move about a foot. Not getting up with the earth moving around like flapjacks in a pan was a no-brainer, so I stayed put, stoned out of my mind. Only later did I learn it was the great San Fernando earthquake, strongest in California's history, about to do more damage than you could imagine in less time than you could comprehend.

Unaware of the destruction being unfurled around me, I lay frozen on the blanket and took the ride. When the rumbling stopped, I was thankful to be in one piece, still on the earth's crust, and not swallowed up into its belly. I took my time rolling over onto my knees. After taking my time to get back on two feet, I realized the old ranch house was still intact, a veteran of many earthquakes.

Billie Nichols, the agent at Louis Busch's Malibu Realty, was thrilled with our $89,000 offer for Lana Turner's 4.89-acre ranch at the end of Winding Way. With $40,000 down there was no bank involved, and Lana carried the $49,000 balance herself. She made a few surprise visits to collect mortgage payments and survey her investment. The small print in the contract specified Malibu's age-old stigma that no land could be sold to a black.

The deed transferred to me anyway, and I stayed in shape by loading my own hay bales at the Malibu Feed Bin, using bailing pins and heaving the big bales off the dock onto the bed of my '71 F150. When I got home, I loaded and stacked them in the barn, which held thirty tons of hay.

My wardrobe shifted from the fancy clothes I wore with the MGs in Memphis to blue jeans, plaid shirts, cowboy hats, and beige Frye boots that went up to my knees. Everyone who had a ranch was wearing Fryes. They offered some level of protection from the rattlers that haunted Malibu's trails with such abundance. Skeeter was not spooked by the snakes and would just speed up when he saw one of the fat females spread out over the road. Not that I was lucky enough to be on the horse for every encounter. There were many times when I was in the brush and a rattler may have been close, so the boots became part of my daily attire.

Though I rode Skeeter western, he was a good jumper since some of the young girls who used him did it English style. I had a deal with my neighbor, Egon Merz, an old German who trained Hollywood starlets to ride, that he could borrow my horses in return for riding and tack lessons. "Yess, I trayyned Elizabeth Taylor to ride for *National Velvet*! I did!" he claimed in his broken English.

Many mornings I heard my horses trot past my bedroom window. They left the ranch early because Egon had sent a pair of young girls to fetch a quarter horse or my Shetland pony. I never minded. The exercise was good for the horses, and Egon always walked and brushed them afterward, not to mention cleaning and replacing all the tack by nightfall.

One day, Egon's daughter, Gina, led us to a trail that sidled past homes in Ramirez Canyon before proceeding under the Pacific Coast Highway into a dark, narrow tunnel that gave access to Malibu Beach. When our horses caught eye of that smooth sand, they couldn't hold back. No pulling on the reins. We let them go, bending our knees, pressing our heels into the stirrups, and hanging on for dear life.

Just like in the movies, trots became gallops, and gallops turned into flying leaps with front hooves meeting back hooves. Skeeter bared his teeth, opened his mouth, and put his head down a little, pumping his neck front to back. Beach houses flew by. Our hats fell off. We gripped the horses' bellies with our thighs. Sweat flew everywhere. The only sounds were four hooves pounding the sand, wind howling, and my pony's lungs whining for air.

The ride home was a victory march. Our horses pulled up and stopped at a huge gully with imposing rocks on a beach too wide to cross. On the left, the gully gave way to a majestic ravine whose water fed the Pacific. I didn't know the beach well enough to recognize where we were. But it didn't matter. The horses knew the way home and picked up speed gradually as we got back to Malibu.

Skeeter was absolutely soaked, so I put a light blanket on his back. He was dripping as I walked him a bit so he didn't cool off too fast before watering. After I brushed him, he galloped off to his stall. Welcome to California!

The year was 1968, and I was embarking on my spiritual journey. In the library of Rabbi Max Vorspan, whose Beverly Hills home I rented while he took his sabbatical, I discovered Ghani yoga, raja yoga, and hatha yoga. I studied graphology, took up astrology, and, before computers showed up and simplified the process, taught myself to do astrological sidereal charts using Greenwich Mean Time. The intricate math was difficult, involving converting birth times geographically from hours and minutes according to a person's birthplace to latitude and longitude. The professional astrologers would do charts, and after I peered at one long enough, the answers to unanswerable questions would "jump off the page." It happened once when a Malibu friend asked me to read his chart. He sat with me and waited. After a while, it told me he had webbed feet. I asked him if it was true. He took off his shoes and showed me his webbed toes. I stopped doing charts for others after that.

Even with all the reading and study, my quest to find meaning and discover my true self was stymied because I didn't know how to meditate. The process was long and tedious, with many side trips that seemed to have no purpose. But eventually, Transcendental Meditation produced results, most importantly by helping me realize the precision my guardian angels had employed when they led me through the door at Satellite/Stax Records.

What a lost soul I would have been without my Memphis music beginnings. What could have taken the place of the security the Stax family provided? And yet, I was unable to resist the temptations to leave. First to Indiana, to study music, and now, trading a solid musical legacy to move to California for the freedom to live on a small horse ranch.

For the longest time, Stax meant nothing to the city of Memphis. Jim Stewart was an insignificant bank teller with the dream of making a fortune publishing country songs. Sorrowfully flawed for the job, he became the nucleus of a musical cooperation of unlikely bedfellows. That slight, frail, country fiddler created a sanctuary, a fortress in enemy territory, where the rules of segregation remained a feeble shadow and where whites and blacks created music together on a daily basis. In that atmosphere of safety, my spirit soared and my heart barely stayed in my chest during recording sessions with Otis Redding and Booker T. & the MGs.

The truth is I was never in it for the money. I loved the people and the music. And the people and the music loved me, and we flew together—on a daily basis. The best-kept secret in the Mid-South, right under the nose of the Crump dynasty. On the same plots of earth where our forefathers maimed each other, we experienced exalted moments together. This is not to say Jim Crow didn't poke his head above ground. Like working on "Maggie's Farm," there were periods when the only pay was the rapturous experience gleaned from the music.

Those eight years, and those people—Jim Stewart; his sister, Estelle Axton; Al Jackson Jr.; Lewie Steinberg; Steve Cropper; Duck Dunn; David Porter; William Bell; Sam & Dave; Wilson Pickett; Packy Axton; Andrew Love; Isaac Hayes; Chips Moman; Floyd Newman; Tom Dowd; Ronnie Capone; Rufus Thomas; Carla Thomas; Eddie Floyd; Otis Redding; Albert King; Wayne Jackson; Deanie Parker; and Al Bell—defined my life. In the prism of music, we became reflections of each other, and over time we came to love each other. Even when we fought. And throughout the whole experience, I was always the youngest, working out who I was and what I wanted to do with my life note by note.

CHAPTER 1

His Eye Is on the Sparrow

MEMPHIS—Summer 1963— ♪ 3

Al Jackson sauntered into the studio. Big grin. Eyes sparkling. Peering directly at me.

"Whatchu got, Jones?"

That was his way of asking me to show him what music we would be working on that day. I was always ready to accept the duty of being the originator of the song material.

I returned Al's gaze with understanding. They needed me to come up with the essence of the song, so, as he always did, he asked, "Whatchu got, Jones?" That plunged me into my musical mind like a deep-sea diver looking for pearls on the ocean floor.

Sweater sleeves pulled up, Al dampened the sound of his snare by plopping his fat wallet onto the snare drum head and securing it with a few generous strips of masking tape. He then stepped off the riser, walked over to Steve, and took a Winston from Steve's box. Lighting the cigarette, he looked back at me. "You ready?"

Having already made a stop at the coffee machine in the foyer, I placed my fingers in "Green Onions" position on the keyboard. When I walked in, I needed an idea, and if I didn't have anything right away, I'd take another sip of coffee, another drag on a Salem, and then dive in and bring up something to show them. Some musical idea would just pop into my head. Usually a pebble, sometimes a pearl.

That morning, I pulled out the same stops as "Onions" and started twiddling the first three fingers of my right hand between a triad and a seventh chord. Good. Great sound from the speaker. Ended up using only three fingers for the whole pattern. Today's song had to be something soulful, and simple. Turned it up so loud, I almost distorted the little JBL speaker.

Jim Stewart entered the studio. "Hi, Booker." His eyes hinted at a smile. "Let's get started." The swatch of unruly red hair on Jim's forehead wrested my eyes away from his steady gaze. His infrequent smile was open, but it had to be earned.

Jim was the founder of the company and the engineer for the day. His nimble, surreptitious shift from country into black music was reflected in his gait, which he often used to amble into the studio late. Sometimes he forgot how hip he had become and went back to the fast shuffle of a white Memphis banker.

This session, which Jim surprisingly showed up early to, would have been started by Chips Moman (Jim's first studio foreman) or Steve Cropper (after the first couple years), and Jim would have to play catch-up to learn the song, or songs, for the day.

He bent over and moved the mike back a little. The banker's jacket slid off his tiny, swaybacked frame and revealed a neck elongated from years of playing the fiddle.

Lewie, meanwhile, moved his chair closer to my left hand to follow the notes and re-create them as the bass line. "That sounds like something." Steve put his Winston out. Al went back to his kit, straddled the throne, and picked up his sticks—a funky, subtle backbeat.

Lewie Steinberg, who picked lightly and faultlessly at his bass, was the daddy of the group. Steve Cropper paid attention to the rhythm. You could depend on Steve for originality and simplicity. You could rely on Al to keep the tempo better than a metronome; he never let songs run away. With this group, you could count on having a great groove no matter what you played.

"You guys got anything yet?" asked Jim, peering through the glass, listening.

Steve threw me a glance. *Nothing worth working on yet,* he said with his eyes. I dug deeper until I finally struck gold with a melody not unlike the ones I concocted on a nightly basis down at the Flamingo. Hours later, after nonstop experimenting and rearranging, Al, Steve, Lewie, and Jim were smiling as we came to the end of the little ditty.

Another day's work at Stax.

At the end of the day, I navigated my way to Jim's desk to pick up the diminutive but always valid check. We seemed to have a good rapport, Jim and I. He respected my musical abilities, my work ethic. But Jim still wrote the musicians' checks fast and somewhat begrudgingly, as if it were dirty work to be done quickly. He often looked off as he handed you the money or had Linda (Andrews, the secretary) do the honors.

Jim was there to acquire ownership of the publishing rights to the songs he recorded. From the beginning, he understood there was small chance of getting rich operating a record company. If he could get country or (later) R & B songs played that were licensed to his company, royalties were paid without deductions from the radio stations. To boot, the annuity lasted for twenty-six years, with a free renewal for another twenty-six years under US law.

This information was hidden from me. I was unaware of the

concept of any profit associated with the writing of a song or that any proceeds were paid to people who wrote songs. At Satellite, I could get upward of five dollars per day to create original music, which I gladly did.

MEMPHIS—Summer 1951— ♪ 2

As I finished second grade, going on seven years old, one of a few public spaces available to blacks in South Memphis was Lincoln Park, which also happened to be the site of my first kite contest. Before participating, I had fashioned a kite from newspaper and balsa wood sticks. It was held together with glue and had a bright blue tail made from Christmas wrapping ribbon. That early June afternoon, a light wind quickly and gently lifted my kite up close to the puffed-up, milky clouds that were waiting in the warm blue sky. It joined the flock of other kites erratically swaying next to each other.

I was so excited for the contest. There was food out on tables, booths with crafts, games, lots of people, and a large band playing on a covered stage. At the time, I had advanced from flying kites purchased at the drugstore to flying ones I had built in a large field behind my friend O. D. Adams's house over on Orleans Street.

Months of effort went into making my kite for that afternoon, but in an instant, none of that mattered. Serendipitously I wandered over to the stage where Al Jackson's band was playing. The blend created by the string bass and Al's kick drum hit repeatedly in my chest, like the dreams I'd had of music late at night in my bed. I was swept away in wonder at the sound of brass instruments dancing with wood instruments. My kite-making friends stayed behind, holding tightly to their strings, not noticing I let mine go. My kite wafted and glided upward while I also floated, just in the direction of the music, my feet skipping. After all that work, the newspaper kite was whirling, escaping, vanishing from sight.

The first big band I had ever heard live overwhelmed me with excitement.

The leader of the band was a slim, well-dressed older man. There were five saxophones in the front row and trumpets and trombones behind them. There was an upright bass, a piano, and a guitar. And there were drums with a very young man behind the set.

I didn't have much to say about the kite contest to my parents when I got home, just that I had heard a band playing in the park.

My parents already knew of my passion for music and, from the time I was very young, supported my endeavors in the discipline. Our small Edith Street house was built in 1945 and was only thirteen hundred square feet. The piano was in the living room, not far from my parents' bedroom. They never complained when I played into the night.

My success as a keyboardist comes from my attempts to emulate and duplicate my mother's style. She was a loving person and bequeathed to me many portions of her musical makeup. She birthed all of me, physically and musically.

The way she played the piano sunk into my being. I was born listening to her. When she sang at church, the room quieted as she gave renditions of gospel pearls and classic arias.

I got a double dose. People at church also requested my father, Booker T. Jones Sr., to sing "His Eye Is on the Sparrow" a cappella. There were no dry eyes when he finished. His sterling tenor voice, with its vibrato and sincere delivery, ensured that.

While I was only three or four when Mama sold her old upright piano, the missing instrument left a gaping hole in my heart. Even if I didn't know how to play then, I'd still get up on the bench and use two fingers to make harmony. Mom and Dad made up for it by buying me musical toys and later real instruments. I was so happy with those. One afternoon, a woman reporter from a Chicago magazine came to our house and sat in the living room, interviewing Mama. "Was Booker always musically inclined, Mrs. Jones?" she asked.

"I never thought of Booker doing anything else," Mama replied.

Piano notwithstanding, it was always the drum, or drums, that harbored an inescapable fascination for me, even before I saw Al Jackson Jr. the afternoon of the kite contest.

When I was a little boy, Mama used to take me to the downtown department stores: Bry's, Goldsmith's, Lowenstein's, and the Black and White Store. Of all the magical things we saw, what captured my attention the most was a toy drum at the five-and-dime store on Main. A delicate wooden thing, with the heads covered in a coarse paper mesh cloth, the drum sounded real. At home, it seemed like seconds before I busted the head, but I got to beat on it and to hear that sound and to hold those sticks.

I played my sticks anywhere I could—on a pillow, on the carpet, the top of a paper cup, anything that would bounce back even slightly. And then it became the sticks themselves that held the fascination for me. Rhythm after rhythm beat out on Mama's beautiful hardwood floor. It did damage the floor, and I got yelled at, but that hardwood responded so perfectly to my wrist movements. I began to play flams and paradiddles before I knew what they were.

Of course, when Dad took me to night football games, I watched Washington High School Drum and Bugle Corps perform.

MEMPHIS—Fall 1953— ♪ *1*

My life was changed forever when I was nine years old and my father surprised me with a brand-new clarinet. The dank smell of the case, the black wood, the beautiful dark green felt that caressed each piece, and the excess glue on some of the pads made a sight I will never forget. Not until I laid eyes on a Hammond B-3 organ was I ever so moved and hypnotized as when my father put that instrument in my hands. Everyone should experience such love and rhapsody at least once in their life.

Mr. McClellan, who was the band director at Leath School, a small school where my dad once taught, was a close friend and neighbor who lived up the street. One Saturday morning, my dad called him and asked if he would give me a short, impromptu lesson.

We went up to Mr. McClellan's house, he came out, and on his steep driveway, he showed me how to hold my clarinet and where to put my fingers to cover up the holes. Mr. McClellan was a short, stout, balding, and likeable man, who—in spite of inadvertently spitting all over me when he spoke—changed my life in just a few benevolent seconds.

We stood there in his driveway, me still holding the clarinet before I let go of the instrument to put it back in its case. It would be the starting position for my hands over that clarinet and many other woodwind instruments, including the oboe, with my fingers glued in place over the holes, like he showed me. Even while walking, I kept my hands in starting position. I cannot thank Mr. McClellan enough. Dad had sacrificed and made a down payment and signed papers for years of monthly payments to buy a clarinet for me.

One Saturday morning when I was nine years old, my dad told me under a bright, warm sun, "Go back in the house and get your clarinet. We're going to get a haircut." I had a slight twinge of anxiety. I'd been to Cade's before. *Why am I taking my clarinet this time? What song will I play? Will I remember the notes?* Dad was proud of me and wanted to show me off. He didn't doubt that I would do OK.

Set back from the street in a building of storefronts that included a beer garden as well as Samuel T. Lusk's watch repair shop, Cade's was so much more than a barbershop. There was a lot of camaraderie and good talk on any subject, and overflowing on the shelves under the big storefront windows were mounds of musty old magazines with curled edges. Overcoats were piled high on a coat rack, and laughter and political posturing were easy to find. Oddly, I loved the tired, pungent odor of the hair tonic in the red and green bottles that had expired months ago on the barbers' stations behind the chairs. It gave the place a unique, recurring reference point from other types of establishments.

Mr. Cade himself was a dark, slight man with a quiet nature. He always had a pleasant disposition while cutting my dad's hair and giving him a shave. I looked forward to perusing the many *Life* and *Look* magazines at the shop and playing the occasional game of checkers with any one of the men who would indulge me. Mr. Cade's son, Kenneth, older than me, was a member of the Washington High School band, playing clarinet, and I looked up to him. I think this fact was one of the things that helped influence my dad to buy my clarinet. God knows he couldn't afford it.

Mr. Macklin was the barber who took care of my hair—Mr. Mac, we called him. He used his strong hands to give my bald head a vigorous massage with aftershave lotion each time my haircut was done. Then he'd unsnap the pin securing the towel and slap and smack my bald head all over with aromatic tonic and talcum powder. "There you go, boy," he said, with another firm smack, and I was free to catch yet another cold with my bald head.

The shop quieted as I began the first notes. The tune I picked was a very popular song I had heard on a TV show, *Skokian*, which I taught myself on my new clarinet. It was the first time I played for an audience—the men recognized the tune instantly. After I played the last note, there was silence.

I was thrown off by this. *Did they enjoy the song? Did I miss some notes?* One by one they started to smile and applaud. They kept clapping. So long that I felt uncomfortable. I didn't know what to do. I made a nervous bow and rushed over to the window to put my clarinet back in its case and sat down close to my beaming father.

CHAPTER 2
'Cause I Love You

MEMPHIS—Spring 1960— ♪ 2

There was a sameness in the way the fresh spring day started. The bell had rung for my second-period class at Booker Washington High, and I was in my seat. David Porter appeared at the door and gave me an urgent look. With a bogus hall pass in his hand, he had a few words with the teacher and suddenly I was out of the room and in the hallway. David told me to grab the sax from the band room before we sped to the studio in the band director's zippy 1957 Plymouth, which David had borrowed. Mr. Martin's car keys always seemed to be in David's pocket.

I walked through the door to Satellite Recording Studios on David Porter's heels, baritone sax in tow, not quite believing I had stepped inside. Before I knew it, I had my horn out and was standing in the middle of the slanted theater floor amid a room of musicians, having heard only a short excerpt of the music and being asked if I could think of an intro for the song.

From somewhere came the introductory notes out of the bell of my horn, and the rest of the band picked up the opening bars of "'Cause I Love You" for Rufus and Carla Thomas, who were standing even farther back in the room, behind a baffle with a small window. The tape was rolling, and in lieu of an algebra class, my career as a session musician started that morning.

For years, I had stood at the bins in the record store in the foyer of the theater, listening to live music come from behind the curtain and longing to be a participant myself. Only my dry mouth reminded me I wasn't dreaming as I looked at the faces of the professional musicians during the playback. This was real. I had made it over the long-standing hurdle through the "velvet curtain" into Stax's recording studio.

MEMPHIS—Summer 1952— ♪ *1*

Years before, I had heard live music coming to me from inside an opened attic window of the home of my neighbor, Mrs. Humes. I felt free to ride my tricycle, then later my bicycle, in her two-lane driveway. She would call out, "Booker T., you'd better watch out. Henry's coming home soon." Then I'd stay clear of her driveway so her husband could get in without issue.

I treated their driveway like it was my own runway. Mr. Humes would patiently stop his car at the front yard when he came home from work so I could clear my trike and myself out of the way. He would pull his '52 Chevy into the driveway and into the ruts in the floor of his garage the same way every day.

Mrs. Humes was quite old and small, but she wasn't weak. I could hear her powerful voice from my house when she called, "Henryyyy!" to come inside for dinner. Many days I could hear the clamor from her chicken coop when she would grab one and

wring it in the air, 'round and 'round by its neck until the screaming stopped. Then she would feather the chicken and put it in a
boiling pot for Henry's dinner.

The Humeses allowed me to enter their house as my own. I felt
free to go into their junky old garage. It had a concrete floor, where
ours only had a dirt floor. I explored Henry's yard tools. There were
dark stairs leading to an attic. What an adventure! In the attic was
a small bedroom, where their grandson, Carl Kirk, slept when he
visited.

Many evenings Mrs. Humes made lemonade, setting the pitcher
on the table before the porch swing, and talked to me for hours
until my mother called out, "Booker, time to come home." Mrs.
Humes had been a nurse, which she liked reminiscing about, as
well as all the other life experiences she'd had. The muggy, moist
night air in Memphis kept everyone in the neighborhood on their
porch chairs and swings in the hopes of catching a breeze.

Sitting me close, she opened up a world of knowledge.

She told me how they milked snakes in Florida, getting the
venom for snake-bite victims. And how one man would hold the
snake while another would let the snake bite the rubber cap spread
over a wide-neck bottle, and the milk would come dripping down
the side. She told me how fish lay eggs and explained that flowers
need the sun to grow.

For a little boy like me, the smells that came from Mrs. Humes's
yard at night were as intoxicating as the stories she told. I would
stay up after dark so I could go over and see flowers she had that
bloomed only at night. I was always just there, kicking dirt around
or piddling with a rock or playing with the grass, listening to her
talk to me. Sometimes she would let me water her flowers. Carrying the big heavy sprinkler can from around the side of the house,
spilling water all over myself and the sidewalk, it was the happiest
I could be in the afternoon there in Memphis.

That is, unless Mrs. Humes's grandson was practicing oboe in her attic. The oboe! Never had I heard a sweeter, more mysterious-sounding instrument. I was introduced to an unlikely but new and exotic nuance of sound and resonance.

And when I heard my mother play "Clair de Lune" on the piano one afternoon, something happened to my heart. Up to that time, I had not heard anything so tender and sensitive. At the other end of the scale was Antonin Dvořák's Ninth Symphony. The piece, with its dissimilar, imposing chords, took my breath away. In spite of having no knowledge or understanding whatsoever of the method Dvořák employed to create such audacious music, I felt a certain empathy and connection to the piece and its conception. As if I were compelled to try and create a similar work. I was so touched, I would have done anything to learn that art.

I heard those very instruments in my own head. I began to absorb all sound. I heard rhythms in machines, in nature, in the wind. I became excited by the music that played in my mind. The promise and the possibilities were endless! Deep emotional passages echoed in my memory as sung by the a cappella black choruses in the Holly Springs, Mississippi, churches.

MISSISSIPPI—1952— ♪ 8

I remember the mud the most. Its tenacity was second only to that of the men who strained their backs to push and pull our cars in and out of it. There were many cars. A long line in succession had driven from the church on concrete city streets in Memphis to the slippery dirt roads in Northern Mississippi, where the old family church cemetery lay.

I was six years old, and my grandmother, Lealer Jones, had died.

She was one of twelve children, and she had four children, including my father. The rain and the storm were so incessant that the grief seemed to take a back seat. The only focus was that of the men to free one tire then another from the muddy holes.

They had no choice. The funeral had to proceed, and the country road had only one lane. Burying Grandmother was a test of the will and strength of her progeny.

The progeny prevailed. When we reached the church, my soul actually stirred at the sound of the voices singing the Negro spirituals to mourn my grandmother's death. The sound praised God in the most basic, undeniably honest way music can act, with the human voice. Sounding as one force. Haunting and yearning, old, used, with a presence I feel to this day, it comforted and scared me at the same time.

Unaccompanied by any musical instrument, the sounds reflected the moans repeated by slaves in the fields for years and moved me beyond description. How much I loved sitting in those hot, country churches hearing those voices! Even before the sermon, it sent my grandmother to heaven for safekeeping by virtue of its sound alone. The mud and the grief were overcome, and the celebration ensued. Thank God for another life, Lealer Jones.

MEMPHIS—1952— ♪ 6

Also engraved in my musical memory is the song of the hot-tamale man singing down Edith Street at dusk while pushing his cart. "Hot tamales," he cried on two notes as the sun went down.

I consumed and digested vast amounts of musical foodstuff in the rich dirt of Memphis, and I couldn't get enough. I always wanted more.

Externally, my searches started to reveal new instruments and their promises of even more sounds and textures. I began to incorporate not only the instruments I was playing and hearing but all sound. My experimental nature unleashed a torrent of possibilities in my mind. At the same time, a silent support group consisting of my parents, teachers, church people, and community musicians made sure I had enough time with instruments to explore my internal world of sound and gave me the freedom to go deeper beneath the surface of the musical river flowing through my young consciousness.

Fortunately, I landed in the second-grade class of Mrs. Gladys McChristion, a lithe and lovely woman, and she started us with addition and subtraction. I began daydreaming, twirling curls in my hair and tuning out the math drills. I remember Mrs. McChristion calling my name, but I was far, far away...looking out the window. The class would laugh out loud when I came to, because there was a little swirl of hair on the top of my head from playing with it while my mind drifted off.

I was thinking about music, always. Rhythms, symphonies. The external world crashed into my internal world early in my life. Uninvited. Dominating and entitled.

It wasn't always pleasant or even understandable, but the river of sound overflowed and found expression. It was where I lived. No music, no Booker. Like my mother had become a musical reflection of my grandmother, I became a reflection of my mother. Not identical, but so lovingly similar. My grandmother was a piano teacher, and sometimes I felt her grief in her playing. The legend goes that Wilson Newell, her husband, was on his knees praying in the woods near his home not far from Holly Springs when a shot rang out from behind him that shattered his skull. That would have been on August 3, 1943, an event most likely unreported to authorities and uninvestigated. However, word of mouth can go on for decades, and this is the story that my mother told me of her father's death. I can only imagine that my grandfather may have misspoken to some white man or woman. Or possibly even some white woman had taken a liking to him, or some white man had a dislike for him. Worse, maybe he was killed for sport. Unfortunately, all these were likely hazards for a black man in the Deep South during this period, and they gave rise to my mother's burning fear for my safety as a young boy.

And though my grandmother took leave to her bedroom, her strength and spiritual belief found a voice on the piano. At this early age, I perceived the conduit between the vast internal reality and the external expression on musical instruments.

MEMPHIS—Fall 1954— ♪ 3

There I was, first day of fourth grade, in the band room. The cutoff for band was seventh grade, yet I was allowed in. I sat quietly amid a cacophony of chaotic sounds, horns, bells, children laughing, when in walked Mr. Walter Martin, an energetic, goateed young man—the first band director at Porter Junior High. He was the one that let me break the school rules and join the band *three years early*. There was immediate order when he stood in front of the class. He looked at each student a brief moment, then turned away and made a resolved face. Silence still.

"Good afternoon. My name is Walter Martin. I'm your new band director."

Yeaaaaaaah! I yelled to myself.

Mr. Martin smiled and looked off to the side as I would see him do a thousand more times. Instantly, the students loved him. He had already seemed to win over the whole school, and we hadn't yet played a note. We had no idea of his qualifications, but we had a teacher, and we would have a band.

"I graduated from Booker Washington, studied band under Professor W. T. McDaniels." No more needed to be said at this point because Professor McDaniels's reputation as a great teacher preceded him throughout the South. "I received my BA in music from Philander Smith College."

Heads turned. There were a few sighs. The class was impressed.

Then, Mr. Martin outlined the rules and procedures for checking out instruments, music, seating, being late—all the things to make his band room orderly and let us know he was in charge. Best of all, he had us put some music on our stands, and together we began to play some elementary scales.

It was my first experience performing in an ensemble, and I loved it! And on the very first day. I'm sure it sounded awful, but you wouldn't have known by Mr. Martin's face. He was genuinely happy to be there. Everything was going to be OK. *And! He had not regarded me as much younger and smaller than all the other students!* I was being treated as though I was three years older!

Mr. Martin was the first in a succession of gifted band directors/mentors, and he was the last for me—as he was transferred to my high school as well.

Ultimately, I remained part of that ensemble because I volunteered to play the oboe, a difficult instrument important to the concert band that none of the older kids would tackle. The oboe possesses a sharp, nasal quality of sound, solitary and lonely in its beauty. This peculiarity makes it a favorite for orchestral solos.

One sat untouched, brand new, in the instrument storage room at school. Mr. Martin trusted me; I was the only student with a key to the storage room, and he let me bring it home. Still enamored with my new clarinet, I took the oboe down to Amro Music, the store where I bought my clarinet, and was informed this instrument was like no other—it was a "double reed" (two quarter-inch slivers of cane must be cut square on top and wrapped with thread or wire in such a way as to curve slightly toward each other; then the two sides must be forced into the center of a small cork in order to be squeezed into the tube on top of the oboe so the lips can be pursed to blow air through the contraption). It required great care and a course in reed making, as the expensive oboe reeds were not as easily obtainable as the clarinet ones.

Before the age of nine, I told myself, "Life was meant to be lived in the key of C." It was the simplest, least complex key. It had no sharps or flats and was beautiful and pleasing to the ear. The flute, the oboe, the piano, the guitar, and the trombone were all created in C, and I believed that C was the natural key for the earth, humans, and the universe at large.

When I was nine years old, I started living life in the key of B flat. A clarinet is one of few instruments that transposes to B flat. That means clarinets are constructed so the note C (in the normal world) is actually D. In other words, to play a C, as you would hear it on a piano or guitar, you must play a D on a clarinet. It is as if the instrument had been musically "jacked down" like a lowrider.

This unnerving discovery wreaked havoc in my young, developing mind—to find out the C was not really a C but a B flat in clarinet world. There were sounds in my musical palette that I had not yet given names. The notes in my mind had positions on the piano or the ukulele, and I wasn't sure what to call them. I was relieved when I took my first clarinet lesson to discover and associate these note names with the sounds (pitches), only to find out I had to learn yet another syntax. I renamed the clarinet sounds in my head to correspond to the ones on the piano.

I learned that other instruments transposed to different keys as well, like saxophone to E flat or B flat and French horn to the key of F. That meant I must develop a supple mind if I was to understand and write music. *An American in Paris* is an example of a piece that whetted my curiosity. Textures, to sound cohesive, must

24

be written in different keys for different instruments, and the concert key was the common language. With original musical passages flowing through my head, I knew I had to master that language.

I played an oboe solo in fourth grade with the school band at a PTA meeting. My mother came, and I will never forget the broad smile on her face.

I was not, however, always happy being the youngest and shortest member of the marching band. I had their smallest uniform—the cap fell down over my eyes. My mom had to take up the pants. The coat dwarfed me, and I couldn't see over the person marching in front of me.

I rolled up the sleeves and tilted the cap back, excited to participate—even though there were no musical parts written for the oboe in marching band. If I was to continue when concert season was over, I needed to make the grade on clarinet. So in concert band, I doubled as an oboist and as a clarinetist, playing the clarinet my dad purchased at Amro Music.

Unlike saxophones, which have a neck strap to support their weight, clarinets only have a thumb grip, a little bar midway down where you put your thumb to hold the instrument. I developed a worrisome callous/sore on the topside of my thumb from carrying the heavy instrument while stepping high and playing in the marching band.

In the concert band, I shared the first clarinet chair with Leo Thomas, a ninth grader. At one rehearsal, Leo pushed me off my seat to get a better view of the music, and we were sent to the principal's office for fighting.

This is part of a pattern that began early in my life where I was always the youngest—granted an exception by older colleagues or bosses. So often, I felt the need to keep to a higher standard because of my age, but the consequence of being good made some people resent me. I responded by trying to be too good to be rejected—

which sometimes backfired. Thrown into a group that was three or four years beyond me, I didn't realize how out of place I was socially. A fourth grader is not a ninth grader.

One afternoon, Jeramy Beard, who was in the habit of picking on me and others in a walkway next to the classrooms—threw sand in my eyes, and I fell to the ground. I was the unlucky kid that Jeramy chose to harass that day. The clarinet case slipped from my hand, but I managed to find and grab it. Even when I was down on the ground, with all the other kids standing over me saying, "Oooh! Oooh!" and laughing, I held on to that clarinet! Another day, Emmitt Smith kicked me in the chest and knocked the wind out of me. I dropped my clarinet but picked it up before he got to it.

Those jerks were cowards. They were jealous. They knew I'd never let go of my clarinet and saw me as soft. Why me? How do you fight with a clarinet under your arm? That's why.

With two hands, I'd have beat the shit out of them. I was strong. Inside and out. Stronger than those bullies. My crusade was chartered, and I became a convert to the life of a musician.

CHAPTER 3
Precious Lord

MEMPHIS—Summer 1951— ♪ 4

In 1951 Memphis, on hot summer days on Beale Street, big-bellied, white-shirted black police officers walked in twos. They were like Abbott and Costello—with big guns high on their hips—sweat dripping. Customers came out of the shops with brown paper bags containing their food or ate at the tables inside. But the officers came out with fat sandwiches, having walked in, stepped behind the counter, and made their own food, leaving without paying. Not so much as a look at the black proprietor.

My dad taught some of these officers in his ninth-grade algebra class at B. T. Washington High School. They were respectful of Mr. Jones, who turned out impeccably dressed in white shirt and tie and addressed the young men and women as Mr. or Miss.

SAN FRANCISCO—1972— ♪ 5

He was so respected that the memory of him lasted in his students' minds for years. In 1972, some twenty years later, I was on my way from Seattle to San Francisco, and the flight had stopped in Portland, Oregon. A young black man about my age took the empty seat next to me. Without introduction, he started to talk to me, opened his brief-case to show, to my dismay, that it was filled with tightly wrapped bills.

He smiled at my reaction and continued to talk as if he knew me. I responded nervously, knowing his type was not one to be standoffish with.

Landing in San Francisco, I put on the speed and, with a brief goodbye, walked swiftly ahead of him toward baggage claim. As I walked, a dark-suited man appeared on my left and seemed to be pacing me. Another suited man appeared on my right. Within seconds a man moved in front, slowing down a bit. I didn't bother looking behind.

I was funneled through a doorway, down a stairway, through a corridor, and into an interrogation room underneath the airport. A detective was waiting near a large conference table. The men stood around as he asked about my "friend" on the plane. How well did I know him?

"Who's your pal with the briefcase?"

"I don't know him."

"What's your name?

"Booker T. Jones."

He frowned. "No, what's your name?"

Another detective stood close. "The man asked you a question—best you tell the truth."

"Like I said, Booker T. Jones!" I said, breathing faster.

Taking my ID, the detective at the desk said, "You Booker T. Jones? You Mr. Jones's son?"

"Yes, yes!" I answered.

"Get outta here, boy! Your father was my homeroom teacher at Booker Washington! No way you're involved in this thing!"

The officers stepped aside, and I bounded up the steps and out of the airport very relieved! I don't know if the money was real or who the guy was, but I'm sure he's still in jail now.

MEMPHIS—1951— ♪ 2

When I was a young boy, my dad and I were always physically close to one another—going places, playing ball, or listening to the radio. Both my parents were loving people, and our home was filled with warmth and happiness. I was protected, looked after, and cared for. When we weren't working, we were having fun with cards or checkers. We relaxed together with long drives in the car. Dad was a huge baseball fan, and we listened to the Dodgers games on the front porch.

I also loved baseball. I played every day. My first glove, which I oiled and cleaned regularly, was my prized possession, save my B-flat clarinet. I slapped my fist into it to shape it up. I kept it wrapped in a curled position with a large rubber band to make it supple and easy to use. When it was ready, Dad threw a ball out to me in the yard. I caught it with my fielder's glove. My pitcher's mitt was my other most prized possession. As far as I knew, I was the only kid on our block to have one.

When we weren't tossing the ball around, we would sit together on the porch and listen to every Dodgers game in the summertime. We didn't speak, just paid close attention to every word from the announcer—it was a bonding experience. When Jackie Robinson hit a home run, we and the rest of the world erupted.

In the unbearable heat of midsummer, in his uniform of tennis shoes, shorts, T-shirt, and a baseball cap, my dad would take his position on the side porch, along with a large pitcher of iced lemonade, away from the sun. I was never far away, most usually sitting on his lap with his hands on both my knees, a position so comforting and serene to me I have never been able to replace it. I knew when to jump down by the pitch of the game... just in time to let him jump up for his holler, "Did you hear that, Leanie?" He had played baseball on a local black team in Holly Springs for years, and in the country baseball was more revered than church.

Of course, Leanie heard that. All of Memphis, the entire nation heard *that*. There was no professional football or soccer or hockey or basketball; there was only baseball, and besides the occasional boxing match, it was all that was necessary. Even when Arthur Ashe commanded professional tennis, baseball kept its place. Baseball. "Whoo, whoo!" you could hear Mama laughing in the kitchen, and next-door neighbor Mrs. Pritchard rolled her eyes from her chair, perched on the side of her porch where she could hear the goings-on in and around our house.

Daddy would holler, jump up and down, and run back and forth out into the street, and his glass of lemonade just sat, unattended, with frost from the ice dripping, on the edge of the porch. His noise drowned out the radio, and Mama and I assumed the celebration was because Jackie Robinson had hit one of his 137 home runs. We went to the screen door to watch. "Whoo! Whoo!" resonated up and down the street in a ritual that had repeated itself more times than I can name. When the Dodgers scored, everyone in my neighborhood for two streets on either side knew because my daddy hollered so loud. Other men in the neighborhood had their radios tuned in to the game and had the same reaction.

It's baseball for breakfast, baseball for lunch, and baseball for dinner. I can't count the times I broke Mrs. Humes's back-bedroom window with a line drive meant to be a homer sailing across the roof of her house. But I had my loving dad, then my paper route, to pay for the broken glass. It happened so many times she stopped getting mad. In fact, Mrs. Humes began to enjoy letting us boys use her backyard for our games. It kept us off the street, and her nephew, Skipper, enjoyed being the center of attention. Even though he couldn't hit a fence with a ball or bat, he was included in every game.

MEMPHIS—Fall 1953— ♪ 4

There were less wonderful moments growing up too, and my father saved the day for me more times than I can remember, such as the time he ran off some thugs down on Lauderdale Street who had surrounded me to take my paper route money. Since it was early on my route, I was loaded down with two heavy cloth sacks of papers over both my shoulders. I couldn't move my arms above my elbows—I couldn't defend myself from boys from south of Lauderdale Street. I was bracing myself next to my bicycle when, out of nowhere, a white '49 Ford screeched to a halt on the other side of the street. A small man jumped out angrily with his fist balled up... walking fast at the thugs. "How you makin' it, boy?" Dad greeted me.

The thugs hesitated.

"Boy, I'll beat the stew out of you!" my dad said to one of them.

They scurried like mice in all directions. He walked to his car, the engine still running, and pulled off. From then on, I was clear to throw papers on Lauderdale.

I was never so glad to see my dad, especially since I didn't learn to fight back until high school, when one day I hit one of the worst thugs in Memphis. They called him Ba' Brother, and he cornered me one night in the basement of our church. My dad was his math teacher and had given him an F. He was just kind of toying with me, and before he knew it, I landed a nice one right on his jaw. He looked at me in disbelief.

Ba' Brother won the fight that followed, but after that, certain thugs became nice and even wanted to hang out with me. A big guy from South Memphis named Levi, who I had been afraid of, even started staying close and being friendly. Word got out that Booker T. hit Ba' Brother.

MEMPHIS—Fall 1952— ♪ 2

At a young age, I felt the need to be busy and self-sufficient, though I had no idea how to do that.

I spent more than a few evenings in the Urban League office where my mother worked, waiting for my dad to pick us up. In the hall was a rack where people passing through from other offices in the building would pick up a copy of the *Memphis World,* a local black weekly newspaper. The *World* was popular but not as much as the *Tri-State Defender,* a weekly paper for the black community.

When I was old enough, I stood in line outside of one of the press's weekly meetings for its carriers and obtained an application for a route. I attended the meetings for months before a route opened up.

There was a two-week apprenticeship with the outgoing paperboy. It was a small route with only thirty-five customers. The only way to get there from my house was down tiny McEwen Street, then left on Mason Street—enemy territory—a gang-infested section one block away from South Fourth Street.

My mentor was a big, streetwise boy who was not intimidated by the gangs. But as soon as he stopped mentoring me, the harassment and attacks started, mainly on Fridays, which were collection days.

Turning left on Mason from McEwen meant passing by Mason Temple. It was on this route that I first heard the Staple Singers through the double-wide church doors, open to the street. I slowed down to see them filling the pulpit in colorful robes. Their father was playing an electric guitar, and their voices were surging. What a sight. What a sound. Guitar in church. What an outrage. God in church.

With only thirty-five customers, my *Tri-State Defender* route wasn't very profitable.

I put in a second application to throw the *Press Scimitar*. I was eleven years old. My new route consisted of seventy customers. I was glad to get it—twice as many customers as my first. The route encompassed a squalid quarter, but it was on the way home from school.

My papers were dropped off at 4:30 p.m. on the lawn of a big church on the corner of Mississippi and Alston. I strapped one bag over each shoulder, folding the papers as I walked. The cloth bags were enormous. I looked like a pregnant boy. When I'd get distracted, I'd stop at the first house on Alston, the home of Memphis jazz pianist Phineas Newborn—I could hear him practicing piano with the screen door open. If I stopped, I would be late delivering the whole route…dallying at Phineas's front yard to fold my papers and listen to him play. Phineas Newborn was a Memphis jazz institution. I didn't know that then, of course.

After a few weeks, I started to solicit customers farther up on Lauderdale Street, off my route, on the way home. I started soliciting all the way to Lauderdale and Walker and added customers to my route, to a total of 120 customers.

To handle this additional volume, I went home after school and got my Western Flyer bicycle with its rack over the back tire.

I folded the papers, stuffing them into bags hung on the sides of the rack before I left the pick-up point, and stood up while riding to throw the papers on the run. This system worked well— except my aim was not as good as it was when I was walking. I tried to land the papers just above the front step—right in front of the door.

It wasn't unusual for me to walk up the steps to a porch on my routine Friday collection trip and find a little girl answering the door, saying, "My mama say she not here."

It was typical for my customers to avoid paying me for a week or two, whether they had the money or not. I would continue throwing to them for a few weeks, trying to collect every week, until too many weeks of nonpayment accumulated for me to keep the customer.

There were numerous challenges. Some houses were up on hills...some had hedges to throw over. Some had fences or dogs to bark at you while you tried to perfectly place those papers on the porch. There were mishaps. I broke windows, overturned statues, threw papers in bushes and puddles.

Parts of my paper route were so poor and squalid that the city would have kept them secret if it could have. (As if there were anyone to keep the secret from.) One gangly old man huddled in a single-room shack by a woodstove and waited for his evening paper. All he had in the hovel was the stove and a bed, as far as I could make out. It was dark in there save the dim light of a kerosene lamp. Built on stilts, the lean-to was higher than others on the alley and reeked of burned kerosene and body odor. The smell was so bad, I could never bear to go in.

But I could not avoid going up the rickety steps to the shanty because the old man could barely walk. He was pleasant and greeted me with, "Hello, paperboy!" He had little money and paid me in pennies and nickels from an old worn-out change purse. Never knew his name and never forgot him, even if the welfare system did. (My customers existed only as house numbers on streets in my journals.) I had to go between houses and through mud to get to his back-alley shack. I gave him every extra paper I had, and it hurt to collect from him.

Others were sex workers, people with disabilities, addicts, homeless people, and church faithful. One afternoon I stood on the front porch, knocking at the door of a woman who had a few men lined up waiting in her living room on chairs and a couch. Through the screen door, I could see and hear her telling a man, "Wait a minute," as he tugged impatiently at her skirt. It was a lesson in life and survival...without hope.

Another such case was the man who never spoke—who, from the days I was a very young boy, sat at the corner of McLemore and Mississippi. He was missing some fingers, and he wore no expression on his face. His pullover cap and clothes were dirty. He never moved. He just sat there on the corner as if it were the only home he knew. If you looked at him, he turned his head away. If you stood near, he left. You would look around, and he would just have disappeared.

Years later, I saw this man. He looked at me briefly. He acted as if he had been caught being alive. I know he remembered me because he knew me as a child. He had seen me thousands of times.

Thirty years on, he looked the same. He was sorry I had seen him. He was sorry anybody had. He looked away again. Just like before. I turned the car around to try and find him, but he was gone. Disappeared, just like thirty years ago. Only this time I was sad he had left. I had more compassion than before.

He was the only thing in Memphis that was the same as it was when I was a child. I wish I knew his name. He had not aged a minute, like he was in a time machine. I loved him more than felt sorry for him. I think about his mother. He must have had a mother, and she must have loved him.

No Name, that's what I'll call him.

MEMPHIS—Spring 1954—♪ 11

In time I grew stronger, developed a good arm and decent aim, and made enough money to buy school clothes and pay for clarinet lessons and piano lessons at Mrs. Cole's.

In addition to the *Press Scimitar* in the afternoons, I started throwing the *Commercial Appeal* in the mornings. I found myself getting up at 3:30 a.m. on Sunday and completing my route with the help of my dad and his car to transport the heavy Sunday paper.

With the extra funds, I could now afford organ lessons in addition to the piano and clarinet lessons I was already taking. I returned to Mrs. Cole. Best thing I ever did in my entire life.

My Lord! She had a Hammond B-3 organ in her dining room! It was a handsome piece of furniture, as were all her dining room pieces. She explained that the organ was reserved for a few special students and that the lessons were expensive.

The first time I saw it, a powerful, irresistible urge to sit at that Hammond organ overtook me. Looking back over my shoulder as I was led to the living room for my piano lesson, I was transported by the sight of the instrument. I played my piano lesson that day rapt with desire and fascination for that entity in the next room.

This was before I heard Ray Charles playing "One Mint Julep"; before I heard Brother Jack McDuff at the Flamingo Room, with only three pieces and playing bass with his left hand; before I heard Jimmy Smith doing "The Sermon" or Bill Doggett doing "Honky Tonk"; or any of the other Hammond B-3 organ masterpieces of the time.

Mrs. Cole and her husband—who would often stand next to the table to watch the students, as if he were standing guard—probably paid more for the Hammond B-3 organ and Leslie speaker in their dining room than they did for their house. In 1955, Hammonds retailed for around $4,000. In 1954, my father paid $6,000 for our modest two-bedroom home.

I told my mother about my discovery. She reminded me that there was an organ at our church and that I could get her friend Merle Glover, the church organist, to give me a lesson for less money than Mrs. Cole would charge. I wasn't excited about taking lessons from the persnickety Merle Glover. During church services, she couldn't make it through an entire service without leaving to go out for a smoke. However proficient at the pipe organ, she was fussy and impatient. I had only one lesson with Mrs. Glover at her home, during which she showed me how to take my shoes off and feel the pedals with my toes and how to push the stops.

One night I went down to the church with my dad when he had a treasury board meeting, and I waited for him at the huge pipe organ in the sanctuary. Staring at the stops in the darkened, scary room, I knew I had to discover where the electric box was in that section of the large church and how to turn the lights on in the huge room as well illuminate the organ riser itself. Where was the key to turn on the behemoth, and was it safe for a small boy to be alone in a room as large as this at night, even with the lights on?

But the sound was different from the instrument at Mrs. Cole's house. It was a pipe organ, and the notes spoke so slowly because of the time it took for the air to go through the big pipes. For a while, I would practice alone at night in the sanctuary when my dad was downstairs in the finance room. But I had to go back to Mrs. Cole's organ. It was so much more accessible musically than the big pipes that extended up into the walls of the church, with all their reverberation and majesty.

I devoured every morsel of training Mrs. Cole had to offer during our short half-hour sessions and ran home happy, looking forward to the next lesson in two weeks. I was enamored with the sound of the Hammond and the Leslie speaker; I had been shown my destiny.

Because the organ has the capability of sustaining notes indefinitely and of getting louder or softer with the expression pedal, it's possible to simulate a singing, melodic effect—and, with the use of the Leslie rotator, a vibrato much like the human voice can be produced. Also, it's possible to simulate nearly any orchestral sound or combination of instruments with a Hammond B-3.

MEMPHIS—Spring 1956— ♪ 3

I added organ lessons to my list of chores. It seemed natural, and Mama had retrieved Grandma's old piano and put it back in the living room, so I was able to at least practice the piano lessons and simulate the organ exercises. I practiced on a real organ wherever I could—at church or anyplace that might have one. Mrs. Cole was a practical, methodical teacher, attentive and old-fashioned. She practiced the technique of tapping a student's finger with her baton, which was more like a dowel. She was very good and could hit your knuckle anytime she wished, so I practiced very hard.

Mrs. Cole demonstrated technique frequently and emphasized straight posture, chin up, and raising the knuckles high above the keyboard. I still try to emulate her figure at the keyboard.

As I matured musically, I considered Memphis to be the headquarters for southern blues and gospel, since so many influential artists headed there from Mississippi, Louisiana, and Arkansas. But if Memphis was the headquarters, then Chicago was the capital. The great Mahalia Jackson originated there, but I didn't know her importance on the day I was called on to accompany her.

By twelve, I started to play afternoon teas on Sundays to pick up some extra change. Most often they were Sunday-afternoon affairs attended by church ladies, held in the large dining room at Universal Life Insurance Company on Vance, a few doors down from my church, Mt. Olive. At such occasions, ample-bosomed churchwomen pulled my young head into their chests after I played a song. This particular tea was held at a private home out on South Parkway West. Upper middle-class Memphis African Americans kept meticulous dining rooms and living rooms for church benefits and meetings. Folding chairs surrounded the ornate, flower-filled centerpiece on the dining room table where Mahalia Jackson stood just inches from me at the piano. Beads of sweat poured from her forehead, and I caught a whiff of the familiar combination of perfume, perspiration, and soiled percale.

The song was "Precious Lord," made famous at Ebenezer Baptist in Chicago and Martin Luther King's last request in Memphis. Mama dug out her old *Gospel Pearls* hymnal, showed me the chords, and helped me learn to play it in all keys. I rehearsed it over and over for days without Ms. Jackson, who would be the first church lady I played for professionally. I brought the raggedy old hymnal along with me for emotional support, although I still didn't read music that well.

It was a beautiful, warm Sunday afternoon, and the home was decorated with flowers. The room was buzzing with intense competition between the hues of all the various rouges and the scents of all the perfumes.

Very soon after the performance began, I realized what a musical giant Ms. Jackson was, due to the immediate onset of emotion and purpose initiated by her commanding, soulful voice and powerful presence. She meant what she was singing. Completely swept into the strong feeling Mahalia created with every phrase, I focused on playing the chords and let her energy guide me through the song. At the end, I wondered what had really happened.

The applause was warm and enthusiastic. Mahalia was gracious, used to that kind of thing. She smiled at me, thanked the women, and moved into the room. I sat motionless at the piano, unsure what to do, like an orphan who had found a home. My hand had been taken.

CHAPTER 4
Havana Moon

HOLLYWOOD—Summer 2017— ♪ *12*

It was good to get back together with my old friend Carlos. It had been twenty-seven years. Twenty-seven years of weirdness. Years ago, at Eric Clapton's Crossroads Festival in Dallas, we had avoided one another. We had even sat in the same movie theater in Marin for two hours and not spoken.

Time passed.

Carlos invited me to play a show with him at the Hollywood Bowl. Like he did so many times in the '70s.

We saw each other in the hallway backstage, and a long, warm hug erased all the years of imagined animosity. We pushed away, still holding arms, and smiled at each other. Neither could find the appropriate words, so we headed off to our respective dressing rooms, each feeling so much better.

Carlos's first words were to my son, Ted. "I want you to play like you don't know how to play," he told him.

I hadn't seen Carlos's son since he was in swaddling clothes at Stinson Beach. What would I say to him when I saw him? Back in the '70s, his father had had the best band in rock. Armando Peraza, Chepito Areas, Raul Rekow, Greg Rolie, Neal Schon, Michael Shreve, Coke Escovedo—all award winners—the best rock band ever assembled in the history of time. And I got to hear it all from backstage. One stellar performance after another. Night after night. I took photos of Carlos sleeping on his rickety old airplane. We were brothers.

The best was one night in San Juan, Puerto Rico. A crowd of fifty thousand watched my little brother soar into the heavens and play like the angel he was. He threw his head back, closed his eyes, and scrunched his body until the notes came out of his guitar. From Carlos's guitar came the loud, high, painful moans of relief and deliverance that filled the night air and cleansed the audience. No one, not Hendrix, not even bandmate Neal Schon, could play with such heartfelt urgency, agony, simplicity, and beauty.

Stax and the MGs limited my contributions, but Carlos was open to my other musical interests, including singing.

SAN FRANCISCO—1981— ♪ 3

I had just finished the two-week control of smoking course at Westwood's Schick Center when Carlos asked me to come to San Francisco to work on his solo LP. The professional help was necessary—I hadn't been able to quit on my own. My car, my clothes, my house, everything made me sick because they smelled of cigarette smoke.

I flew up and checked into the Holiday Inn on Eighth Street. Carlos was outraged that I was staying there and had his people check me into the Fairmont.

I had dinner every night with Carlos, Jerry Wexler, and Barry Beckett—the other producers on the project. We ate at San Francisco's finest restaurants. Jerry, who was staying at the Clift Hotel, would pull out a fat roll of one-hundred-dollar bills to pay for dinner, which made me very nervous that he was walking around so close to Turk and Eddy Streets with that kind of money in his pocket. The danger didn't seem to bother him, though. Jerry kept a perpetual smile on his face. Sometimes Barry and I would even hitch a ride in Jerry's limo.

We were working at David Rubinson's Automat down on Folsom, in an area of big studios west of Market Street. It had a great reputation. There had been a big buzz in the early '70s when David was building the place, and I had always wanted to see if the result was worth the hype. It was at these sessions that I witnessed Jerry doing his famous heebie-jeebie dance. His legs anchored and spread wide, his hands grabbing his hips, his thighs, his head, wherever, his whole body jerking and twitching, eyes closed in rapture. Guaranteed the funniest thing ever in rock history.

The session marked the beginning of a period of creative freedom for me. "One with You," the song I composed in the studio with Carlos and the musicians, flowed freely. A first take. A piano credenza, conga flams, more congas, then rhythm, intoxicating, into the open mikes and back again through our headphones, like splashing out onto an open sea.

I swooned when the rhythm fell in, lost my bearings, hypnotized by the Latin-ness of the thing, but kept my hands on the keys.

The congas followed lazily along, like children straggling on a mountain path, but solid, and so right. Jerry was in the control room minding the knobs, and all was well. Everyone in the band stayed silent until they felt it was time to play, and all went as planned, without a plan.

Then, words surfaced. They danced off my tongue.

"Angel, I want to be one with you. Spread your wings and let me in."

After the verse, the music flowed. Then Carlos spoke. Congas responded. He spoke again. The whole band responded. Barry Becket was on electric piano. He created a warm, dark, purple hall for the music to abide in. A strong, quiet background presence. His essence was similar to the electric piano part Spooner Oldham created for Aretha Franklin when she sang "I Never Loved a Man." So soulful. So simple.

Fran Christina on drums. Carlos knew how to put a band together. Kim Wilson on harmonica. Usually loud and aggressive, Kim was subdued and melancholy, playing everywhere, never in the way. Jimmie Vaughan on guitar. Who plays guitar on a Carlos Santana solo album? The unassuming Jimmie Vaughan, that's who. It was all about Mexico, and love.

Carlos is one of the most independent, creative musical souls I have ever known. Not unlike the spirit of Maurice White, with whom I set out on my first musical journeys in Memphis.

MEMPHIS—Fall 1958— ♪ 1

If you were a young, aspiring musician in Memphis in the late fifties, it was assumed that you would play jazz. There were no other options. Classical music and blues were there, but classical offered no future. A little money could be made in blues, but it didn't present the intellectual challenges of jazz or classical.

Memphis's young musicians were to unwaveringly follow the footsteps of Frank Strozier or Charles Lloyd or Joe Dukes in dedicating their lives to the pursuit of excellence. Memphis had produced Booker Little, Hank Crawford, and Phineas Newborn. Joe

Dukes was the standard bearer. He left Memphis and was sought out by great jazz musicians in New York and Detroit.

My crew was no different. My high school music buddies Maurice White and Richard Shann and I yearned to become jazz proficient on our instruments.

Aside from the five-piece Booker T. Washington Combo, some of us formed our own group: Richard Shann on piano, Maurice White on drums, Frank Easley on bass, and me on guitar and tenor saxophone. I was a sixth-grader practicing in the band room one day when Maurice, an eighth-grader, walked in and said, "Hello, I'm Maurice White." We discovered we lived not far away from one another and started hanging out at his small LeMoyne Gardens apartment or in the den at my house, usually listening to music.

When we met Richard Shann from South Memphis and began playing sax, piano, and drums together in my den, we became a threesome. I left school with other friends or my girlfriend but somehow always ended up with Maurice and Shann before the day was over. When I wasn't around, Maurice created another trinity of close friends with Shann and singer David Porter.

Maurice was the first person of my age group I'd met who was really committed to making music and had the skill to become a virtuoso. We ended up playing live or practicing together nearly every day for what seemed like years. He was usually on drums, and I was on piano or some other instrument. As a result, we became like soul brothers, neither of us having a natural brother our own age.

One sweltering summer Saturday night, our first paid gig ever, my dad packed his car with my musician friends and instruments and drove us across town, across the Memphis-Arkansas Bridge and into the Arkansas country for a gig at a broken-down, ramshackle, one-room club on a back road; the job paid a pittance, barely gas money. Frank's upright bass hardly fit in my father's 1949 Ford.

All the instruments were sticking out the windows and the trunk. During the gig, my dad sat in the car and waited to drive us home. The sight of us all piled in there, Maurice laughing at the sound of my mother shouting, "Booker, you forgot your peanut butter and jelly sandwiches!" as we were pulling out of the driveway, the broken wooden planks on the floor of the dilapidated backwoods club, made the entire experience feel like a trip into the future.

Because he cosigned the loan for the drums, loaned us his car, and believed in us, Maurice and I were both deeply indebted to Mr. Walter Martin, the band director. You could hear a reverence in his voice when he spoke Maurice's name. Maurice and David Porter were always running around town in Mr. Martin's fast 1957 Plymouth two-door with the 127 engine.

With Mr. Martin's help, Maurice's grandmother managed to get money for him to buy a small set of drums. We loved that set. My dad brought it home in his car, from the music store downtown to Maurice's apartment. It was gold, and the drums were small, but they sounded great. Maurice was so proud. Many times we carried those drums on foot down Mississippi Avenue, all the way from the Elks Club on Beale to Maurice's apartment, a little more than a mile and a half. Frank Easley didn't have a bass, but since I was student assistant band director by tenth grade and kept a key to the band room, we borrowed the school's upright bass.

Playing for peanuts became the order of the day. We couldn't have been happier. We were performing music like our heroes. Maurice loved Max Roach (drums), I loved Hank Crawford and Leroy Cooper (saxes), and Shann loved Bobby Timmons (piano). Each of us favored the respective instrument(s) of his hero.

Shann was our leader. He was the jazz aficionado. Lazy, elegant bebop lingo poured from his thin lips like warm, creamy soup. His beige face was stuck high up on a frame supported by lanky stilts. He sat sideways and picked at the keys as though taking notes on a pad.

From our perspective in Memphis, Shann was the bohemian who could have been from New York. As committed as he was, he could have hung out with Monk or smoked dope with Miles. But he was there with us, attending Carver High School, where my mom was a secretary. Thin as a pole, Shann walked everywhere—he had no money for bus fare. It was an hour's walk from his house through unsafe Lauderdale Sub to my place.

Shann spoke in the slowest possible deliberate southern drawl. He sounded more white than black, save for what he was saying: "Seh, Boogah Tee, may'n—U'm comin' over yo' house—'round seven—play some tunes, hear? I'll be over there, may'n." He would show up, and so would Maurice, with bundles of LPs to play on my turntable for hours.

Shann sat sideways with his legs crossed, tinkling the keys on my mother's piano with one hand, trying to imitate Bobby Timmons. Shann and Maurice and I listened and tried to play what we heard. They regularly listened with me to the albums I brought home from the Satellite Record Shop but seemed to harbor some disdain for the studio. To my knowledge, Maurice and Shann never entered the building—maybe because they considered themselves jazz musicians and not R & B session players.

Shann's parents were more permissive than ours; he would stay as long as he wanted and wear whatever he wanted, his head often topped by a maroon beret. He was always polite to my parents, but he seemed on course for destruction. He never used drugs, but he gave the impression of being a likely candidate because of his nonconformity. I wondered if Richard could achieve the high standards he dreamed of. Nonconformity was such a rare thing in Memphis in the late 1950s. Maurice and I joined Shann in his other world as he doodled at the keys and compared himself to Bobby Timmons or McCoy Tyner. He was the most original, authentic, and uncompromising dreamer of dreams I knew.

Richard Shann, the jazz piano player from South Memphis.

I was in a similar position. Could I approach the level of Jimmy Smith or Brother Jack McDuff, my idols on the organ? The answer, at least at the time, was no.

MEMPHIS—Winter 1961— ♪ 6

One night early in 1961, we saw our guiding light. Jack McDuff was playing at the Flamingo Room in Memphis with one of our contemporaries, Joe Dukes, on drums. Joe Dukes had been Maurice's idol. McDuff had come to Memphis, heard Joe, and pulled him out of high school to go on the road with him. That must have been Maurice's dream at the time.

At the Flamingo Room that night, Brother Jack McDuff was on fire, as he was prone to be. He played his own bass on the lower keyboard like Jimmy Smith, or with his feet on the foot pedals, and he was very much in charge. And charge he did. With Joe on drums, the music had an energy that was unforgettable. A challenge that was undeniable. An excitement that was irresistible.

The three of us sat there in the audience listening. We were imagining ourselves on that stage, immersed in music and in a moment that would change our lives forever. Inspired and motivated, we started booking gigs.

Ramsey Lewis heard Maurice play when he was on a visit to Chicago to see his father, and Maurice left his grandmother, us, and Memphis to play drums in the Ramsey Lewis Trio.

Maurice's departure when I was in the eleventh grade took the vitals out of our little trio. This was a new kind of feeling in my heart, one I'd never had before. I drove slowly to the train station with Maurice and DeLois (his girlfriend) crying in the back seat. Maurice's big old wooden trunk was about one inch too tall for my dad's Buick, and Dad found some rope to tie it down. It bounced annoyingly on the ride. Illinois Central's train, *The City of New Orleans,* perched up high on the tracks in brown-steel splendor, blew steam like a dragon from both sides of its guts. The City, as we called it, was the major means of escape for blacks fleeing the South.

I didn't say much. I just stood there watching the lovers part—pushing and kissing and pulling like a cell dividing.

"All aboard!" a man in a red cap screamed.

Maurice pulled himself away from DeLois and reached out his hand to me. The handshake turned into a quick hug, and he walked up the car's shiny metal steps. DeLois and I were quiet on the ride home. She lived a few doors away on Edith.

I wouldn't be seeing Maurice's adopted mama anymore; she'd "done the work the good Lord wanted her to do." His "Mother Dear," his real mother, dropped him off at "Mama's" as a newborn, and he hadn't known her. His father was also in Chicago. Maurice had to go. It was 1961, an early introduction to emptiness.

Maurice later went to LA and formed Earth, Wind, and Fire. It was the first significant separation in my life.

That we were truly brothers became glaringly apparent in 1976 when I first heard "That's the Way of the World," by EWF. The song struck me deeply, like no other had before. I realized our separation had been necessary. Neither of us would have reached our full potential had we stayed together because just as we supported each other, we limited each other. The Supreme was at work, as always, setting things as they should be, even if not apparent to us. Maurice was doing the work of his life, as was intended.

CHAPTER 5

C Jam Blues

NEW YORK CITY—Fall 1962— ♪ 9

If you listen to "Baby, What You Want Me to Do," by Jimmy Reed, you would think the song was by a rational, heartbroken man, but that was not the Jimmy Reed I found myself with at New York's Roseland Ballroom one night in 1962. The MGs were opening for Jimmy and backing Otis Redding and Ruth Brown.

After Otis's set, there was a long delay in the show, and someone in the crowd threw a bottle onto the stage. After we played, a rumor started in the crowd that the show would not continue. Scheduled to go on next, Jimmy grabbed a pistol out of his guitar amplifier backstage and started waving it onstage.

I panicked. "Jimmy, what you doin' with that gun?"

"I'm gon' shoot!"

"Shoot where?"

"Out there!" He pointed to the audience.

"Why?"

"That's where the bottle come from, ain't it?"

The crowd got more upset. Everyone was upset. Jimmy and Ruth were threatening not to go on. The promoter, LA's Magnificent Montague, was nowhere to be found. Had he left the premises with all the money? Would any of the artists be paid? The night drew on, and we all waited backstage for Montague to show up. He never did. Montague had surreptitiously vanished with the box office cash. No one got paid.

Chagrined and down in the dumps, we walked back to our hotel carrying our drums and amps. The next morning, we used gasoline cards to pay our hotel bills.

Montague, who was powerful enough a DJ to have his way, set an example and made a statement. "If you want your records played, you have to go through me."

Welcome to the big time.

MEMPHIS—Fall 1959— ♪ 1

When I was a tenth-grade student, just starting to play bass around Memphis, I hung around the clubs near Beale Street.

A carnival atmosphere prevailed. Jazz and blues music, gambling, drinking, grills, pickpockets, thugs, theaters, voodoo. All lit up to entice customers into this other world.

One sultry night, I wandered over to the corner of Beale and Hernando, where I heard music coming out of an upstairs window. I was standing on the sidewalk below Club Handy, listening to the blazing Hammond B-3 organ sounds of "Blind Oscar." I got a glimpse of him as he was led from the club. Thin and tall, he looked like a blind Malcolm X in his black suit and bow tie.

The club's entrance consisted of a forbidding set of wide, dark stairs whose ascent was guarded by a well-dressed bouncer standing at the top. The Godfather of Beale Street, Andrew "Sunbeam" Mitchell, granted entry to the stairwell and ultimately to the club. His perch was an open window where he kept watch on the street below his club. Most nights the staircase was filled with people pushing to get in.

I hesitated until the steps emptied to go up, but permission was denied me because I was only fifteen, underage. The Handy was Memphis's most frequented black nightclub, and Blind Oscar became a major influence on my organ playing. His chords rushed through the second-story window and down onto the street where I stood, filling the night air with such furious gusts of wind and fire that I wondered if the music might burst into flames.

On Beale Street, the bandleaders were kings, but there was one queen, Evelyn Young. Slight, owl-eyed, in long-sleeved shirts and suspenders, Evelyn played alto sax and remained the lone, undisputed bandleader at Club Handy.

Club Handy was gritty. I got inside once, during an afternoon rehearsal of Evelyn Young's band. I was promptly kicked out (one look pegged me as too innocent to stay). But I got the picture. Club Handy—named for composer W. C. Handy, the father of Memphis black nightclubs...no white faces...undiluted blues and rhythm...black life chord changes...red dirt country...pleasure and pain. Dark, loud, and wild—suits and neckties...promiscuity.

Across the street, at the Flamingo Room on Gayoso, a younger, dapper club owner, Clifford Miller, came down to the street. "How you doin', young fellow?" Clifford asked, and led me up the steps to his club. His bass player, Frog, was sick. Cliff Miller put me onstage at the Flamingo despite my age.

I strapped Frog's bass—a beautiful, heavy Gibson with a bright red finish—onto my shoulder and found myself in the throes of a hot set, standing less than two feet in front of Memphis's foremost drummer, Al Jackson Jr., and about to play four hours of tunes I did not know. Baritone sax player Floyd Newman and bandleader Bowlegs Miller glared at me. Tenor saxophonist Gilbert Caples looked the other way, refusing to condone or condemn my harassment.

There was no dressing room. There was a big parking lot out back and below the club. Musicians had to walk up a long fire escape to the back door that led to the stage. That rear parking lot was where all the activity was. All the drug deals, whiskey sales, equipment loading, patron parking, employee parking—with a big floodlight exposing every bit of it.

In front of the club, at the curb, there were only a few parking spaces. They were taken by the better-looking, later-model cars— convertibles and so forth. The jalopies were parked out back. I drove my dad's Buick, parked the car in front, and walked up the steps of the front entrance like a respectable patron.

Clifford instructed his brother Jasper to pay me the standard seven dollars a night. At four in the morning, Jasper handed me the crumpled bills with orders to come back the following night at 9:30 sharp. I had taken Frog's job.

The resident pianist at the Flamingo Room was a pudgy African American woman named Mamie Dell Meriwether. She was charged with calling out the names and keys of the songs the band would play each night. Because of her short, stocky, and bespectacled appearance, her piano was positioned nearly out of sight at the back of the stage. Whichever band played there was obliged to use her on piano. The talented Mamie Dell was the true bandleader— not Gene "Bowlegs" Miller, who took the credit.

Mamie Dell barked the chord changes at me from the side of her mouth through a cigarette, so precisely timed that I had only a fraction of a second to react. She would say, "'C Jam Blues,' F sharp!" She chose weird keys and called out changes at the last second for her own amusement, not wishing to play in certain keys. I wondered if she ever played "C Jam Blues" in C. You had to know the song, originally written in C, but you had to transpose it on the spot into the key of F sharp, or whatever key she chose, which was no problem for her. She took great delight from knowing the musicians had to squirm and scramble to decipher notes, missing the count-off.

Mamie Dell taught me by challenging me. She liked to provoke musicians by calling out numbers in this devious way—especially if there was a young new whippersnapper on stage. There were no fake books, no music. You had to learn songs by ear and remember them from night to night. Before I knew it, a few bars of the complicated jazz piece in the awkward key had already passed me by. Mamie Dell grinned and showed the wide gap between her front teeth before she took off playing. You would have thought Mamie Dell had had four years of music theory classes.

MILLINGTON AIR FORCE BASE, FRAYSER, TN—Spring 1960— ♪ 4

Driving north on Highway 51, you could easily miss Frayser at night, even with the sign. I made a U-turn more than once to get to the club in the country north of Memphis, a joint on a long dirt road off Highway 51 near Millington Air Force Base. On this windy spring night, I was onstage playing the usual set of hot, sexy blues. Late into the gig, the white sheriff walked in, in full uniform, picked out a voluptuous black woman, and started dancing with her in the middle of the floor. This being business as usual, the other patrons continued to dance surrounding the couple. This all went on to a slow-boiling blues rhythm that never skipped a beat; we played an extended version. After a while, the sheriff and the woman slipped into the night.

This was an example of the arrogance displayed by white authorities before black musicians at nearly every gig on any given night. Memphis whites were so insulated and convinced of their "goodness" to the Negroes that it never occurred to the majority of them that it might be an imposition to take a black woman against her will—in front of a black man, or men. By 1960, the white mentality in Frayser, where the incident occurred, was "How much, how very much, we've done for the Negro." The music played on.

MEMPHIS—Fall 1960— ♪ *9*

Al Jackson Jr. was the drummer on all my early stints at clubs in professional bands. He was there when I sat in on bass for Willie Mitchell at The Manhattan Club on Bellevue. He was there when I borrowed Frog's bass to fill in for him at the Flamingo Room.

"Get on the goddamn beat! Young motherf—er!" Al yelled. "Can't play shit! Get off the goddamn stage!" The taunting was so insistent—from so many people—it was like water beating down on a rock. That taunting caused a tenacious strain to form in me, which has helped me survive the music business. Like Floyd, Al was well dressed, with cuff links and loafers. I wore a yellow seersucker suit from the Dollar Store, but I had managed to buy a pair of quality leather shoes with the money from my paper route.

My father let me return only in the custody of his trusted former student, Floyd Newman. Suave and snazzy with straight black hair, he was the baritone sax player that had glared at me.

"Gotdamn! Little young motherf—er!" Floyd yelled at me in the car all the way to the Flamingo while I worried about him missing stoplights. He was nonplussed at having been given the job of transporting me to the club and back. Clifford Miller and my father had an agreement that Floyd had to honor.

Floyd was not the only one.

Frog got his job and his bass back when Bowlegs added another horn player at the Flamingo—me, playing baritone sax in the band. Once again, I found myself standing in front of Al Jackson Jr. with him shouting expletives at me as I blundered my baritone sax parts in Bowleg's four-piece horn section. I was positioned on the edge of the six-foot-high stage, in front of Al's drums on the far right of the horn line. I was always afraid of teetering off the tall stage and onto the floor when we did our steps. The older guys yelled at me, but deep down they were on my side.

Passionate about music, I was doing what I loved, and in the process, I took on too much.

I was managing a lot of activities for an adolescent. I had my evening paper route, Christian Youth Fellowship on Wednesday nights at church, piano and organ lessons, and my job at night at the clubs. At Booker Washington High, I was commissioned as a first lieutenant in the National Defense Cadet Corps and was assistant director of the band, where I played first trombone. The band played at the football games and provided music for assemblies and for all other school events, like commencement. We marched in every city holiday parade and provided music for a few charity events. It was at one of these events that my picture was taken as I sat up in a tree playing my trombone—and the photo was published in the *Press Scimitar*, a local newspaper.

On top of everything else, I was also a member of the school dance troupe, and we gave concerts downtown at Ellis Auditorium three times a year.

There were evening and weekend sessions at Satellite Records.

I kept a full social calendar too, hanging out with my friends, playing sandlot football on Saturdays, basketball in my driveway and at the school gym, and dating regularly.

Then, on Sundays, I had to start at four thirty in the morning, with my dad's help, to get the heavy Sunday *Commercial* delivered on time. Still, it was a fun time for me. I was doing the things I wanted to do.

By the time I got to Satellite in 1960, music had become a regular second source of income for me, next to my paper route. Out McLemore Avenue to Thomas Street, Thomas Street to the club where I spent so many nights playing bass with Ben Branch, Currie's Club Tropicana.

At the time, I was so young my dad made Johnny Currie, the club's owner, promise to bring me home every night himself. He would begrudgingly pile me into the front seat of his Lincoln, and I could see the big long .45 next to the flashlight and the money from the night's sales in his glove compartment.

I got swept up in all of this. The Flamingo Room was open four nights a week, Friday through Monday. Monday nights were called "Blue Monday" and were a popular evening at the club. Also on Mondays my algebra teacher gave out formulas for us to study for the weekly test held at nine the following morning. Mrs. Gloria Callian's room was next to my dad's classroom on the mathematics floor at BTW. These Tuesday mornings followed Blue Mondays, the last of my four-night week at the Flamingo.

One Tuesday I hadn't paid attention to the homework assignment. Mrs. Callian caught me cheating on the test. Cheating— next door to my dad's classroom. Mrs. Callian stopped the exam. She had me stand up and fold my paper. She marched me next door and interrupted my dad's class. We stood there. I don't remember words being spoken. My parents had tried to raise me with love and integrity. I was devastated. Dad was surprised and embarrassed. My only memory was looking at his immaculate white shirt and tie while his students watched in silence. I couldn't bring myself to meet his gaze. Mrs. Callian stood at the door behind me.

All the BTW teachers were so much more than coworkers; they

were a society unto themselves. They ate lunch together at the same table, they watched over each other and their families. They socialized apart from work—they shared the same values.

Time froze. I had really done it this time. There was no way to make it up. In our world, you just didn't cheat on an exam. With a slight nod, Dad excused Mrs. Callian, his good and trusted friend, and me. He let us know the incident was over and we could leave. My father stuck with me. He saw how the experience shattered me.

Dad didn't demand that I quit playing at the club. His support for my music continued, but he insisted I carve out adequate time for schoolwork. The three of us sat down in the living room. We never sat in the living room. It was an intervention.

"Booker, I know you've worked hard for a long time to build up your paper route, and it means a lot to you, but it's just too demanding," Mama said. "You need to make time to do your homework and practice and get enough sleep for school."

I interrupted, "Mama, but I—"

"You've got too many responsibilities," she said, "working for Chips at Stax, the Flamingo Room. You're doing too much, son."

"Yes, ma'am, I know," I answered. "It's just that I—"

"Your father and I worry about you. You're going to have to give up the paper route."

Only a person with day-to-day knowledge of the situation, someone like my mother, who loved me as much as my mother, could see that I was overbooked. I was so relieved that she was my advocate. Relieved that she approved of letting go of my paper route—a job I had started at age seven and worked so hard to build up. I had to let it go. At the paperboy meeting, sitting on the top ledge with my feet between the two boys on the bench below me, I raised my hand. "Mr. Sullivan, as much as I love my route, I'm going to have to let it go. I have two other jobs as a musician."

"Booker, I hate to see you go," he said. "You waited so long for this route, and you built it up."

The money I was making was also crucial for our family. My income rivaled the $392 a month my dad made as a teacher. I bought my clothes and my lunches and gave my parents a little money.

But the way Blind Oscar put his hands on a Hammond B-3 was the way my parents put their hands on me. They had faith in Providence, in me, and in my gift. Along with the Memphis community, they trusted me and granted me freedoms.

I was admitted into nightclubs even though I was years under the legal age, as if I were unusually mature.

I was permitted into studios to record music of my own design, as if I had exceptional musical aptness.

I was allowed to follow my passion at a tender age, like getting an early driver's license.

My folks and the community worked hard and went to great lengths to provide these opportunities, never doubting my abilities. I seized the moment at every occasion and ran with it for all it was worth.

CHAPTER 6
Green Onions

NEW YORK—Fall 1965— ♪ 7

Quincy called. It was as if God was on the phone. "Yeah, man, come to New York. I want you to hear something." I rushed home, packed a few things, and went to the airport. I flew in.

That night Q met me in the hallway. I tried to peek into his dark, luxurious suite. Ulla came right to the door. They were dressed to the nines. I was out of my league. Ulla smiled graciously at my suit. She was in an expensive black sequined dress, and she looked like—well, she looked like Ulla Jones, Quincy's wife. "Let's go right downstairs; the car is waiting!" Q said. I followed them down the hall, feeling like a southern country hick. I squeezed into the back seat of the black stretch between Quincy Jones and his beautiful wife! *How lucky could a young twenty-one-year-old man be? Damn!*

The car pulled up to a club with a brightly lit marquee. Everything had become like in a dream. The doorman grabbed the handle, looking past me. "Mr. Jones! Welcome to the Vanguard!"

I looked up, but I wasn't the Mr. Jones he was referring to. The marquee flashed "The Village Vanguard." Way upscale. The dream continued. I stayed on my feet. We were led to our table, heads turning as we pushed through the crowd. Drinks came. Q smiled at me. "Just wait."

The Thad Jones/Mel Lewis Orchestra was revealed to applause when the curtains parted, and Q whispered, "Now this, Booker, is music."

It was bebop. The jazz precursor/equivalent of rap, which I hadn't heard before. It swang. Made you move your body with the chords. Fine art.

Then it was over. I hardly remember the drive back to the hotel, saying goodbye, the flight home. I was a changed young man. The music had transformed me. I had to learn how to do that. My new teacher had taught me a lesson without saying a word. Five years before, at Booker Washington, I was the only student in Mr. E. L. Pender's after-school music theory classroom, and I went from there to Quincy Jones in New York City. *Damn!*

MEMPHIS—Late fall 1961— ♪ 11

In addition to exploring the musical world around me, I was still keeping up with my educational priorities. After deciding against a full scholarship to Beloit College and determining that UCLA was too far away and too expensive, I applied to Indiana University Music School in Bloomington. Hoagy Carmichael, one of my musical heroes and the composer of "Stardust," "Georgia on My Mind," and "The Nearness of You," some of my favorite ballads, had attended Indiana.

In order to increase my chances of being admitted, I took music theory classes after school. Professor Pender was the choral director at Booker Washington, and like the generous band directors, Mr. Pender made an invaluable contribution to my musical understanding. The very act of experimenting and exploring with my newfound knowledge led me to change one note of the scale from a major third to a minor third, which ultimately led to the second chord change in "Green Onions."

The theory lessons taught me the rules established by the masters. Knowing the laws and operating principles of chords and melodies gave me the confidence and tools to experiment and forge new ground in jazz, R & B, and classical. Once I understood the rules, I felt free to change them, and that unleashed a flow of ideas in my head.

Late in the fall of 1961, I arrived at Memphis's Christian Brothers College to take the entrance exam for Indiana University. Leaving my father in the car, I crossed the sidewalk and stepped onto a long, adobe brick archway lined with apses and niches.

My dad was also intimidated by the building. Black people didn't go into buildings like that. Memphis, the most segregated of southern cities, had no black students at Christian Brothers College at the time. Dad sat in the car outside. Countless times my dad waited patiently in the car—whether I was studying at the library or playing a gig at a club in the Arkansas back country. Dad was there for me.

Walking alone, I forced myself to put one foot in front of the other and finally arrived at the door of a cavernous hall. The room was one and the same as the hall in the movie *The Blind Side*. Not only was I the only student; I was literally the only person in the room, except for the person administering the exam.

After a terse exchange with the administrator, I was seated and handed the exam materials. I looked at my answer sheet and felt that my shirt was too tight. The plaid button-up that I had worn a thousand times was pulling at the middle. *Why, of all times, am I now concerned with my shirt?* I lost my focus. Suddenly, unexpectedly, all the knowledge from my weeks of preparation on various subjects went missing. Vanished. So did my ability to recall. I panicked. I spent fifteen minutes of time I did not have just pulling myself together. This was not a music test. The subjects were the stuff of college exams that I had practiced in study hall when nothing mattered. It became a test of my will. The bell rang. I submitted the answer sheet and walked quickly to Dad's car. Knowingly, lovingly, Dad never said, "How'd you do?"

I had no sense of the likelihood of my passing such a test. I had done some preexam study—generic, comprehensive college entrance exam–type drills, but they had done nothing for my confidence. I don't remember any single aspect of the exam, just being in that huge room all alone.

Around the time I completed my entrance exam for IU, I began working in the Satellite house band, playing sessions nearly every evening after school.

MEMPHIS—1961— ♪ 2

In November 1961, I had been called over to Satellite to play organ on a song by William Bell called "You Don't Miss Your Water." Chips Moman was at the console, and he was also the producer. Rufus Thomas's son Marvell played piano, Ron Capone from Pepper Tanner Studios played drums, and Lewie Steinberg was on bass.

Nervous and uncomfortable for the session, I sat at Satellite's Hammond M-3 organ, isolated in the deep, dark room. The organ was beyond the piano on the slanted theater floor, in front of where the screen would be and visible from the control room window.

The sounds from the instrument were pumped to the men's restroom, to a speaker that was placed on the floor next to the latrine. Heavily tiled, the room's echo was miked and sent back to the control room, where it was mixed into the recording, giving the organ a reverberant sound.

Marvell started the song. There was no printed music, but his self-assured lead was easy to follow. The song was in an easy key for the organ, F major. I sat out the first verse but came in on the second, answering William's entry phrases, which seemed to need repeating, in a call-and-response between the two of us. "I kept you crying"—organ refrain—"Sad and blue"—organ refrain—and so forth until the song ended, "You don't miss your water till your well runs dry."

No sooner had it started than it was over. The recording seemed to take no time at all. *What happened in so short a time?* Riding on the music, we drifted to another world. The three-quarter-time track was our ship, the chord changes and melodies were our sails, and William's testimony was our purpose.

When we returned, we filed into the control room for the playback. The smiles on Jim Stewart's and William's faces said it all. We had recorded a hit—on the first take, no less. So much chance, work, and talent had converged in a magic moment. "You Don't Miss Your Water" became Stax's first southern soul classic song, and the first indication there might be substantially more "water" in Stax Records' "well."

BLOOMINGTON, IN—Spring 1962—♪ 1

In the spring of 1962, my dad drove my mother and me from Memphis to IU in Bloomington, Indiana, in our 1955 Buick and checked us into the Van Orman Hotel with an Esso gas credit card.

It was the first time any of us had ever checked into a hotel. We slept and ate next to wealthy white folks for the first time.

Growing up black in the Deep South ensures your awareness of your inequality. What you cannot do, who you cannot be, how successful you cannot become. You take on a smallness of stature, an unwillingness to overcome obstacles. Worse than fear, because you can't justify your existence, death bears little consequence. As soon as you are treated as an equal, however, the sky turns a brighter shade of blue. That gnawing feeling of lethargy disappears, an unfamiliar sense of well-being takes hold. A new energy is found.

The next day, I went to audition for the jury that would decide if I could enter the school. My music sight-reading skills were lacking, short of acceptable. For years, I had fooled people with my ability to play and re-create something I had heard only once. Now I had to look at the page and read by sight. My entire previous experience consisted of writing out a few lead sheets for Stax Records to get copyrights. But my jurors saw potential and took a chance on me. For that, I am grateful to them.

In Memphis, the producer of "Fool in Love" was a white, rockabilly-influenced guitarist named Lincoln Wayne "Chips" Moman. The owner of the record company was a bank teller named Jim Stewart. A country fiddler based in Brunswick, Tennessee, Stewart's ambition was to record and release records. Chips was turning the bank teller on to a few of the local groups around Memphis.

At sixteen, I found myself alone with Chips in a thrown-together recording studio. He held his guitar, and I sat at the Hammond M-3 organ. The M-3 was the smaller, lesser version of Hammond organs. The studio had yet to obtain a Hammond B-3. "Play something for me," Chips said. I played "Slumpety Slump," a tune I'd learned onstage with Ben Branch at Currie's Club Tropicana.

On the organ, I played the same guitar line that Ben's guitarist, Clarence, used to get everybody up on their feet for our first song every night.

Chips watched me from the corner of his eye, his lit cigarette hanging loosely from his lip. He played a few choice licks on his guitar, a cross between rockabilly and blues—clean, sharp toned, the notes of an experienced master. Real southern riverboat guitar. Chips was one of those people who moved up in the world, by hook or by crook—mostly the latter. He wasn't lacking in talent or style. Something about him said there was a derringer in his bag. In the end, he got the best of me.

MEMPHIS—1961— ♪ 9

I was just a wet-behind-the-ears kid, in a room with the equivalent of an experienced boxer who had won championships. Chips was seven years older than me, and he got his nickname from his penchant for gambling. He would become the producer for Carla Thomas, Rufus Thomas, the Box Tops, B. J. Thomas, Aretha Franklin, James Carr, Waylon Jennings, Bobby Womack, Merrilee Rush, Willie Nelson, and Elvis Presley.

Chips's uncanny survival instincts included the ability to sense what cards a man might be holding on the other side of the table. I was too naïve to understand that I was going into a business situation. My concern was with making music. Had I understood songwriting, publishing, and copyright, or known that Chips was recording the performance for commercial release, I would never have shown him the tune.

On my next recording session, I didn't get to play the simple blues changes that were going through my mind, and I didn't get to formally meet Prince Conley even though we were in the same room. He was stationed near the top of the theater behind a baffle, and I was way down at the bottom in front of the control room. What I remember most about the session was that I was playing hooky from school and that it would pay me all of fifteen dollars!

I was enthralled listening to the song, and when time came to play, I wasn't ready. As if someone else was going to play the solo. But I quickly got my act together and made the fastest fifteen dollars I ever was paid in my life.

I was still a recording neophyte. I should have been flattered, but I didn't understand why they didn't want me to play in the body of the song, only perform the solo, and no more. It seemed strange to me then, but in retrospect I realize I was given a premier spot to play. The song was "I'm Going Home" by Prince Conley, which Charlie Musselwhite later told me was regarded as an unsung gem by blues pundits. It has been called a "cryptic pearl" by some soul music stalkers and diggers.

MEMPHIS—1962— ♪ 7

For years, most Sundays, in the morning, I would be in church...without a doubt. Since I started working at Stax, however, that pattern started to fall off, and it felt strange. We were the only people in town who weren't in church—and we should have been! There were no cars on the street, and there was a kind of lonely, hollow feeling to the neighborhood around the studio. The record shop was open, but it seemed sacrilegious. Satellite had become my new priority, and my parents had given it their blessing, as had everyone in the community who had heard the music we'd been making.

On one Sunday afternoon in 1962, Billy Lee Riley packed up and left the studio. Riley was an ex–Sun Records rockabilly artist who was trying to revive his career. After he left, the four musicians who had been hired to play on his session were free to utilize the recording studio for the rest of the afternoon. Al Jackson Jr. was on drums, Lewie Steinberg on bass, Steve Cropper on guitar, and me on Hammond M-3 organ.

I started picking out a phrase on the piano that I had been playing at a club out on Parkway with my little combo with Jerome Miller on drums and Errol Thomas on bass. I was playing the melody on the organ. It was like I was subconsciously talking with my fingers when playing the melody or solo line. I didn't really have much awareness of what was going on; it was very relaxed. The song was a slow blues that I made up trying to imitate Ray Charles's organ style. The others joined in, and Jim Stewart hit the record button.

As we played, I really liked the sound the organ was putting out. It was low and gritty coming out of the speaker between my legs. I hadn't played this organ very much, just once before on the William Bell session, where I used mostly high vibrato sounds in answer to his vocal phrases. I never knew you could make an organ sound like this before. It was so funky, so growly, and yet so clean and clear. Lewie started a walking bass line, just like he did in the clubs, and Steve started playing guitar chinks on the backbeat with Al's snare. It started to flow and feel good.

Jim thought the cut turned out great. So much so that he wanted to put it out as a single. All agreed. But this new 45-rpm single record, "Behave Yourself," as named by Jim's sister, Mrs. Axton, needed a B side. Cropper suggested I show them my other song. "Booker, what's that little tune you've been playing on piano?"

In my music theory class with Mr. Pender, I thought, *What if the contrapuntal rules applied to a twelve-bar blues pattern? What if the bottom bass note went up while the top note of the triad went down, like in the Bach fugues and cantatas?* Sitting at my mother's piano

68

at home, I had played F, A flat, B flat, F—using the contrapuntal chord triad structural rules from eighteenth-century Baroque Bach. A little swing and blues changes, and the song was born.

I moved from the piano to the Hammond, since I had played it on the previous song. Jim Stewart hit the record button.

During this second recording, I started speaking on the keyboard with my right hand—a simple musical exposition—a sentence in sparse musical notes. It became the first solo of the song. Then I returned to the original twelve-bar pattern to use as accompaniment and let Steve have a guitar solo. He played an aggressive, simple exposition also—so perfect! All the while Lewie and Al laid down a relentless rhythm based on the original phrase.

Al Jackson's drums were the cohesive element. Lewie's bass and Steve's guitar played the deceptively simple rhythm with a relaxed magic that created a new sound and a new groove that became one of the first instances of the Memphis sound.

We finished the cut, and everyone rushed into the control room, excited to hear what we had done!

When Lewie Steinberg heard the playback, he said, "Man, that's so funky it smells like onions! Funky onions! We oughta name it 'Funky Onions'!" Mrs. Axton came back to the studio, heard the playback and the proposed title, and exclaimed, "You can't name a song 'Funky Onions' in this day and time; why not call it 'Green Onions'?" Everyone agreed.

When time came to give the record an artist name, Al Jackson spoke up.

"We gotta call the group Booker T. and..." He looked out the back window at Chips Moman's British Leyland MG parked out in the lot. "The MGs! That's it—Booker T. and the MGs!"

With my high school diploma, I was free as a bird, about to make a beeline for college. My newfound knowledge of music was a double-sided coin: preparing me for the tasks ahead at Indiana while also establishing a bond with Memphis as a more sophisticated, capable songwriter, session man, and producer. So in reality, a continuing link was constructed between Indiana and Memphis.

But before I bade farewell to Memphis, there was one more significant person I had to meet.

CHAPTER 7

These Arms of Mine

MEMPHIS—Summer 1962—♪ 12

I stepped outside the studio to get some air and spotted a big man gently and meticulously unloading suitcases and instruments onto the street from a vehicle parked at the curb. When I was ready to go back in, I took my seat at the organ to find the session winding to a close.

As I prepared to go, a man sat down right next to me and started singing "These Arms of Mine." It was the guy who had been unloading all the luggage and instruments. He was the driver and gofer for the next band setting up in the studio, Johnny Jenkins and the Pinetoppers, a group from Georgia. Although I hadn't played a note on the organ, the driver, whose named turned out to be Otis, started in right on key in B flat, as if he had perfect pitch. I knew he was special.

Instantly, I got lost in the emotion of the song, being that close to his voice and him emoting like he did, similar to what happened when I played for Mahalia Jackson. I came to myself and started playing chords in B flat. All dictated by his voice. He had an intuitive understanding of music. Beyond the limits of classroom education. It was a moment so colorful that I want to paint it brown for earthy. That's the color that comes to mind when I remember those moments.

Then, I had to go. I hadn't counted on meeting a man of such musical sensibilities that he would change my life. I had a regular gig at the Flamingo Room, a commitment I had sacrificed to obtain, so I got up to leave. I had Otis Redding's emotional, anxiety-filled, angst-ridden pleadings still in my head, and my heart. I had made a new friend. He was twenty, and I was seventeen.

Regardless of age, though, none of the singers I worked with on Beale or heard on the radio sang with the emotional power or had the melisma of Otis Redding. To have a musical force that strong and so physically close affected me. There was just so much feeling and power in his delivery.

Otis's heartfelt approach fit right in with our simple, no-frills regimen. I walked to my car, pulled myself in, and drove to Beale and Hernando and stepped onstage. But I was different now.

Meanwhile, Otis drove back to Georgia as he had driven to Memphis, a hired hand, but he had moved from the back seat to the driver's seat, so to speak.

MEMPHIS to BLOOMINGTON—August 1962— ♪ *3*

I pointed my car in a different direction. It was a route I came to know like the back of my hand. Every turn, every hill, every stretch. I also knew all the farmhouses, all the bridges, but not the hotels. I never stopped. Always the four-hundred-mile stretch, pulling over only for gas.

First by Greyhound bus, then by copying the route in a series of cars I drove. Starting with my little '61 Ford Fairlane, every Buick my dad owned, and ending with my own '66 Buick Special. The same road that took me to school as a boy, Porter Junior High, B. T. Washington, and church, Mt. Olive, took me to my new school, Indiana University. Wellington turned into Thomas Street and headed north toward Kentucky.

I drove that route so often that I stopped looking at the familiar waypoints: Currie's Club Tropicana, Millington Air Force Base. And as I paid less attention to the scenery, more music began floating into my mind. One song after the other. "Soul Dressing," "I Forgot to Be Your Lover." Whatever the muse decided to serve up. By the time I got to Bloomington, I had a plethora of musical ideas that had accumulated from the trip.

I stayed true to the Greyhound bus route because it was open twenty-four hours and I could fudge a cheap meal by ordering toast and filling the two slices with jelly or mayonnaise from the counter. I knew every Greyhound stop and station—Millington, Covington, Ripley, and Dyersburg in Tennessee were stops. The next station was Paducah in Kentucky. I would try to time my appetite to be hungry when I got to a station.

BLOOMINGTON, IN—Fall 1962— ♪ 7

No sooner had I set foot on the Bloomington campus than I got a call from Arne, leader of Arnie and the Soul Brothers. Ironically, Arne was Jewish, but his band was called the Soul Brothers. Arne had the fraternity party scene on lockdown at IU, and I was immediately in the band. There was Stan on sax, Lawrence on trumpet, Bob on drums, me on keys, and Arne on guitar.

The group was not the MGs musically but was equal to some

other bands I had played with in Memphis. They were well established on campus, playing a lot of gigs. And it was quick, easy money that really helped with tuition and expenses. "Green Onions" sounded different with Arne's group. No one would ever play it like the MGs. Other songs, covers of the day, were fun with Arne's band.

I was moved by the historic old campus and startled by the modern architecture of Teter Quadrangle, where I stopped to drop my bags and take a quick peek at my room. I opened the door and was greeted by the oddest character. He looked at me as though I had invaded his private sanctuary. Big, surprised eyes told me I had the key to the wrong room. As far as I knew, the dorms tended to pair students of similar race, and my new roommate appeared never to have laid eyes on skin black as mine. I for one had never laid eyes on skin white as his, so the mistake was verified without a word. Mingling races was OK with me, since I had associated with whites at Stax in Memphis.

He was studying at his desk by the door, glaring at me through huge, thick eyeglasses. He was dark-haired and studious, a collared shirt and open IU sweater draping his thin frame. The next second, I was distracted. My gaze was diverted to the large window on the other side of the small room, cracked slightly open at the top. Inserted into the window from outside the room was a thick black insulated wire that stretched out and extended across the middle of the room, ending underneath my new roommate's desk.

This spectacle stopped me in my tracks. With my bags still in the hallway, I found the nearest exit to the street. I scanned the building and located my room. Sure enough, there was a black wire stretched all the way over and across the access road from Teter Quadrangle to Wright Quadrangle, a large dorm, up to a room on the fourth floor. Cars and trucks were driving underneath it. Unbelievable.

I had been paired with an inventive, unusual young man who had rigged some kind of communication network with an equally unusual student. I was sure we were mismatched. I went straight to the resident counselor, leaving my bags in the hall and my car on the access road. *Did she know who I had been assigned as a roommate? Did she know him? Had she met him? Was he clinically insane, and had I been paired with him because no one else would room with him? Had she seen the wire?* The counselor gave me a look that said there was no hope. All the rooms were assigned. Unless I wanted to try for a hotel in town. First day on campus. Frankly, I was probably spoiled. My parents had indulged me with my own room all my life, and I wasn't looking forward to sharing such a small space with a deranged roommate.

A number of weeks passed. I spent all my time outside the room, studying, meeting new people, and hanging out in the dorm's common room. I shared the lounge's piano with a fellow from South Bend, Indiana, named Dick Short. Sleeping was the only activity I did in my room, and for a while my roommate and I managed not to step on each other's toes. Or wires.

At last the counselor informed me of an opportunity to move to another room. I accepted without any questions or qualifications. My new roommate also had strange habits. Every night he used massive amounts of skin care products with scents so strong that the smell became unbearable. He had a mirror at his desk and sat for hours primping his face and eyes, gussying up his skin with cleaners and oils. We had a distant relationship. Polite and respectful, but we didn't speak much. At night, I came to the room in my pj's and robe from the shower and climbed into the top bunk, leaving him to sit with his cosmetics.

MUSIC BUILDING, IU CAMPUS—1962— ♪ 1

My trip to the music building was a much better experience. It was a circular structure with floors and floors of practice rooms and a huge music library underneath, which was available on a twenty-four-hour basis. In other words, heaven on earth. My first instructor, Buddy Baker, was an angel on earth. A young man just starting a family, he was the protégé of the famous Professor Thomas Beversdorf, the head of Indiana's trombone faculty. Walking into Buddy's office made me feel so comfortable, I knew I had arrived and the next four years were going to be great. He showed me pictures of his wife and children, and I too fell in love with them. He handled the photos with so much care, I felt like it was my family too.

Getting serious, Mr. Baker picked up a trombone and instructed me to get mine. The training was going to be rigorous. I was doing many things incorrectly, but time would fix them. Mainly, I had to develop what Buddy called an embouchure, strength in the muscles surrounding the upper and lower lips, so for days I was walking around looking like an idiot with my lips pursed all the time.

For no reason, I took a detour leaving the music building— wandering the campus. Thought I might take a walk down East Seventh Street to downtown Bloomington. There was an inconspicuous dark brown door down the steps leading to a side entrance to the huge auditorium in the middle of the campus. Boldly, I opened the door and went inside. There were rows of empty chairs behind music stands facing a conductor's podium. I should have read the campus map.

I had found the band room under the auditorium. I was so not ready for what was ahead. Dr. Ronald Gregory was like the Otis Redding of Indiana University, except he had a cadre of little Dr. Gregorys arrive at school early to whip the band into shape before he appeared. In shape we got, and appear he did.

I swear, we were in better shape than the football team (who were the only other folks to arrive on campus two weeks early). The drills started early in the morning. On the football field, with no instruments. It took me a while. All the freshmen were sucking wind. *Aren't we going to play music?* Yes, but not until we were able to pull our knees up to our chests as we marched across the field at a breakneck cadence, at the same time staying in line and paying attention for hours.

Days later we sat down in the band room with our instruments to learn the music with the assistant director. It was a relief just to be sitting down.

Dr. Gregory appeared, smartly dressed and smiling. Looking everyone in the eye, expecting everything to be perfect, first time. When disappointed, Dr. Gregory tended to look away, which felt worse to us than getting chewed out by his assistants. The band sounded incredible on and off the field.

After football season, we became a concert band, and I had some of the best musical experiences of my life under the direction of Dr. Ronald Gregory. Symphonic music, operatic music, and finally, big band jazz, my favorite. I was fortunate to play trombone in the jazz band alongside talents like Randy Brecker (trumpet) and Jamey Aebersold (sax). Many of the charts were by David Baker, Indiana's famous jazz trombonist/cellist/professor.

Jazz band rehearsals and classes were set at reasonable hours— 2:40 in the afternoon and such, unlike music theory class times.

I had music theory class at seven in the morning. Five days a week. Getting up that early was crazy. Since I was in tenth grade, my shift at the clubs had been 10:00 p.m.–4:00 a.m., Thursday through Monday, so my body clock was that of a night owl. And now, getting up before dawn, I had to walk, sometimes through the snow, to get to the building. You couldn't be late because they were blind drills. The instructors would sit behind an upright piano and play something, and you had to write it down. If you were late, you missed out and got an F or a D. You couldn't get a friend to tape-record it for you. This was the requirement for the bachelor of music education degree I was seeking.

The program was so challenging and grueling that you could be assured if you ever met someone who graduated and got the music degree from Indiana, they were likely to be a cut above the field.

MEMPHIS—Fall 1962— ♪ 7

One of the first sessions I played as I began commuting to Memphis was William Bell's "Any Other Way." I played piano, widely spaced chords that William answered with his lyrical phrases. The chords were evocative of those I had learned listening to Horace Silver play piano. "Please Help Me, I'm Falling" was William's cover of the Hank Locklin country song, which featured a Floyd Kramer–style high piano part. On William's record, I played organ, and the fills were reminiscent of Floyd Kramer.

"Green Onions" was originally issued in May 1962 on the Volt label (a subsidiary of Stax Records) as the B side of "Behave Yourself" on Volt 102; it was quickly reissued as the A side of Stax 127.

Steve Cropper took it to Reuben Washington, the drive-time DJ on the Memphis station WLOK. He gave it a spin and said, "That's pretty catchy!" Then he played it again—but this time live on air. The phones lit up. Everyone wanted to know what this record was and where they could get it.

"Green Onions" entered the *Billboard* Hot 100 the week ending August 11, 1962, and peaked at number three the week ending September 29, 1962. The single also made it to number one on the soul singles chart for four nonconsecutive weeks—an unusual occurrence in that, on the soul singles chart, "Green Onions" fell in and out of the top spot three times. "Green Onions" was ranked number 183 on *Rolling Stone*'s list of the five hundred greatest songs of all time.

With the success of "Green Onions," it was decided we should record Stax's first ever LP to capitalize on the song's success. The first attempt was an almost exact cover of Dave Baby Cortez's "Rinky Dink." Same key, except I played the organ an octave lower. Al Jackson, probably on his second-only Stax session, replicated the drum fills from Dave's record exactly. Steve did the same with the rhythm: *chink, chink, chink.* I guess we just didn't know any better and should have come up with something more original.

There was something of a residue that I picked up in the air. I felt a hint of resentment from the MGs and other Stax people that I had walked away from the whole thing just as our record hit number one on the R & B chart in September. I had left in mid-August for Indiana, just after the record was released, and it was enjoying phenomenal success, which I was ignoring. I didn't want anything to interfere with my obtaining a music education and a college degree like my parents and grandfather wanted. It was my legacy—in stark contrast to the designs of the record company and my bandmates.

When the Mar-Keys record hit big, they rented a van and traveled the country in support of the record, and Stax fully expected the MGs and me to do the same. Only an idiot or a maverick would even think of doing anything different. But there I was, already out of place, taking music courses at Indiana for four weeks running. *Will I quit now? Now that "Green Onions" is number three in the nation?* Nobody had the nerve, or the gall, to make that case to me directly, but they managed to make me feel like I was an idiot not to be at least considering it. In spite of the conflict, I left each Sunday session and drove all night back to Bloomington.

The whole *Green Onions* album was recorded this way—with a contentious feeling between me and everyone else. But the music got better as we went along. "I Got a Woman," the Ray Charles song cover, got a drum intro from Al Jackson and a new unique key as well as a little more life in the arrangement. We were starting to get the hang of this song-cover thing.

But the whole affair seemed rushed to me. I quietly felt, *What's the big hurry here?* I was not at all savvy to the music business strategy and didn't understand that we needed to get the album out soon to capitalize on the hit song because *this may never happen again.* They must have cursed me. I didn't quit school. My ears were burning, but I knew I needed the training. Back at the Stax studio, on "I Got a Woman," I was struggling to keep the tempo. I closed my eyes and saw Ray Charles at his electric piano, shoulders all hunched up to his neck, smiling at the effort it took to play the rhythm to this song in time, not missing a note or a beat, with such precision, every note exactly in place, singing at the same time! And here I was, couldn't even play it in time. Not only did I not know anything about the music business but I was also no professional organ player. *Where are my original ideas when I am soloing? And where are the original songs? Why are we recording other people's songs?* I had a long way to go. And I knew it. Back in the car. Back to school.

BLOOMINGTON, IN—Fall 1962— ♪ 3

Liberal Indiana was a breath of fresh air compared to conservative Memphis. Restaurants and buses were not segregated, and you could sit where you pleased in the classrooms. White people were generally friendly, and there was opportunity. I felt free to regard myself and my fellow blacks as whole people whose liberties weren't compromised on a daily basis. Not social underlings, undeserving of society's best. But the line was thin, and blacks ate together and had separate social groups.

I missed Memphis. My family. The barbeque. Pizza, which I'd never had before, was all over Bloomington and became the sub-stitute. Everyone in Indiana ate pizza. With beer. I gained twenty pounds. These, however, were the least of my problems.

MEMPHIS—1962— ♪ *12*

Shortly before and during this period, Isaac Hayes began stopping by the studio. It was after I replaced Joe Hall and Marvell Thomas on piano. Frequently, like a phantom, Isaac would quietly appear, standing behind me when I played. If I didn't look to the side, I didn't know he was there. I began to hear my triad placements and chord voicing on songs like "Hold On, I'm Comin'."

A man of amazing aptitude, skill, and patience, Isaac took over the piano seat by looking over my shoulder. I started moving to organ when Isaac was around—whichever one he wasn't playing. We became a keyboard team. On "When Something Is Wrong," by Sam & Dave, we switched roles, with me playing organ. It was intuitive between us.

After the *Green Onions* LP, we decided to start recording originals. I was excited and thrilled, and we knew this would take more time than *Green Onions*. At this time, the pattern was set where I would bring in the core, original idea of the song, and the other band members would add their contributions.

The chords to "Soul Dressing" came to me on the highway while driving back to Memphis from Bloomington. The melody came just as I sat down to the M-3 organ and played the chords. Because Satellite Studios had not yet obtained a Hammond B-3, the tone was very basic and thin. Al played an intriguing but complex and elusive rhythm throughout.

"We need a break somewhere, Jones," Al insisted.

"Let's just play the song through from the head," I replied.

Just before Steve's solo, it became apparent Al was right. A four-bar break introduced Steve's solo.

Steve played like his heart had been broken, and sweet "Soul Dressing" became an instrumental blues over jazz changes.

When time came for my break, I tried to do the same thing Steve had done. I went for broke—having no idea what I would play or how it would turn out. It was a relief to get through those four bars and arrive at the gentler C section, where the chords were smoother and just skated along. We returned to the original theme to take the song home, and it was quite the emotional roller-coaster ride for me.

After first hearing the Beatles' "I Want to Hold Your Hand" on a jukebox at the IU Commons, I monopolized the box, encircling it and draping my arms over it, and played the song until I ran out of money. It was the first time I heard the Beatles, and I would never approach music the same again. I had also just heard Philip Upchurch's "You Can't Sit Down," and it too had mesmerized me.

I rushed back to Memphis.

"Can't Be Still" was the first time Cropper and I played a *melody* together. Then we turned around and played the *rhythm* together— just the reverse of what we always had done. We became a little two-man rhythm machine on this hectic little tune. Just like the title, it was really hard to stay still when we played it, and we had to hold back physically just listening to Al's beat and Duck's bass line.

A guitar song in the true sense of the word, "Plum Nellie" (which foreshadowed "Melting Pot" with its organ swells) was our first excursion into sound experimentation. The elements of our other songs were there: distinguishable bass line, solid groove, and twelve-bar blues. However, "Plum Nellie" was built on the old Bill Justis guitar tradition, made to make you get out on the dance floor and strut your stuff. Steve played the melody on the low strings.

We used standard song form: two verses, solos, with a horn ensemble/breakdown, go home. My solo was very percussive; I tapped the organ like a drum—bouncing and dancing. The horn ensemble (I overdubbed trombone with Wayne Jackson on trumpet) featured long, unison E notes that segued into guitar trills.

Then, like lightning, the last guitar trill exploded! A fleet, acrobatic, musical stunt you have to hear to believe. Listen closely. As if the notes left the fretboard, past Steve's hands, up into the air, in a blinding flash. A tour de force. Not to be repeated. Steve was never able to replicate that lick. This is how Steve Cropper became Steve Cropper. We were lucky the tape was rolling. After the take, Al Jackson said he "plumb nearly fell over his dick" when Steve played that lick. Hence the title "Plum Nellie."

KNOXVILLE, TN—1963— ♪ 10

Lewie Steinberg's brand-new white 1962 Cadillac El Dorado with the pointed tail fins was teeter-tottering on the landing three-fourths of the way up the steps leading to the Knoxville Coliseum, itself brand-new. Passing concertgoers gawked at the car, laughing and gesturing. Maybe they thought it was a promotion gimmick for the show.

Lewie, ignoring warnings from the stage crew to back out the way he had headed in, had surged the big car forward to exit the loading ramp, plunging into the entrance area where the audience enters the building. I was speechless, frozen.

The massive steps, built in groups of landings, imposed a rude halt on the long car at the second landing, and it balanced there in the middle of its gut with the engine still running and the lights on.

Lewie was arrested and taken to the Knoxville jail for being abrasive with the police, booked on reckless driving and driving under the influence. With less than an hour before the show, there was no time to go downtown to bail him out.

Looking down from the equipment landing stage, I grimaced, wondering how I would get through the show without a bass player. I had backed my own car down the ramp after unloading, and the events of the next few minutes were shocking.

We played the show for the dubious crowd, with only three pieces, me playing the bass parts on the lower keyboard of the organ. It was a natural swap out because at each song's inception, my left-hand notes were the indication to the bass player of what he should be playing. No one mentioned we were missing the bass player, but the dangling Cadillac they saw on the way in to the show alerted the large, wary crowd.

It was our last performance with Lewie Steinberg. Steve Cropper had wanted to introduce his friend and bass player Duck Dunn from the Mar-Keys into the band for quite some time, and this last-straw blunder by Lewie was the perfect chance.

And so, as luck would have it, the fate of the man who played the great, rock-solid bass line on "Green Onions" would be left dangling, like his car, at the inception of our career. Unfortunately, Lewie was left to his own devices that night in Knoxville, and Duck Dunn took over as bass player with Booker T. & the MGs.

None of us went downtown to bail Lewie out or discussed it.

Still, the guilt for not getting Lewie out of jail ate at me. I should have driven straight to the police station and made bail for him with the money from the gig. The next morning, however, I drove back to Memphis, leaving Lewie in Knoxville.

Mama, me,
and Daddy
(Artist Collection)

On the stoop of
my childhood
home on
Polk Street
(Artist Collection)

My childhood buddies.
From left: Greg, Rudy, me,
and Skipper
(Artist Collection)

My dear mother, Lurline Jones
(Artist Collection)

Dad's classroom at Booker T. Washington Hig]
(Artist Collection)

First promo photo of the MGs, in Memp]
at the first Holiday Inn: me, Steve Croppe
Duck Dunn, Al Jackson, Jr. *(Courtesy of
Stax Museum of American Soul Music)*

My sister, Gwendolyn Golden, in her green 1954 Buick convertible
(Artist Collection)

My next-door neighbor, Mrs. Humes, in her garden
(Artist Collection)

My Edith Street childhood home
(Artist Collection)

Looking into the future with my bandmates
(Courtesy of Stax Museum of American Soul Music)

Memphis boy keeping time *(Courtesy of Stax Museum of American Soul Music)*

On the south side of Chicago *(Courtesy of Stax Museum of American Soul Music)*

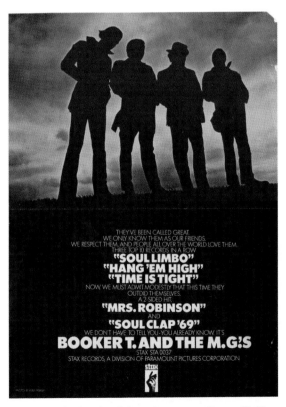

Dusk on the bank of the Mississippi River *(*Billboard *magazine)*

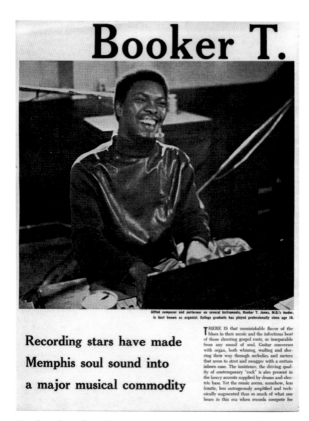

Booker T.

Gifted composer and performer on several instruments, Booker T. Jones, M.G.'s leader, is best known as organist. College graduate has played professionally since age 14.

Recording stars have made Memphis soul sound into a major musical commodity

THERE IS that unmistakable flavor of the blues in their music and the infectious beat of those shouting gospel roots, so inseparable from any sound of soul. Guitar converses with organ, both whining, wailing and slurring their way through melodies and meters that seem to strut and swagger with a certain inborn ease. The insistence, the driving quality of contemporary "rock" is also present in the heavy accents supplied by drums and electric bass. Yet the music seems, somehow, less frantic, less outrageously amplified and technically augmented than so much of what one hears in this era when records compete for

Studio shot for *Ebony* magazine, April 1969 *(Ebony Magazine)*

Onstage with my Ibanez guitar *(Artist Collection)*

At the Winding Way Ranch in Malibu *(Gems / Getty Images)*

Skeeter and me, Malibu,
California *(Artist Collection)*

Jules, the boys, and me on the Culver City lot *(Artist Collection)*

Pouring concrete forms for my Comptche house *(Artist Collection)*

CHAPTER 8
Higher and Higher

CHICAGO, IL—Spring 1965—♪ 9

In the spring of 1963, the current formation of Booker T. & the MGs—Lewie Steinberg (bass), Steve Cropper (guitar), Howard Grimes (drums), and myself (organ)—piled into a rented station wagon and drove to Chicago to play a show for E. Rodney Jones, a disc jockey for WVON. The compensation? Airplay for "Green Onions." Howard, filling in for Al Jackson, received road pay.

The Regal Theater, on the south side, with its velvet drapes and plush carpet, was the city's most important venue for blacks and a sight to behold. Booker T. & the MGs opened the show. The main attraction was Jackie Wilson. I was among the many who were excited for his show. His songs, "Doggin' Around" and "Lonely Teardrops" and his stage energy were legendary, and I was going to be within a few feet of the singer who had replaced Clyde McPhatter of the Drifters. The spectacle I saw that night forever changed my perception of what a live R & B show could or should be.

From the moment Jackie Wilson faced the stage, he became the definition of electricity. He lit up, both literally and figuratively. You could *feel* the energy coming from him. Not Sammy Davis Jr., not James Brown, not Prince, not even Elvis Presley could have held the stage with him. And the *women*. The women went crazy. The ample crew was ready for the onslaught. But it was to no avail. They were going to get their hands on Jackie Wilson, and they did. When he spinned, split, and dropped effortlessly to his knees, a throng, a gaggle of females swarmed the stage, ripping what sweat-drenched clothes were still on his back. It was a melee. He left the stage with only his pants and shoes.

And the music. The *music* was captivating, hypnotic. The dynamic band and horn section was seriously kickin'. When he broke into "Baby Workout" at the end of the show, I had to dance. Backstage. Even the laconic Howard Grimes had a big smile on his face and moved his feet a little. I became even more of a fan. I was a freshman at Indiana, and the guys drove back through Indiana to drop me off at school.

Four years later, Jackie made "Higher and Higher," and it was perfect in every way, but my imagination presented me with another vision of the song. Slower, a loping bass line, straight eighths instead of triplets, with melody and lyrics the same. In California, I bought some cheap studio time for a demo session and hired John Robinson, Paul Jackson Jr., and Chris Ethridge to record my version of the song. My wife, Priscilla, and her sister, Rita, came with me and sang background parts to my vocal.

LOS ANGELES, CA—1974— ♪ 8

A few years later, the arrangement on this demo of "Higher and Higher" prompted Rita to ask me to do an arrangement of the song for her debut A&M Records album, and the record got extensive airplay and sales. Rita's vocal rendition, as well as the arrangement, was an exact copy of my demo.

Rita's producer, David Anderle, made use of the laissez-faire approach to record producing. He called the musicians and put the other elements together. I directed the musicians and vocalists, chose the keys, set the tempos, and wrote out the arrangements on the score for the strings and horns. I arranged the background vocals and wrote the chord charts and played piano and organ.

The arrangements had to be on the copyists' desks by 7:00 a.m. for a 10:00 a.m. session, so I was on the road from Malibu by six. There was a boy standing in the alley behind Wallach's Music City at Sunset and Vine to receive scores from arrangers and rush them upstairs to the waiting teams of copyists. You couldn't leave your car in the alley and go into Wallach's because it didn't open until ten. The music was delivered to the studio. I waited the hours out in the lounge, consuming inhumane amounts of coffee and doughnuts.

I wasn't offered producer's credits, but as a compromise, I received two deal points and label credit for my arrangements.

NORTHERN CALIFORNIA, Highway 101—1974— ♪ 5

In the fall of '74, in our orange Datsun station wagon, traveling north on 101 past Santa Rosa, eight hours into the drive from Malibu to Mendocino, Priscilla, who was driving, turned to me. "I can sing circles around Rita. I've been singing since I was twelve. Why haven't you cut a song like that on me?"

"It's not about who's the better singer," I said.

"Then, what is it about? I can hit notes she can't even hear."

"David is Rita's producer, not me."

"Why don't I have a deal?"

"Priscilla, please."

"Who are you f—ing?"

"Please, Priscilla."

"You're f—ing Rita, aren't you? You're f—ing her at the studio."

"Priscilla!"

"Who else are you f—ing?"

I thought, *Maybe she thinks I'm being unfaithful because I met her by cheating on Gigi with her.* Or worse, *Maybe she's projecting guilt from some infidelity of her own.*

The argument escalated beyond the point of no return. Driving in the dark on our way back from Malibu to our Northern California ranch, I was quiet, riding in the passenger seat during a lull in the fighting. I noticed that Priscilla missed the turn to go northwest on 128 at Cloverdale and continued north on 101. I sat up in my seat.

In silence, we drove another thirty minutes. This type of thing had happened before, when she would do something outrageous to ruffle my feathers and upset me, but this seemed different. After Ukiah, the road began steep grades and long descents. *Where are we going?* When we reached a straightaway, Priscilla glared at me, pressing the accelerator to the floor. "I could kill us right now and no one would know."

I put my hand on the door handle, not knowing what I would do. She looked at me again, with hatred and disgust on her face. *She's going to kill us tonight.*

With my hand on the door, I couldn't do anything. It was an intense, scary situation. I certainly couldn't jump out at that speed, and I couldn't say anything to her to inflame the situation any more. I had to just sit there and wait it out or suffer the consequences.

I won the standoff. At Willits, Priscilla took the exit west on

Highway 20, a full two and a half hours out of our way to get home, but not before scaring me out of my wits one more time on a straight stretch of Highway 101 before Willits. When we made it off the winding road from Willits back to the Pacific Coast Highway at Fort Bragg, she pulled over and let me take the wheel. I was never so relieved. I drove the rest of the way on Highway 1 south, dreaming of having a new, different life someday. I dreamed that dream for five more years until that fateful night in Malibu when Priscilla piled her things in a limo to go live in New York with Ed Bradley.

MEMPHIS—1955— ♪ 9

I didn't have a lot of luck with women in my life. It started back when I was in junior high. All along I was socially naive, and even when I got older I didn't know myself, drawn to women who weren't a good fit.

I had wanted to kiss Jocelyn Glenn since I first saw her. She sat in the front row of the youth choir at church every Sunday. I looked at the back of her head until she turned around during the service to stare at me.

I planned the time for when we both had to leave the choir pit during service to go downstairs to the bathroom. The spot I planned to kiss her was in the cafeteria of the church bordered by the men's and women's bathrooms. There was no one there. I took her hand, pulled her close, and kissed her on the mouth. It was my first kiss.

After service, Justine Brown came up to me and said, "I heard you can't kiss." Jocelyn must have said something. Justine stood there waiting for my response. So many things raced through my head. All the kids who must have known this by now. What a bad choice I made for my first sexual venture. Embarrassment. Embarrassment.

Suddenly, Justine grabbed me and put her tongue in my mouth. I had no idea of my innocence before that. She stepped back and smiled. I never kissed Jocelyn Glenn again.

MEMPHIS—1956— ♪ 1

My earliest girlfriend was Marie. It seemed we might spend the rest of our lives together. The relationship lasted five and a half years, until I met Willette, my first wife. I was twelve when I met Marie, and I was never the same again. Everyone—all my friends, my parents, my family—saw the difference in me once I met Marie. People thought we would get married and live happily ever after.

She was wearing a blue dress, one of a few she had to wear to school. Diminutive, with short hair, bright eyes, prominent cheeks, and an hourglass figure, her personality was contagious—she was loved, or hated, by everyone in the school. Talkative, smart, and energetic, Marie had her own clan that included both girls and boys. They lovingly shortened her name: "Mau-Ree."

Marie, whose absentee father was a musician and composer, had a way of walking very quickly that I found irresistible. I was more than smitten. She was impish, cute, vulnerable, and openly crafty.

The first time I kissed her was at the bottom of the steps after school, with what seemed like the whole seventh-grade class looking on or peeking around the corner. The only obstacle: she didn't live around the corner.

The bike ride to Marie's was a long one. It was fifteen blocks west on McLemore, instead of Trigg, to avoid gang territory. For years, my Western Flyer bike provided a way to get around—from my prepubescence. A smooth conduit from trike to sedan.

MEMPHIS—1962— ♪ 2

After high school graduation, I spent my last summer in Memphis before heading to college at Indiana. Marie told me she was going to Nashville for a few weeks to stay with friends at Tennessee State University, presumably to explore the campus with regards to enrolling that fall. She said goodbye and gave me a Nashville address to write her.

After a few days, I wrote Marie, asking how her visit was going and telling her I missed her. My evening route finished up at Walker and Lauderdale, and I remotely knew the family that owned a small grocery/restaurant at the corner of Wellington and Walker. I had a couple of customers on Clack Place just a few doors away from the store and was rounding the corner at Walker to head back home.

"Hey, Booker T., when are you coming over?" It was Veronica Waltham, the store owner's daughter and a friend of Marie's.

"Well," I answered, "I hadn't planned to. Why?"

"Marie is staying with us. Upstairs. We thought we might see you sometime."

You could have knocked me over with a feather. *That's why my letters have gone unanswered!*

Then Veronica looked at me as though she knew something. She did know something. It was either Levi, a Lauderdale Sub thug who had mockingly befriended me, or it was a guy from North Memphis, E. J. Washington. When we were seniors, everyone at school knew that E. J. Washington had told Marie to quit me, but she didn't have the courage. So in the hall, or at recess, she would stand close to me, with him watching, and mouth words as if explaining something: "Uh, Booker T., uh, you know, uh, uh…"

My mother was not surprised. My father rolled his eyes.

I had a natural gift for choosing the wrong women.

BLOOMINGTON, IN—1963— ♪ 4

Willette Armstrong, nicknamed Gigi, became Willette Jones, my first wife.

We were sophomores getting breakfast on our trays in the cafeteria at Teter Quadrangle one fall morning at Indiana U. Picturing an idyllic life together, I managed to get her to sit next to me for breakfast.

Our first date, at her request, was on Sunday morning. We went to Trinity Episcopal Church on Grant, where she wanted us to attend. I was raised CME, or Christian Methodist Episcopal (originally Colored Methodist Episcopal). The service was so formal, like the Catholic church, and it was awkward sitting with Willette that morning because I had spent the night before with a senior girl the first evening I was on campus.

Cute, extremely smart, popular, and sporting a little feminine swagger that was as irresistible as it was endearing, the senior girl arranged for a friend to drive us (along with her friend's freshman date) forty miles south to the small town of Bedford, Indiana, where we checked into two rooms. On the ride down, we sat in the back seat and listened to Smokey Robinson and the Miracles. Very reserved, she didn't kiss me; she just looked over and smiled from time to time. In the hotel room, she took me with her slip on. I was seventeen; she was twenty-one.

I never saw her naked body. To turn me on, she merely stripped down to her bra, but that was enough. I don't know if she loved me. She never said she did, but I thought I loved her. She seemed to enjoy my company.

This particular morning, with the girl already off to classes, I found myself sitting at breakfast with Gigi. The girl's friends were all around us at the table; she was very popular. It was the custom for the African American students to sit together, apart from the white students. There were always a good number of people who knew each other dining together.

I did not try to hide my relationship with Gigi from the girl. They knew about each other. It was a small community of black students on a large campus. Gigi would ask me about the girl, if I would break up with her. I found out I wasn't the girl's only lover.

The girl and I had a ritual; on any given day, I would check in to an old downtown hotel, the Van Orman, call the girl, and give her the room number. She would leave class, stop by Sam's, and join me later in the hotel room.

This time we talked; she said she would meet me there later. Ten o'clock came, twelve o'clock, one o'clock. No girl. She never came. That was the way she was. Lesson learned.

A few times during the semester, I had phone conversations with Gigi's roommate at Morrison Hall, Becky, where she hinted maybe I shouldn't be dating Gigi.

Gigi moved into Sycamore, and Becky stayed behind at Morrison Hall. One evening, I met Becky in the Morrison lounge.

"I don't think seeing Willette is a good idea."

"Why?"

"She's not good for you."

"What are you talking about?"

"You don't know her."

"Gigi's fine. I'm going to marry her."

"You don't know what's good for you."

Becky stood and went up the stairs to her room.

Hardly suspicious, I was a big man on campus, with a brand-new Ford Galaxie convertible and a balance of $5,000 showing on my checkbook due to an advance royalty payment for "Green Onions." I remember Gigi's eyes bugging out when she saw the balance on my checkbook. She broke into a big smile and made it no secret she had come to Indiana looking for the "Mrs. Degree."

Becky appeared to be a concerned friend who was in no way interested in me, but I wasn't sure where she was coming from. So on New Year's break after Christmas, I drove to Gary, Indiana, to spend those days with Willette Armstrong. I took her to a hotel, and we spent a few days after New Year's 1964 together. It was then that our son, Booker T. Jones III, was conceived. He was born nine months later, October 6, 1964.

I could tell from her body, though, that she had been with someone else over the holidays while I was in Memphis at my parents'. She told me she had "scratched herself" as the reason for the abnormalities.

Without my asking, Gigi insisted the child was mine, and in my heart, I knew that was true. I had "sensed" the moment of conception. But something was not quite right.

Walking down Pennsylvania Avenue, on the way to my car, Gigi's tall, red-headed, light-skinned schoolmate noticed me on the sidewalk as he picked up the morning paper. He turned as he headed back to his porch.

"Hey, man. What's happening?"

"Good morning; everything's cool."

"Are you—are you Booker T.?"

"Yeah. I'm staying with my girlfriend, Gigi, two houses down."

"Oh, yeah, yeah, Gigi! What, you're a couple now?"

"Yeah, man, we're getting married!"

"You're what?" He threw his head back in laughter. "You're what?" Uncontrollable laughter. Composing himself, he said, "Yeah, man, congratulations, she's a nice girl—nice girl." He closed the door, still smiling.

I couldn't get the scene out of my head, on the neighbor's porch, his laughter. *What does he know that I don't?*

A few months later, a justice of the peace in Crown Point, Indiana, married us. When we got back to the hotel, Gigi jumped up on the bed, dancing, and screaming, "I'm a liberated woman! I'm a liberated woman!" I was nineteen years old, and I thought, *Have I done the right thing?*

She was from Gary. Gary, Indiana. The American capital for steel mills and murders. Her father was murdered.

We tried so hard, Gigi and I did. She loved to laugh, and we would make pork chop sandwiches and hit the road—stopping at cheap hotels, chuckling to each other as the doors would open and shut throughout the night.

She was the happiest sad person I ever knew. I never did figure out what was eating her. Something deep down inside that she wouldn't face? Her dad's drinking, or something in her child-hood?

She was a good person. I loved her, and I still do. I just couldn't live with her. And couldn't now, either. I didn't try to then, and there went our little family.

BLOOMINGTON to GARY—Fall 1964— ♪ 2

She went home to have the baby—to be near her mother and to enlist the services of her doctor, Dr. Georgia Lutz, for the delivery. Gary is about a four-hour drive from Bloomington, and I got the call at about one o'clock the morning of October 6, 1964.

I had a white Ford Galaxie 500 convertible, black leather seats, and a 390 under the hood. I had to leave it in front of the hospital in Gary. I was so anxious that I burned up the engine on the four-hour drive from Bloomington.

It's not easy to burn up a '63 Ford 390, but there was no one on the highway at that hour, and I wanted to be there for the birth. I missed it—by minutes. They were wheeling her down the hall to her room when I walked in, and I'll never forget that satisfied glow and the look of accomplishment on her face that morning. She said it was the first thing she ever did right.

She did indeed do something right. He was perfect. He was ours, and he was a boy. I stood there looking at him in amazement for so long before I remembered his mother needed attention too.

I had brought her flowers and thanked her for having the baby. All of a sudden, I could see the toll the birth had exacted on her. Like the roses I had brought her, this once young flower had bloomed and blossomed, and it had made her tired. I tried to hold her and stay close to her.

And I did. For a while.

CHAPTER 9
Bootleg

SAN FRANCISCO, CA—1963— ♪ 4

Bill Graham bought my first ticket to San Francisco. At the airport, I saw an Indiana School of Music classmate getting off the plane wearing a very expensive fur coat in a very nonchalant manner. It startled me to see her trappings of wealth. At school, I assumed she was struggling to get by, like myself and other students from Indiana, barely managing school tuition, clothing, and necessary expenses. Maybe being from San Francisco, not Memphis, was a different story.

Bill had us play his new club, the Fillmore Auditorium. Our hotel was on Van Ness, walking distance to the Fillmore. After sound check, walking back to the hotel, I was stopped by several black men who blocked my progress on the sidewalk west of the Fillmore. They allowed Duck to walk past, but he stopped before turning on Geary toward the hotel.

"It's not his nature to love you," one of the men said to me.

I didn't respond.

"It's better for you not to play here tonight with them."

I pushed forward and around the men, ending up on the east side of the street, and joined Duck on Geary. We continued walking toward Van Ness. They didn't follow. At the show, I looked for them but never saw them in the crowd.

After the performance, we went to our dressing room, elated at having played what we felt was a great set for a large, enthusiastic crowd. We ordered drinks and sat around waiting for the bill. A lot of time passed. No one approached us about being paid. I was sure Jim Stewart at Stax had arranged some type of compensation, as we always got at least a little money after gigs.

I went out into the hallway and asked to see Bill Graham. I was led to a small upstairs office.

"Look, Booker, I bought you tickets from Memphis and Bloomington to San Francisco. I rented instruments for you. I put you up in a nice hotel. You just played a great show for your first West Coast audience. You're going to be stars on the West Coast after this. No one else could have done this for you. What do you want me to do?"

The feeling came over me that I had just met Bill Graham. Someone I had not previously known but who was presiding over the music scene for this part of the country. He had the strength to lean back in his chair after addressing me and say nothing, looking me unerringly straight in the eye, as if to say, "You owe me, young man."

I couldn't find any words. None at all. I got up and left the room and went back to the MGs' dressing room.

I said to the guys, "I didn't get any money."

Al said, "C'mon, Jones."

Duck said, "Where my money?"

Steve began to look at me with a knowing half-grin.

I always got paid. I had stared down hefty New York club owners who told me they lost money when the floor was packed and come upstairs with cash or a check. Many times before. I got paid.

But this man was different. He was Bill Graham.

I flew back to Indianapolis. The others returned to Memphis.

BLOOMINGTON, IN—1963— ♪ 9

Back in Bloomington, there were so few African Americans compared to white students that most of us were at least somewhat aware of the others. The Commons, a restaurant at the Indiana Memorial Union, was the only place African Americans gathered on campus, and you could always find someone there. All the blacks came to know one another by frequenting this campus restaurant. The white students allowed it to remain exclusively black.

During my freshman year, I was at the Commons so much it's a wonder I made my grades. My girlfriend was a math major, a skillful whist player, and a demanding partner. Before I got to campus, she and a couple of other smart girls established a winning tradition at the whist tables, so I whipped myself into shape to sit across from her as her partner. The worst part was learning to keep score. Even if you knew how to bid, and won, scorekeeping went by turns, and mistakes were costly. Not money but bid whist determined African Americans' social status on campus as well as whether they were Greeks or GDIs (God Damned Independents). It was more desirable to be a Greek.

Social status was more important than academic status among blacks at Indiana, so I spent my time on campus at the music building or at the Commons during my freshman year and soon made the decision to pledge a fraternity. I met Roosevelt (Rosie) Williams, the charismatic young president of Kappa's Alpha Chapter, and he had talked to me about the social advantages of going Greek, especially with his frat, Kappa Alpha Psi, which, according to Rosie, the women preferred over the Omegas and which had a beautiful frat house on the north campus.

In order to become a Greek, you attended mixers, called "smokers," to earn the right to be regarded as a social inferior in the fraternity you wanted to join. The smokers were held during "rush week" and gave the senior frat members a chance to look at you and decide if you were worthy of becoming an underling (or pledge) of theirs for a week of harassment and hazing. If you were deemed worthy, you had to do everything from getting coffee for your "big brothers," to taking their clothes to the cleaners, to allowing them to "lose" you in the woods at night, or whatever humiliating prank they might dream up. A senior member of the frat was assigned the task of seeing the pledges through hell week duly unharmed (or duly harmed, whichever he saw fit). The pledge captain was entrusted with the fraternity "paddle," a large piece of plywood, for the purposes of "managing indiscretions" among the pledges. The suffering of these indignities, along with the unperturbed toleration of such humiliations, would purportedly cause the lowly pack to huddle together and become "brothers for life."

Pledges slept together on the floor in one room. We walked to school together too. We sat at the same table for meals. We washed the dishes. We swept and mopped the floors and cleaned the windows. We mowed the grass and washed cars. All in addition to our regular studies. We took notes and ran errands for the big brothers. We carried books to classes. We took on the unmistakable haggard look and demeanor of pledges—just like hundreds of others on campus.

If by chance your group sacrificed enough for one another to the satisfaction of your pledge captain, the group was initiated in a formal ceremony, became members of the fraternity, and were honored at a big party. In practice, however, most pledges, by the end of hell week, were so tired and disillusioned they couldn't have cared less.

When the pledge process was complete, I took leave of Teter Quadrangle and moved into my new home on East Seventeenth Avenue. It was the Kappa Alpha Psi fraternity house, where my new roommates paid me as much deference as my parents had in Memphis. There was a grand piano in the living room, and they indulged my constant playing. They tolerated and even encouraged me to play all hours of the night.

I spent an equal, inordinate amount of time in the music library underneath the music building. It was open twenty-four hours a day, so I didn't have to put academia on complete hold, but I didn't get much sleep most days.

In addition to the music education at Indiana University, I used to sneak away with friends on the weekends and go up to Indianapolis to see the bands play in the clubs, and that was a different kind of music education. That's where we could catch the Isley Brothers. Yeah! The Isley Brothers! They had a sideman on guitar named Jimi Hendrix.

Jimi melded in seamlessly, both musically and visually. I think they got their dress code from him. He seemed the most relaxed of the group.

I made new friends at Indiana, but I missed my old buddies in Memphis. Every time I came back, there was a new face in the studio. Brilliant new people were coming onto the Stax scene, making our sound even better.

MEMPHIS—1964— ♪ 8

Had I known I was in the presence of the man who made all the great records I idolized as a kid, including Ray Charles and others, I would have been in awe of him. But as it turned out, he was just another one of the guys, some motherf—er from New York that Jerry Wexler sent to meddle. In my experience, there was no more modest or hardworking engineer than Tom Dowd. In addition, Tommy was a musician. He gave you no choice but to like him, with his affable personality. We started to look forward to sessions with Tom Dowd.

When Tommy walked in and saw our setup, he must have thought we were cave dwellers or something. I had no idea what he was talking about. But he showed up with a high-intensity lamp and a bunch of technical electronics and sat on the floor with his glasses falling down on his nose. We left him there that first night. I don't know if he went to his hotel and slept. I found out he had built a basic fader console from scratch overnight and was anxious to use it to record some music.

I assumed Tommy made millions because he was a vice president at Atlantic in New York and hung out with Ahmet Ertegun and Jerry Wexler. But his demeanor was that of a painter or a plumber. He just wanted to help fix things. And if something wasn't broken, he just smiled and walked away.

Tommy did his share of walking away (to the control room), and he did his share of pacing in the studio, talking about the music. His unassuming way made sure his ideas got heard—he acted like he didn't know what he was talking about. He was also adept at dealing with the egos in the room, which were unspeakable.

Tommy's nonchalance allowed him to sit at the organ and doodle or go to the drums and fiddle around. He had studied conducting and orchestration, but he didn't let on that he could read music.

Tommy wasn't pretending modesty; he was modest to a fault. The results were extraordinary. Like a magic trick. "Look, Mom, what we did today at the studio." People like Tom are born gifted with a creative urge so strong their work appears effortless, and they achieve the ultimate. Others, looking for fame and money, put out more and achieve less success. Tom's career dwarfed all of Stax's and Atlantic's other producers, mine included.

STAX CONTROL ROOM—1964— ♪ 5

On one of my trips back to Stax, Steve Cropper approached me in the foyer.

"Hey, Booker, come on back to the control room—I want you to hear something."

Al Jackson slipped into the room after Steve.

Steve put a tape on the machine. "Listen to this!" he said proudly.

It was the attention-getting, opening solo guitar chords to "Boot-Leg."

A powerful-sounding bass, an inventive, danceable beat, great bass line. I smiled big. Just before the rhythm, I heard the organ. Playing the melody. Not an organ stop I had used much, but great sounding! Curious. Then, catchy horns playing the second verse. *The Mar-Keys,* I thought. That wasn't me playing organ; it was Isaac Hayes.

"It's the new record by Booker T. & the MGs," Cropper said.

It was one of those moments in life. Something you knew came out front after hiding. Once again, I went silent. I loved the song. It was great. But it revealed to me a truth I had been denying.

How can you be the leader of a band, one that's named after you, that records without your knowledge? What's the message? What does it say to you?

The seed was planted. They didn't need me. Maybe, just maybe, I didn't need them. "Boot-Leg" was already recorded and released under the name Booker T. & the MGs without my prior knowledge or consent.

Rather than disagree or fight, I have often turned my back on conflict. It was my coping mechanism to avoid facing unpleasant realities. I've lost many battles because I never fought them. Duck Dunn was the bass player on "Boot-Leg." There was no denying Duck's playing was more urgent, more demanding, if just as sensitive as Lewie's. And Lewie persisted in being difficult outside the studio. In the studio, both Lewie and Duck followed the notes of my left hand with equal aplomb. On the other hand, the choice of changing bass players had been made in my absence, without consulting me. At best, I could continue, lick my wounds, keep my mouth shut, finish school, and see what my future held. At worst, if I raised objections, I might bring about an early truncation of the life of Booker T. & the MGs.

This event marked the first crack in an interracial group that seemed so tight from the outside looking in. It was a chip on the smooth glass when I first heard Al Jackson say, "Jones, I'ma knock that motherf—er out," referring to Steve. In fact, Al's frustration with Steve became something of an ongoing threat. I provided an ear, but I kept quiet. Like it or not, we had been brought closer together by our touring and success, despite our differences in upbringing and outlook.

Jim Stewart, Al Bell, and other Stax principles kept exhibiting the premise that Booker T. & the MGs were prized artists, but the group was more valued as the company's workhorse house band. Any other front would have been counterintuitive.

Not a single moment was ever taken out from the work schedule for the MGs to rehearse a show. We winged it onstage. Even substitutes were not rehearsed.

There was no manager or permanent booking agent. All those chores fell to me, and I was bound to the wishes of the other band members; accepting the highest offer for the closest gig was the norm. Booker T. & the MGs were virtual orphans on the road, without guidance or preparation. That point was driven home the time Al lost all his belongings in New Jersey.

NEW JERSEY—1967— ♪ *10*

The MGs were crammed into a rented station wagon, and I was driving south on I-95 from New York to Baltimore, my first time on a really big, busy interstate freeway. At the rental car company, we vainly tried to fit everything into the interior, but a couple of suitcases had to be placed on top and tied down. The rental agents were less than sympathetic to our requests for tie-down rope and less than eager to help us find a solution. *Bring less stuff.* Someone's belt was used in place of rope.

In New Jersey, I-95 was territory over which semis exerted unquestioned authority.

Aggressive truckers drove the semis fast. In our overloaded little station wagon, I rarely pulled in front of one of those behemoths.

One time I did pull ahead, and through the back window, I noticed an object fall from the roof of the wagon. From the driver's side rearview mirror, I saw a striped wooden suitcase rolling over and over behind us. Righting itself finally, it came to a stop and stood squarely in the middle of the highway. Then, back in the rearview mirror, I saw a semi change lanes. I pulled over to the right before the approaching truck set its sights on the suitcase, maintaining speed. The big truck never veered.

Bam! Wood scraps, cologne, and underwear flew all over the highway!

Inside the car, there was explosive laughter, including mine. No one had been able to take their eyes off the spectacle. The truck glided past us with a happy vengeance. The plucky driver smiling slightly.

At the hotel in Baltimore, I loaned Al underwear and toothpaste. He was upset with me for days over the heartiness of my laughter.

If there were plane reservations to be made, the job fell to me. If we needed a hotel, I booked it. I collected and distributed the road pay four ways and paid taxes on the whole amount. I interacted with the booking agents and filled out the union contracts. After gigs, when there was money to be collected, I went upstairs, or downstairs, and haggled with the promoter. None of the MGs ever told me to do these things; it was just assumed that I would. I did the interviews and rented the cars. I earned my one-fourth share. I wasn't "little young motherf—er" anymore, but I was the kid.

DETROIT—1964—♪ 9

We never had a road manager, and I usually handled settlements. But one night in Detroit, the promoter handed a large wad of cash to Duck and walked away.

We made it to the airport in Detroit and gave the skycap a tip for checking our luggage and amps. I heard Duck say, "Shit!"

Duck forgot he had the large wad of cash in his pocket and quickly stuffed it in the back of Charlie Freeman's guitar amp. Now he was watching that amp go down the ramp with the rest of the checked baggage.

You should have *seen the faces* of the skycaps at baggage claim when they saw Duck pulling that big wad of cash out of Charlie's amp at the Memphis airport!

There were very few times on MGs road trips when we didn't end up driving a rented station wagon in an unfamiliar city. We took turns driving. After misunderstanding for the umpteenth time whether the navigator was indicating a left or right turn, the MGs worked together and came up with "bear right, tiger left" as a way to solve the problem of which way to turn. Before this solution, we often found ourselves lost somewhere in America's back country. On a long driving trip to Houston, this came in very handy.

HOUSTON, TX—1964— ♪ 5

I had seen fights in clubs and at dances, but this time I was really worried. It was the first time I had ever played this far from home. We had driven all the way to Houston, Texas. Steve, Duck, and Al seemed OK with it, but I was unsteady. Beer, blood, cowboy sweat, and chicken-fried steak combine for a distinctive stench unique to saloons in the Lone Star State. Sound check went OK, but when we came back to play the show, there was chicken wire separating the stage from the audience. Chicken wire. I was nervous. Were we in the wrong place? Who would protect us if something went wrong?

The night passed without incident. There was a small crowd, but they listened to the interracial group with mild enthusiasm. I was relieved.

Next time we played in Houston, we flew. We took a young Memphis singer named Carl Simms, even more of a neophyte than me. We played the gig and jetted back to Memphis.

At the airport Carl asked Duck for a ride to the bus station.

"Why do you want to go to the bus station?" Duck asked Carl.

"I'm going back to Houston. I met a girl there," Carl replied.

"We just left Houston. Why didn't you just stay there?"

"Because I had a round-trip ticket, and I thought I had to use it."

STAX—1964— ♪ 10

Charlie Freeman combed his hair just like Steve Cropper's. Nobody ever asked me if Charlie was Steve Cropper when he played with the MGs. It was Charlie who taught Steve how to play the guitar. Neither the surviving members of the Mar-Keys nor Jim Stewart would deny that Charlie taught Steve to play. He helped out whenever and wherever he could.

Charlie Freeman had the best sense of humor of anyone at Stax. Even over Don Nix or Duck Dunn. Charlie was always on the phone with his wife, laughing, telling her he was f—ing another woman. (He wasn't.)

BLOOMINGTON, IN—1965— ♪ 3

The Marching Hundred came first. Over classes, over holidays, over trips to Memphis for sessions, over health, over college studies, over relationships, and over marriage. All the married members of the band, and there were a few, knew each other, because we commiserated. Our Saturday mornings and our weekends weren't spent like other parents, pushing our toddlers on swings at the park. We were on buses headed to Iowa, Illinois, and Northern Indiana.

One of my white friends in the trombone section was a parent too. We lived in the campus trailer park. He had a truck and got by doing odd jobs during the week. At least I could drive to Memphis, do a couple of sessions, and pick up thirty bucks, enough for a month's rent and expenses.

Married housing life in the trailer park was different than on campus or in town. The park was a small, close community, with an insular social life made up of young couples struggling with extra demands—small children, sleep deprivation, and the vagaries of being grown-up. The trailers were hideous army-green rejects with tiny entry steps and fogged-up windows. Identical, and excruciatingly small, the units were perfectly aligned in rows along two short streets. Our best friends, Lorenzo and Liz Ashley, arrived on campus two weeks early like us, and we were the only ones in the park. We got together regularly in their trailer (ours was too junky). Lorenzo was a football star, and we laughed, drank, and partied harder than I ever had at the frat house. We always ordered out pizza and beer, and sometimes, life was really good.

With all this juggling, some balls hit the floor. The stress and conflict of taking care of my family and yielding to my independent, creative young nature became too much too often. Instead of paying attention to my relationship with Gigi, I went to the studio and wrote a song about not paying attention to your relationship with my writing partner.

Gigi hadn't signed up for dirty diapers, laundry, and isolation with a little one in a small trailer. She checked the box for partying, drinking, and sleeping in late at the dorm. She was overwhelmed. The place was a mess. There was a constant heap of clothes and other items blocking the path to the bed and blanketing the floor. She grappled with postpartum issues, going from exhilarating happiness to deep lows. Her only example of homemaking had been a steelworker father who cooked on weekends. Her schoolteacher mother took the dirties to the cleaners every week. Alone, she struggled with making a home for us and enjoying her new baby while I was on the marching field, in class, studying, or on the road to Memphis.

CHAPTER 10
B-A-B-Y

LOS ANGELES—2018— ♪ 8

It was a beautiful, sunny, bright LA afternoon. There is something so special about showing off your progeny to elder family members, and because of this, it was one of the happiest days of my life. I had just reached age seventy-four, reason enough to be happy, but on this day my daughter Olivia was driving us to Crenshaw with Nan, and my grandchild, Dylan Jones Barber, in the car to meet my older sister, Gwen. We crested the hill at Angeles Vista, and the city revealed the aesthetic glory of its landscape for our eyes—the Hollywood Sign, downtown LA, all the way to Glendale. A view I had seen a thousand times.

Olivia won Dylan's car seat on *The Ellen DeGeneres Show,* and it was the biggest one in the world. A baby could survive a car bomb in that contraption, and it was hanging behind the passenger side where I sat.

"No, Dad. You can't move the seat back any more," Olivia said again, unapologetically. It was the happiest scrunched-up car ride

I'd ever taken. I couldn't see my grandson, as he was facing backward behind me, so I was missing all the baby smiles and cooing Nan was seeing from the back seat.

Olivia has always impressed me with her fierce determination and graceful personality. Now becoming a mother, these qualities are amplified, and any child in the world would benefit from her care. Continuously giving of herself, the strength she showed during the birth, keeping herself together, the joy she finds in motherhood is what the world needs more of right now.

Gwen was standing on the front porch when we pulled up at 12:40 p.m. I told her we'd be there at noon, and I guess she had been standing there the whole time. She had the biggest grin on her face I had ever seen.

At Gwen's house, I got in front and lifted the front wheels of the stroller up the steps while Liv pushed from the back. We almost had the stroller on the porch when Gwen reached in, lifted the baby out, and took him into the house. Small and diminutive, Gwen is ninety-two years old, and Dylan weighs nineteen pounds. Gwen's son, Floyd, started suggesting she might sit down in one of the generous chairs in her living room, but Gwen continued walking, baby-dancing around the room, smiling, and kissing Dylan all over his body.

Olivia tried to follow Gwen around, coat still in hand, periodically reaching out to take the baby, but Gwen never turned him loose, exhibiting the strength of a weightlifter, the happiness of a grand-aunt. Dylan gave Gwen his most beautiful, sincere smile, so finally, we all just sat down to take it all in.

MEMPHIS—1944— ♪ 2

Gwen was eighteen when I was born. She took care of me so regularly while my mother worked that she was like a mother to me.

She gave me the nickname Jun-T because I was Booker T. Junior. I really came to see her as a second mother after her daughter Sandra was born, and Sandra and I were close enough to be sister and brother. Gwen's husband, Floyd, was among many black Memphis airmen and infantrymen who, upon returning home from the war, had barely doffed their uniforms when they realized the unlikelihood of succeeding in Jim Crow Memphis. Floyd studied photography with Earnest Withers before he and Gwen joined the first throng of young marrieds in a sweeping movement of blacks from Memphis to Los Angeles in the early 1950s. Mama was never quite the same again after Gwen moved 2,500 miles away.

TRIP TO LOS ANGELES—1955— ♪ 1

To visit Gwen one summer, my mother and I boarded a Greyhound bus.

We took the three-day, nonstop ride from Memphis to Los Angeles. The city of El Paso, Texas, has always held a mystic appeal for me, mainly because it was the first rest stop on the long bus ride. At least long for an eleven-year-old. Greyhound buses, unlike Memphis city buses, had just been desegregated by a national commission, and my mother and I were free to sit where we pleased, a freedom we were unaccustomed to.

We took our seats, a little forward on the right side, and I turned, standing up on my knees, craning to discern some reaction from the other passengers about our choice of seats. Mama seemed unconcerned, but I glanced at the back bench, expecting to see black faces. On most of the ride, I was unsettled, anxious, and out of place—as if I were sitting in the wrong class. Finally, in the huge bus terminal at Los Angeles, Gwen's smiling face and the sight of her fancy green convertible parked nearby put me at ease.

MEMPHIS—1964— ♪ 5

It was a disruptive time. Kennedy was dead. Johnson was in office, and we were invading the Dominican Republic. People were wondering where our country was headed. "Where are the good times?" The heartfelt, soothing strains of "I've Been Loving You Too Long" were just what was needed on the radio airwaves in black neighborhoods drenched in societal uncertainty and impending hardship. The loss of Kennedy destroyed the sense of upward, forward motion that had begun to take hold in the early sixties and made music more important than ever in our community.

The idea of a love with no end was a theme that sold itself. Otis soaked the vocal with feeling. The recording was one of give and take—where we, the musicians, waited on Otis to express his feelings and supported him with buildups and swells, and diminuendos, or letdowns, in the music. Recording "I've Been Loving You Too Long," all of us reached the highest highs and the lowest lows, together. The piece was crafted by the best soul crooners of the day, Jerry Butler and Otis Redding, and playing piano on the cut made for one of the most special, emotion-filled moments of my recording career.

I had just enough training in the subtleties and nuances of musical form and structure to play a building progression on piano, twelve notes, starting on low E and ending on A, to push Otis emotionally out onto a soaring high—"You are tired! And you want to be free"—to produce the summit, the culmination, the peak, the climax of the phrase. It was just the right timbre. Just the right sound, resonance, tonality. Unafraid, Otis hit the note squarely on the word *tired,* with unabashed emotion and sincerity, and with a dose of undeniable honesty. It was a step forward, moving soul music into a realm of its own.

And there I was. All of twenty-one years old. Married three

years. Helping give rise to a powerful testament to deep, endless love in my work and all the while harboring a deep, inward need to find such love for myself. I came face to face with what was missing in my life. I wanted a woman who meant everything to me, who made me feel like the guy in the song, someone I loved so much I would beg or do anything for her.

LOS ANGELES—1965— ♪ 4

Not long after the session with Otis, I found myself once again in Los Angeles. Naively, on the set of the TV show *Shindig,* I asked Billy Preston how much money he made. "Oh, I guess around fifty thousand."

My God! I thought. *I haven't made that much since I started working!*

Billy smiled. "Go join AFTRA."

"That will be nine hundred dollars, thank you." I was standing at the counter in the offices of AFTRA on LaBrea on my last day in LA, and I needed to be a member of that union to collect my check from the TV show. *How am I going to get nine hundred dollars before my flight back to Memphis?*

It was 1968 before I saved enough cash to join that union. They saved my checks, and I walked out of there with over $3,500 in payments from past TV shows. By that time my dues had grown to $1,800, but it was still profitable for me to join.

I never forgot Billy telling me he made $50,000. I was making $125 a week at Stax. Billy had a Cadillac; I had a Ford Galaxie. Sure enough, first year I moved to California, I made more than $50,000 and bought myself a ranch and a new Mercedes-Benz.

California was starting to look like the Promised Land. Not only for me but many others in the music business, including the promoter that burned me, Ruth Brown, Otis Redding, and Jimmy Reed in New York. He turned out to be the same Los Angeles DJ, the Magnificent Montague, whose slogan had become "Burn, baby, burn!" By the time we made our way to LA's 5/4 Ballroom for two shows, the shameless hero had driven the phrase into the jargon of South LA, and it sifted into every black neighborhood in America.

August 11, 1965, the day we opened at the 5/4 Ballroom, was the day LA's finest chose to cross the *thin blue line* once again by beating up a pregnant black woman on the street, igniting an already too-short fuse and ensuring the city would "burn, baby, burn" for certain. Fittingly, we played Phil Upchurch's "You Can't Sit Down" and "Soul Twist," written by King Curtis.

Ahmet Ertegun called my sister, Gwen. Wanted me up on Sunset Boulevard at ten the next morning for a recording session. The artist was Bobby Darin. It's a mystery how he got her number. Gwen let me take her car and told me how to take Arlington and how it turns into Wilton to Western and to drop down to Sunset to avoid traffic and the freeway. The studio was Sunset Sound. The charts were done by Gene Page, and they were stacked up on the organ when I walked into the studio. *These guys were sight-reading the arrangements!*

The studio was full of people. I could see the Blossoms in their own private vocal booth. I spotted Ahmet in the control room. I never got my bearings because I had barely parked Gwen's green Buick convertible, walked in, and sat down before Gene looked over at me, counted one-two, one-two-three-four, and the red light went on over the control room. We were recording. The song had started. I spotted Al Jackson over by the wall next to Hal Blaine. They were both on drums.

I scrambled to find my chart and the place on the music. It was baptism by fire. My first Hollywood session. The pianist looked over at me with a congenial smile. I found the place on the music.

I don't know how. I followed the chart. I didn't usually come in until the second verse on songs anyway. Thank God. I played. The music was exhilarating. Bobby was rock's Frank Sinatra. *Did I turn the car off?*

On the break, I ran to the parking lot and checked. Ignition off. Whew!

After the session, we walked outside to see smoke in the skies. Los Angeles was under siege.

I called Gwen.

"Booker, stay over there! Don't come over here! Bye, baby!"

Word came that the California National Guard wasn't allowing any autos south of Wilshire. I was in a war zone, and I feared for my life. The sky was black with smoke.

One of the Blossoms, Jean King, saw me standing by the phone booth out back of the studio as she was pulling out. She rolled down her window. "Get in!" I squeezed into Jean's little sports car and spent the night on the couch at her apartment in the Hollywood Hills. Jean was concerned but stayed calm. The next afternoon, we heard on the radio the curfew was lifted. I was still scared to death. I felt I owed her my life.

Montague, meanwhile, struck again. This time in a way I never suspected. He went into a partnership called Pure Soul Records with Packy Axton's mom, Estelle, for whom we all would do anything, and persuaded us to go into an LA studio. There was no music; we were told just to jam. Al was on drums, Johnny Keyes on congas, and Leon Haywood on Hammond B-3. I happily provided the first lead verse on piano, which was repeated for the third verse, and Packy played a sax solo in between. Johnny put a conga break in the middle section. "Hole in the Wall," the instrumental by the Packers, was a massive hit. We got writer's credit but no royalties and no publishing. Pure Soul went out of business before it paid any bills. Houdini could have learned a thing or two from Montague.

GARY, IN—1966— ♪ 4

Bloomington was starting to feel like home, but it was already time to choose a place to do student teaching. Roosevelt High School in Gary was the obvious choice. Gigi and I were spending part of our last semester on campus in married housing, after which we moved to Gary and rented her parents' upstairs apartment on Pennsylvania for the final half of the school year. It seemed like a perfect situation. Mr. Williams, Roosevelt's band director, was happy to have me do student teaching under him. He was a smart, well-dressed, experienced teacher in his forties and regularly left me in charge of the band and the daily classes as well. The students were well behaved and cooperative. It was a student teacher's dream come true.

Willette wasn't thrilled about moving back into her parents' building. She had visions of us living far away from her folks. The rent, however, was affordable, and I needed to student teach at a school in Indiana. It was our only reasonable choice.

She didn't get on with her father. Our apartment was messier than her room had been, and she and her parents fought about that and other things. The mess was disturbing to me. You had to step on, or over, all the clothes that were strewn all over the floor in a large pile, and it was impossible to walk around the room. *Is this an indication of Gigi's inner turmoil or just the basic absence of a need for neatness?* Her mother and father weren't much involved with our child, Booker III, and he was often sick when we were in Gary.

I couldn't afford to pay too much attention to the situation at the Armstrongs' duplex, as I was in my last semester of college and had to make a go of my student teaching assignment at Roosevelt High School. Mr. Williams, my supervisor, decided to retire and started leaving school early, entrusting entire days to my instruction.

The band decided to give Mr. Williams a trophy as a sendoff on his retirement. Along with the band president, who was an attractive, mature, senior girl who played clarinet and sat in the front row, I was elected to go downtown and purchase the trophy. We went shopping for it at recess in my car and obviously were spotted by one of Gigi's friends, who assumed we were having an affair. Soon after, I drove the band president home and stopped short of getting involved with her.

That evening Willette confronted me with what she felt sure was my infidelity. I couldn't convince her otherwise, and the truth was, I did find the young lady attractive even though we weren't involved. My relationship with T's mom was in trouble.

Our first big argument came after Gigi took me to a club to introduce me to her friends, and I ended up feeling like she was showing me off like a trophy she had won. By ourselves, in our quiet moments, I wondered if Gigi was aware of me. We didn't customarily exchange words of affection or exhibit fondness. There were no smooches or warm embraces. She looked forward, however, to the takeout food I fetched every night and to the moola from the gigs and the checks I brought in from Stax. *What have I gotten myself into?*

Instead of Bloomington to Memphis, my trips became Gary to Memphis.

MEMPHIS—1966— ♪ 3

For the Carla Thomas session, I left Gigi in Gary with her parents and the baby, and I stayed with my parents in Memphis.

Everyone at Stax was having affairs. Some were more elegantly veiled than others. The innuendos came out in the music, through the songwriting and the vocal deliveries. Betty Crutcher stayed out of the fray, as far as I knew, but she was one of the best at exposing this nuance in her songs. She and her partners wrote "Who's Making Love" and "Somebody's Sleeping in My Bed" for Johnny Taylor.

One of the best examples of this tendency, and one of the sexiest songs ever recorded at Stax, was Carla Thomas's "Let Me Be Good to You." It's hard to imagine Carla wasn't singing the song to someone in particular. As with a lot of Carla's songs, I found myself at the piano on this one. The arrangement took on a whimsical, playful feeling and became (in my opinion) a novelty due to its 3/4 shuffle rhythm.

This was a period of artistic change for Stax artists that coincided with political nuances and advances brought about by the new popularity of rock. Most Stax artists embraced the new music from America's hippy culture and Europe.

Otis and the Stones admired each other. I loved the Stones just as much but found playing piano on "Satisfaction" felt odd to me. Any way you cut it, "Satisfaction" is a guitar song, and a keyboard player has to dumb it down either with quarter notes or Jerry Lee Lewis–style eighth notes. I knew this because I was a closet rock guitar player. And even though my guitar playing was openly discouraged in the studio, I sometimes played anyway, with Otis, William, and Eddie and when Cropper wasn't around.

The electric guitar was given a new authority in the music industry by rock. A clout that blues couldn't muster on its own. Like the rock David threw to slay Goliath, the Rolling Stones' opening guitar to "Satisfaction" claimed undisputed, uncharted musical territory for rock and roll till the end of time.

There was no getting around "Satisfaction." It was an anthem. We cut it in the same key, but with nowhere near the clarity of tone on the guitar as on the Stones' cut. Our weapons were the horns, tight rhythm, and Otis's ability to preach rock and roll. Where the Stones left space, we put keys. Maybe nobody had the guts to tell me to lay out. The Stones' record bounced and danced along. Ours stomped, left, right, left, right, and smashed you in the face. Who covers the Rolling Stones, anyway? The self-assured or the dense. I like to think we fell into the first category.

There is no song in my recollection, Stax or otherwise, that I put more effort into, in terms of trying to come up with an arrangement, than Carla Thomas's "B-A-B-Y." I tried everything. Every rhythm, every tempo, so much trial and error that I got sick of the thing before playing the high piano chords that finally began the song. Carla was done with it. Finished. She didn't want any more of David and Isaac's song, "B-A-B-Y." I didn't give up on it, though. I know my persistent nature has driven people mad, but David and Isaac were our proven best songwriters, if not arrangers, and there was something in this tune. Somewhere. Maybe a more Motown feel. Motown? At Stax? Nah. Nah. Maybe? Yeah! Why not? Finally, I came up with a Motown-style bass line.

Next morning, I tried my idea out on the band with Carla in the vocal booth. It worked! It worked! People were dancing in the control room! Carla had a big grin on her face when she was singing. She loved me for changing the arrangement! It was a big accomplishment for me! All the elements—the changes, the melody, the structure, and the lyrics—were there from the beginning. I just rearranged them.

STAX'S WRITING TEAM—1966— ♪ 12

A few weeks later, I was in my office working on an idea, or at least trying out an idea, when I heard some chords coming from the office next door, David and Isaac's. I tried to focus but found myself standing in the hall, listening. "When Something Is Wrong with My Baby" came wafting through the crack underneath the door.

This was something different. I lost concentration on what I was working on. Right next door to me, a true song was being written, and I could not take my attention away from it. A picture formed in my mind of a man committed to his woman to the extent depicted in the song. This was why we were here. This was why I studied music and what we were dedicated to. Depicting life and love in its most beautiful state. This was one of the greatest purposes of music.

The song was delegated to Sam & Dave, of Miami, Florida. On the day of the session, Isaac sat down at the piano, which meant I would play organ. We worked the arrangement up at the piano and took places for the recording. Cropper played the four simple opening chords. Leading chords, suspended on A flat, after which Duck played three grace notes leading to the first down beat—the canvas was set. "When Something Is Wrong with My Baby," accompanied by traditional rhythm and blues piano triplets, and Isaac and David's dream became a reality. In the second eight of each verse, I played a counter-melody on the Hammond B-3, a longing, wistful line that threads its way into the song's fabric from the inside. The organ tones shone golden in color and mixed with the gospel church piano chords, soulful Lowman Pauling–style guitar, and honest vocal testimonials and harmonies. All this held together by a faithful 6/8-time signature that swayed from side to side. Dave laid down the first verse with support from Sam in the background.

There was a respite after the first verse, a quieting, where all the elements settled down for the second verse, as if the song's mood and place was established, and now it could relax for this next part. Beginning the second verse, Sam appeared determined to take his time. And this is where Duck Dunn played his famous "falling" bass line, from B flat to G flat. With the vocal, Sam sang his heart out, and when the chorus arrived, it came as a relief, and a release, deliverance in the power of love. That feeling was experienced by all involved in the recording and never forgotten.

BLOOMINGTON, IN—1966— ♪ 2

Time came for me to choose pieces to play on trombone for my senior recital. It dawned on me these would be the last days I would come to this little room in the music building for my weekly applied lessons with Buddy Baker, my teacher, who, over the past four years, had gradually become more than an instructor, a mentor and guru. So much had changed since I first entered this room at age seventeen. Most important, Buddy had lost his young daughter in an accident in his home swimming pool. No one who knew him will ever get over that. Especially not his students. First, he was second-rank trombone professor at IU. Professor Thomas Beversdorf was department head, and his roster was more than full. Buddy's office went vacant during the tragedy, and Buddy's students had to walk past going to class; it was always a reminder.

The recital day arrived, and Mama was able to make it to Bloomington, even though she was recovering from neck surgery. I muddled through the difficult program, having spent more time studying business or biology than practicing music, but such was the nature of graduation with a liberal arts degree as opposed to an applied music degree. Music education wasn't available as an applied music course at Indiana University, and I wanted to learn to teach as well as play, so I had to go for the bachelor of music education degree. I marched with my class in June, and my parents were so, so proud, and I was so happy and tired.

It would be difficult for someone who didn't have musical training and education to appreciate the full value they afforded me. I gained the knowledge, the confidence, and the security that came with it. I acquired the ability to transcribe music and musical textures to a written score. By virtue of my proficiency on, and knowledge of, the ranges and capabilities of brass, strings, and woodwind instruments, I became a regular arranger at Stax, to my benefit and others'. Knowing the history of music made me more capable of creating future music. That's the value of studying anything.

MEMPHIS—1966— ♪ 2

"Sad songs is all he know, y'all." Although the tune was not his biggest hit, I feel that "Fa-Fa-Fa-Fa-Fa (Sad Song)" is the one that captured the true essence of Otis Redding. I mimicked his vocal on the piano, playing along with a dancing rhythm of thirds up high on the keyboard, practically dancing at the piano myself. The dichotomy in Otis's music and what we were doing at Stax was never more apparent than on this session—playing sad music to make us happy. Everybody had a ball that day.

In an effort to make Otis's star even brighter, Phil Walden, his manager, sought a way to get Otis on the big TV shows and into the big nightclubs. He suggested Otis try recording "Try a Little Tenderness." I was surprised, but the inventiveness of the idea piqued my interest.

"Try a Little Tenderness" was proven material, and with the musicians' help, Otis managed to turn the lyric into a truly powerful, honest exhortation as to how to treat a lady. On the first run-through, like a good theory student, I played a leading, descending piano run down to an A minor chord on each verse in the eighth and ninth bars, and Otis waited each time for me to do that before he whispered the lyric.

As always, an air of experimentation pervaded the first run-through, but quickly, ingeniously, Al began pecking rim shots quietly. I probably looked up at him like he was crazy at first but soon realized those taps were in rhythm and possibly the precursor of something more exciting to come. Never underestimate the creativity of Al Jackson.

Sure enough, he played a big fill leading into the first turn, and I hit a B in the left hand, an inversion leading to the E7 turn, and instantly we had a turn, a build that was about to explode into something. Otis stomped out from behind the vocal booth into the middle of the room.

Otis said, "You got ta!" (Now marching, left, right.) "Squeeze her! Tease her!" (Full-out stomping, arms flailing, waving side to side.) "Never leave her!" Otis jumped in front of the drums and glared at Al. Al played a fill, inciting the band to break. The band broke. (Silence.) Al glared playfully at Otis.

He responded: "Nigh, nigh, nigh! Nigh, nigh, nigh! Nigh, nigh, nigh! Try a little... *tenderness!*" Otis shouted.

We all hit the downbeat together.

It was a release. A musical explosion.

Then, we walked the chords down, back down, to the same place as the first turn, and it became apparent *it was going to happen again!*

"Nigh, nigh, nigh—Nigh, nigh, nigh!"

The tension built again. Al stood up.

And again, I played the leading, descending piano run down to the A minor chord, and we were off! This time everybody but Al leaned hard on the backbeat, playing the upward chord progression.

On the way up, Otis interjected, asserted, and demanded, "You got ta...squeeze her!" Pause. "Tease her!" Pause. "Nigh, nigh, nigh—Nigh, nigh, nigh! Try a little—"

When we got to the top, another *explosion!*

"Tenderness!"

This time Al was standing up at the drums, banging out snare hits, answering Otis's exhortations. We used four beats of G, four beats of F, and two bars of E7 to bring us down from our high, but we had reached the zenith, we were at the top, there was no denying that because we felt the exhilaration. And as luck would have it, tape had been rolling the whole time. The whole time! Jim was recording us!

I had waited seven years to see this expression on Jim Stewart's face. It was possible to satisfy this man, a notion we doubted from time to time. He loved it. He was moved.

CHAPTER 11
Born Under a Bad Sign

MEMPHIS—Spring 1968—♪ 2

Writing the guitar part for Eddie Floyd's "Big Bird," I was visualizing. Trying to simulate the action of the wings on a big jet when they cut the first piece of air on takeoff. How that first sliver becomes a slightly larger stream that pokes over the wing, and finally under the wing, until a vortex develops with such force that the heavy body of the big jet comes into view and lifts off the ground into flight.

I started picking the pattern on an E on the B string with my third finger, in the fifth position, then added the open E top string into the pattern so as to have two E strings playing together. Moving to the seventh position, I kept the picking pattern on three strings simultaneously to form a D chord with the top E still suspended. Then, a C triad in that same position, moving to an A7 chord without the bass note.

Finally, for the part where the big 747 lifts off the ground, I played four beats each of E, D, C, and A, then the E rhythm pattern for four bars.

Eddie waited patiently for all this introduction to happen, dancing expectantly behind the vocal booth. After we *took off,* he starting singing, "Open up the sky! 'Cause I'm comin' up to you!" *Are we still at Stax? Is this Detroit? Isn't this a little esoteric? Mystical? Symbolic?* Yes, to all. We had moved into the Age of Aquarius, and Eddie was right there with me, even when I moved to California and started recording at Leon Russell's house, where we wrote and recorded "California Girl" and "Never Found a Girl" with Leon's crew. Eddie was the only one willing to join me in LA.

In Memphis, there was subtle, and not-so-subtle, pressure to stick with keyboards. Even so, I never gave up my Sears Silvertone guitar. It was second nature to me.

MEMPHIS—Fall 1966— ♪ 9

One day I arrived at my office at Stax to find a letter waiting for me on my desk. It was from a woman named Anne. The handwriting was big, elaborate, and ornate. In the letter, she simply said, "Dear Booker T., Please come f—k me." She signed her name and wrote her phone number.

My girlfriend was out of town, and my wife was mad at me. What could I do? I phoned Anne. She spoke in a low, clear, deliberate voice. She lived out in Douglas. I thought I had seen her before, walking down the street near the Sears store. I told my wife I had to work late and went to Anne's house.

She had huge brown eyes, so big that it took an extra second for her to blink. Short hair and long, slim legs. She drank scotch, but I never saw her drunk. Her mother peeked her head in for a quick hello, then retired to the next room. It was late, we had barely met, and Anne took me on the couch in her foyer with her parents in the next room.

It did not seem to bother her that they were so close, because this happened many times. They never intruded, or maybe they weren't there; I'm not sure.

Anne told me not to hurt her. I did. I went back to my girlfriend, and Anne slapped me hard against the face when she found out. She was irresistibly beautiful, with the large eyes and a long, sensual nose. I saw her until we realized we would destroy each other, and then we kept our distance.

After Gigi moved to Memphis, during the day, we went our own ways, but we slept in the same house. The question became not if I was going to bring dinner home after I left the studio but what barbeque place I was going to get it from. Blacks weren't allowed inside legendary restaurants like the Rendezvous, but it didn't matter because blacks and whites considered Culpepper's, on the south side, unbeatable in the barbeque realm. The fact that it was fifteen blocks out of my way didn't stop Gigi from insisting our plates come from there. Unlike the great barbeque place on South Parkway, Culpepper's plates were five or six large ribs pasted with their proprietary sauce, five slices of bread, and a small helping of slaw. The only healthy takeout for blacks came from the Four-Way Grill on Mississippi, routinely consisting of fried chicken, collard greens, yams, corn on the cob, and cornbread.

We both had dependencies. Mine were music and women. Gigi's were, well, I wasn't certain. Definitely alcohol.

After a short road trip, I was somewhat taken aback to find Gigi had installed a well-stocked bar in one corner of our rumpus room. I had a scotch or a beer every now and then but was nowhere near a serious drinker and hadn't known that Gigi was. Her father and his brothers, however, had a long history of alcohol abuse. She said she had some friends over "now and again" who "liked to have a drink or two." What I was unaware of was that there were parties at my house when I was at the studio or at the Lorraine Motel.

I guess I was a knucklehead.

As a kid in Memphis, my friends and I had fun doing "the hambone," a leg/knee-slapping dance resembling a stomp to the rhythm of a mouth harp, or harmonica. It was common for me to have one in my pocket from the time I was around seven.

One day at Stax, our young protégés, the Bar-Kays, had just finished "Soul Finger" and needed something to back it with. I happened to have my harmonica and pulled it out of my pocket, playing a melody to one of their rhythms. They decided to mike my harp, and the tune became a lively dance stomp, "Knucklehead."

MEMPHIS—Spring 1967— ♪ 7

I became a full-time Stax employee. The studio was home.

I was so heavily influenced by Dave "Baby" Cortez. "Booker-Loo" was evidence of that. The B-3 organ, so flexible, could be used to produce sounds of joy or sadness. Cortez's song "The Happy Organ" presented the Hammond in the happy category. My main influences, Jimmy Smith and Bill Doggett, demonstrated the serious side of the instrument. I guess I've pictured myself on both sides of the coin.

The title "Booker-Loo" came from Al Jackson's play on words with the boogaloo dance craze, featuring a similar tempo.

The whole thing started out with an inverted drum beat. Just the opposite of how you think the drums should go. Then, Duck hit the dancing bass line, with Steve providing chinks on the backbeats.

For the melody, I reached up midway high on the swell manual for a comfortable first inversion of the D chord, while the left hand kept the bass pattern and my body moving. Duck doubled what I played on my left hand. Instead of usual twelve-bar blues changes,

I laid the song out on a twenty-bar pattern in the key of D. We played a full eight bars on the first D. The first change went down to the major sixth chord (B flat) for four bars rather than up to the four as in blues, then back to D for four more. For the turn, it was back to the major sixth, then down to the four chord, finally settling back home for a break on the D and a two-bar drum fill that led us into the guitar solo.

I dropped down to the lower manual to play a percussive rhythm behind the solo. Steve did his simple, one-note dancing thing, like he was balancing up on a tightwire with his arms stretched out for balance. He came down a little bit for the B-flat section, then it was right back up there again when we got to the second set of D chords.

In the funky, easy key of C, "My Sweet Potato" is an example of the Ramsey Lewis influence on me. Not only did Ramsey take over my piano psyche, he stole my drummer, Maurice White. I wasn't bitter, but I did listen to the Young-Holt Trio instead of Ramsey sometimes.

All three of the other MGs were as influenced by current bands as I was by the Young-Holt Trio. In particular, Jackson, Dunn, and Cropper loved New York's Young Rascals, whose "Groovin'" rivaled Sinatra's "New York, New York," the other popular song that screams *The Big Apple!* Booker T. & the MGs' "Groovin'" is a laid-back instrumental cover of the Rascals' song.

When we recorded the tune, I imagined myself in a top-down convertible, cruisin' on a crowded New York avenue on a warm Sunday afternoon, pretty girl sitting snuggly close, with nowhere to be and no time to be there, and the Rascals' cut playing on big interior car speakers.

Multitrack recording made it possible for me to put old-school-style piano triplets down before laying down the melody on the B-3.

EUROPE—Spring 1967— ♪ 1

Rushed visits to Lanksy Brothers to have suits tailor-made for the European tour was the first time any attention was paid to what we would wear.

We landed in England. How could this be? Me at such a young age and this so, so foreign land feeling so familiar so soon? The home of Chaucer, Shakespeare, old lore, and legend. But it was real; looking out the window, I saw the countryside, and the wheels underneath the big jet touched the ground.

It was an event that would repeat itself many times in the years to come, each with that same eerie, familiar feeling, but with me older only.

I was traveling to meet my unexpected extended family. Fans I would come to see for many years. Were they coming to see me or I to see them? They started bringing their children to the concerts, and all the things that can come between people who have something in common started cropping up. Language, distance.

They drove and drove. Promoters drove up ticket prices. But to this day we value one another. Overcome the obstacles and grow old together, with the music. Old and new—now we email, call one another by name, and wait. Until I once again...land in England.

Touring Europe with Otis Redding, Sam & Dave, Eddie Floyd, and Arthur Conley, we acquired a loyal group, mostly girls, who would follow us from city to city, hotel to hotel. One particular groupie, Rubie Cowell, was homosexual, and her nickname was "the Vamp." She was thin, with short blonde hair and sharp features.

Rubie and I became friends. She usually dressed in black masculine clothes and loved the long thin silk socks I wore, which were not available in London. I gave her several pairs from my suitcase. Rubie's best friend was a girl named Nicky. Rubie introduced me to Nicky one night at a club, and I started seeing her not long after the tour began.

One night when the entourage was at a club in London, Rubie was with a beautiful Alaskan girl named Chaya. On the dance floor, Chaya was wearing a primitive-looking short coat with a fur lining around the neck. Her miniskirt was London-era short, and her shoes were f—k-me shoes. Being homosexual, Rubie couldn't get on the dance floor with Chaya, even though they came together.

Rubie noticed me looking at Chaya as we were dancing. When we left the club, standing outside on the street waiting for our taxis, Rubie, standing to my left, balled her fist and decked me on the left side of my chin, right there on the street. Everyone, including me, was surprised. But everyone had seen me eyeing Chaya. She was attractive to all the guys, but Rubie made an example out of me.

Rubie and I stayed friends, and I kept my distance from Chaya.

Settling in for a considerable stay in London for rehearsals, London's trendy Mayfair Hotel on Stratton Street in Chelsea became our home away from home.

Because the presumptuous maids at the Mayfair made a habit of barging in without knocking, my roommate, Al Jackson, and I took to the habit of sleeping nude with no covers. When the maids burst in, they had a full-on view of both of us. After a few days of this, the intrusions stopped.

SHEFFIELD, ENGLAND—1967— ♪ 4

There was a knock on the door at 3:00 a.m. Then, the hotel night clerk and the security guard used the house key to let themselves into the room. My English girlfriend pulled the sheet up over her when the bright ceiling light came on. We were told to pack our things and leave the hotel—immediately.

The officious clerk made no pretense of believing the room empty, as nothing would have prevented the cagey manager from visually confirming the white skin of the woman in my bed. Neither was there any duplicity concerning the cause, or justification for, our expulsion in the middle of the night.

Out on the cold English street with our suitcases, we walked until we found a fish-and-chips restaurant where we could at least sit inside to wait out the rest of the dark morning. We ordered fish and chips over and over again until time to walk back to the hotel to board the bus and rejoin the tour for the ride to the next town.

COPENHAGEN—1967— ♪ 9

As this particular mix of whiskies played in my stomach, I don't remember feeling much more than the sting of the slap her large Nordic hand made on the side of my face. The large Danish blonde was angry with me as she lay in my small hotel bed because I was unable to get it up in my inebriated state.

This was the first and the last time I was ever drunk in my life, having imbibed at the kickoff party for the Stax-Volt tour of Finland, Sweden, and Denmark. Choosing from the variety of liquors available, I partook of all of them before I ended up in my room with the beautiful fair-haired European version of an Amazon. As it turned out, she would never get to taste my southern delights because my drunken stupor lasted a full five days—even without another drink.

Bandmates, tour managers, and friends took turns bringing food to my room and urging me to eat at the smorgasbords, hoping I would get sober enough to play the organ at the big concert on Friday night.

We were onstage playing "Green Onions" when I sobered up.

Oh my God! Where are we in this song? How much have I played? Does it sound all right? How did I ever play it this far? Stop thinking about that, and concentrate on the fact that this arena is full of people listening!

All those thoughts raced through my mind, which had not done much thinking the past week, as the bright lights produced a black-and-white glare in my eyes.

PARIS—1967— ♪ 5

On my first trip to Paris, Annika Sole was waiting for me at the airport. It was like she had picked me out of a lineup and had chosen me. She grabbed my arm and stayed with me the whole time I was in France. She must have been the most beautiful girl in Paris.

After the show, she came back to my hotel to spend the night with me.

I had given all my love to Nicky in London the week before. Annika and I just held each other through the night, and I boarded a plane for Denmark the next morning. She rode with me to the airport, and I never forgot her face, or her touch, or how she cared for me and my things. She carried my case, ordered my food, smiled quietly at me, and never let go of my arm.

Annika spoke no English, and I spoke no French.

Who can speak the language or hear the voice of life when it decides fate should make a move?

When a storm is brewing, the atmosphere changes. Leaves tremble, people and animals behave strangely, a sallow pall envelops the sky. And just before the squall, an eerie calm that's easy to miss.

I missed all the signs. People complained privately about Steve, but I never expected the "intervention."

I heard a thud. Duck (just out of Steve's sight, on the couch in front of the speakers) fell off the couch and onto the floor, trying to suppress his laughter.

Al ran to the door, hit it open, and dragged me out to the street. "Jones, I swear, I'm gon' knock that motherf—er out! I swear!" Apparently, Cropper had said something that sparked this behavior.

My fear was that it would fall on me to try to stop Al if he did go after Steve.

The experience was embarrassing. Bill Halverson, the engineer, heard Steve, but he didn't comment. Here's Steve, this guy who worked his tail off and contributed immensely to all the processes, including mixing, negating the good effects of all his amazing handiwork in the blink of an eye.

Even if Steve really was telling the truth, or believed he had been, it was this kind of "revelation" that he was continually prone to, as well as other frequent musings and behaviors of his, that provided the incentive for the infamous "meeting" in Al Bell's room.

The stated purpose of the "intervention" was to "rein in Steve Cropper's ego" or something of the sort.

I don't remember the tension between Al Bell and Steve being discussed openly. It was a rift that could have split Stax Records with a fatal rupture.

I walked into the room and seemed to lose my sense of time. I looked briefly at a few faces—Deanie Parker, Al Jackson—took a seat in the crowded room, and then kept my eyes on the rug. I felt Steve's eyes on my dropped head. Al Bell was in the armchair on my right. There was no chatter. People were waiting quietly for more principal players to arrive. It was somber.

I think if I had been called to such a meeting, I would have turned and walked out of the room. Even before a word was spoken, there was no doubt who the alpha male was. This process was just a formal verification of the changing over of power in the company.

Joe Arnold came in, looked around, and stood by the door, realizing he was the last to show up. His face told me I wasn't the only one to feel sorry for Steve. But, then again, Steve had asked for it. As I often did in uncomfortable situations, I let my mind drift to events outside the room. I was good at that.

The allegations were bona fide. Steve's vindication was unlikely, and I stayed quiet during the thrashing. I didn't add to the complaints about Steve. He was still a member of my band, the MGs.

If the intention of the intervention was to change Steve's behavior, it failed miserably. He left feeling he had been the victim of a mass betrayal. The company he'd busted his balls for had just slipped through his fingers, unfairly. He'd been the first to unlock the studio doors and the last to leave at night for years. And this was his reward?

On the other hand, I can't imagine any organization that Al Bell was a part of that he didn't rise to the leadership position. He was a born leader. It was his nature, and he slipped easily into the role.

As far as I know, nobody helped Steve lick his wounds.

MEMPHIS—Spring 1967— ♪ *7*

A funky unison organ/guitar introduction, a double snare/slap, a brusque, and commanding bass pickup introduce the undeniably infectious dance groove that is "Hip Hug-Her"—quite possibly the funkiest groove ever to come out of Stax Studios.

The hallmark of "Hip Hug-Her" is its bass line. The funkiest thing you ever want to hear. Not to mention the sound, which makes it seem like Duck is going to break the string on every note, he pulls it so hard. His amp is turned up so loud it distorts, and he plays like he will never get to play another song again. Ever.

So for the first few bars, we just lay back and play rhythm to Duck's bass.

The organ melody, with its oriental tone, sets the curious, mystical character of the tune. Right out of my subconscious, and my fascination with things occult, the melody is searching for its purpose. Finding no answer, our musical path gravitates to the four chord, with the same result, so we go back to the one chord, the tonic. Finally, instead of going to a standard five chord, we stay on the one—searching, we find the minor three, then the major six and down to the four! It makes sense. Resolution! Thank God! You can really dance now, as Al rocks out and we play the rhythmic phrase triumphantly on the familiar one chord. Steve bends back, pushing the really high strings up top in minor thirds—crying! His guitar is crying!

MEMPHIS, Edith Street Home—1964— ♪ 11

William Bell and I were staff songwriters at Stax, a revered position that allowed us first dibs at the label's artists. One of the most prized acquisitions was bluesman Albert King.

William and I were informed that Albert was coming to the studio and needed a song ASAP. That night, we went to the piano in my den, much to the discomfort and chagrin of my wife, Gigi, and wrote the song. It was rumored that Albert King kept a big pistol in his guitar case. I remembered my experience in New York with Jimmy Reed and wondered what tomorrow's session might be like. Turned out he was the sweetest soul ever to walk into that studio.

Learning from composers like Wagner and their use of keys for emotional impact, I knew for instance that a song like "Born Under a Bad Sign" (by Albert King) would be much stronger in C sharp minor than in, say, B flat minor. One of the most significant things I learned from Wagner was the powerful emotional value of the use of a key such as C sharp minor, which was the key of my choosing for Albert King's blues classic, "Born Under a Bad Sign."

On the piano, I started to play the signature line on the lower notes, G flat, A flat, C flat, D flat, F flat, D flat, and so on, and William started singing the words of the title line above what I was playing. We looked at one another and smiled. We had a song.

Next morning, in the studio, I had the thrill of my life. Sitting at the piano, after having taught the main bass line to Steve and Duck, Albert pulled the strings and made the first bent wail of his introductory guitar solo, and it was like electricity struck! I never dreamed I would work with such a master craftsman of the blues. I knew for sure I was alive, because my heart was making movements I'd never felt before, and I was playing notes on the piano I'd never played before. It was just so exciting! I was in the same room with, and at that moment playing with, the inimitable, peerless blues legend. It was a moment I will never forget.

Of the Kings, there was of course B.B., there was Freddie, and then there was Albert, who was left-handed. That gave him an advantage: he could *pull* the strings instead of *push*.

Trusty David Porter, always willing to work behind the scenes, hung back behind the vocal booth, whispering William's words into Albert's ear, saving him from the embarrassing admission of not being able to read.

Albert was a contortionist. Sacrificing his body for the sake of making notes on the guitar. I have no idea why he was so feared. If Albert ever threw a guitar, or a person, across the room, I feel certain it would have been justified. He was the gentlest man I encountered at Stax.

I don't remember if I got paid for the session, or much else about that day, just that I felt, well, successful, happy, and accomplished.

The experience created a special closeness between me and Albert that lingered until he died.

The song, and the cut, marked the end of an era. An era of free-flow creativity at 926 McLemore. Soon after, Al Jackson was named Albert's producer, and we fell off into the crevice of having separate producers for each song.

MONTEREY—June 1967— ♪ 9

In the conspicuous absence of Joe Arnold, who played tenor on the European tour, and Otis himself, Wayne said, "How are we s'pose to do this?" referring to the impromptu rehearsal in Andrew's room for what was to be our biggest show to date in the States: the first Monterey Pop Festival. We hadn't played with Otis since Europe, weeks ago, so there was nervousness and trepidation, especially since we only had time for a hurried run-through with no bass, drums, keys, or guitar. It had seemed like the whole affair was trumped-up from the beginning. "Why hadn't we been offered the date sooner?" We could have been more prepared. Good thing we had just toured Europe a few weeks earlier.

The first day was a gorgeous one, with sunshine, and I was awakened by the refreshing ocean mist. Walking around Monterey alone, I was struck by the absence of police and by the offering of free sandwiches at restaurants, even people offering to share their hotel rooms, making for such a new, unique environment for an American city. People didn't hide their joints and smoked grass on the street.

The front desk called. "Ginger Baker would like to say hello." It was one in the morning.

"Send him up."

There was a knock on the door. Ginger Baker was surrounded

by people. I looked down the hall and it was packed—all the way to the elevator. As many as could followed him into the room, and they made themselves at home. Ginger had an entourage. It was my first experience with that phenomenon.

Quiet and respectful, Ginger was a large ball of hair. It was everywhere on his body, but mostly his head. He smelled like a bouquet of Eastern fragrances. He was wearing thick glasses and custom leather clothing with fringes and sandals. I had my pajamas and bathrobe on. His reputation preceded him. I wished we could go to a studio and play because I knew he could make a drum set sound like an orchestra.

He stayed about an hour, and we talked quietly, with references to Max Roach or Philly Joe Jones, Blakey, drummers he admired, becoming friends in the process. When he left, his court left. My room, and the hall, were suddenly empty. I had been visited by either the Art Blakey of rock or the king of England—I didn't know which.

From our hotel, we were escorted by a large cadre of Hells Angels to the fairgrounds amid a deafening roar from their motors.

Then there were the teal-green mohair suits from Lansky Brothers, which seemed such a good idea in Europe. There wasn't a suit in the whole town, except ours, and we didn't have anything else to wear.

But more important, what would they think of our music? How would they be affected by our groove—which was anything but "Somebody to Love," a song being played nonstop all over San Francisco radio? The crowd was a far cry from the audiences that so warmly and enthusiastically received us in Europe. They were hippies, a counterculture with long hair who embraced tie-dyed clothes, psychedelic drugs, and no sexual inhibitions.

I was the only person in fifty miles who didn't take or smoke anything. I refused joints that were offered me a gazillion times.

Everywhere. At the hotel. At the festival. I didn't need to take or smoke anything—I was so sensitive to the stuff, I was on a contact high. People offered their hotel rooms for me to share, and room doors were generally left open, but I went back to be alone every night. Even on the third and last night, when it seemed I had a whole hippie family sleeping in my room.

Still reeling from the Hells Angels escort to the fairgrounds, I searched different faces in the dressing room, trying to get my bearings. I missed most of the concert. It seemed like the right time to meld the divergent cultures, so I stayed backstage talking to Jack Bruce, who I erroneously assumed was one of the performers since he was backstage. Before Otis came on to close the show, we played nervous renditions of "Philly Dog," with Wayne and Andrew, "Booker-Loo," "Hip Hug-Her," and "Green Onions."

It was the first time I was faced with a shaky performance from the band. It had been awkward starting the Mar-Keys song, especially with only two horns. I wasn't sure what to think. Maybe it was the unfamiliar crowd and the cold night. But they warmed up considerably when Otis came on.

There was no feeling like being onstage with Otis Redding doing "Shake," with Al Jackson on drums. You just wanted to get up and dance. And sometimes I did. Standing right there in front of the organ. The crowd went crazy. Otis had that warm, inviting smile, and they felt it. He hadn't been able to wait to get out on that stage. Even in the cold drizzle, with the sickening teal-green mohair suits on, we just started to have a good time! You couldn't help it. Otis was shouting the provocative, *"Shake! Shake!"* like a possessed man. What a song! It earned us instant acceptance. People rushed the stage. You just had to be in the moment. You didn't have a choice.

The show went on, and the weather got worse. What luck. We started "Respect," and it seemed the crowd ignored the drizzle. It was such a demanding beat, with Otis stomping and the horns bleating, nothing was lost from the energy of "Shake," and the groove continued without a break. By the end of "Respect," the rain was pouring, and Otis was reminding the hippies that they were "the love crowd," which brought us to "I've Been Loving You Too Long," a natural selection for the love theme. Otis begged his way through the song, pleading from the bottom of his heart, with our steady rhythm embracing every triplet with loving care.

When it became apparent we needed to end the set, and the concert, immediately, we did a quick stomp through "Satisfaction," followed by a painfully stubborn rendition of "Try a Little Tenderness." At that point, they would have to *physically remove us from the stage*. Otis had won the game, and he correctly called the shots. *Don't speed this one up. Don't cut it short.* We left the stage victorious! Soaked! And cold! Spent and drained!

NEW YORK CITY—Summer 1967— ♪ *11*

I insisted on having only people directly involved in the recording process present in the studio. At Stax, my wish was honored, as if they realized how visitors and onlookers distracted me to the point of writer's block.

It was decided, however, that we would record "Slim Jenkins' Place" at Atlantic Records' fifth-floor studio in New York, with Tom Dowd at the board.

The tracking session went well until, just before I started to over-dub an organ part, a young man entered the studio and sat on the floor with outstretched legs crossed. I hesitated. The fellow didn't look at me or say anything. Tom came on the talkback: "Ready, Booker?" Cropper, Dunn, and Jackson were in the control room. I was outraged.

"Who the f—k just walked in on my session?"

I got up from the organ, walked past the man and into the control room, with *WTF?* written all over my face.

"Oh, it's just Eric," Tom said. "Don't mind him."

In the hall between the control room and the studio, I paused, half pondering catching a cab to LaGuardia and a flight back to Memphis. Instead, I returned to the studio and overdubbed the descending melody and solo the best I could—completely distracted, eyes on the strange visitor the whole time, who never once looked me in the eye or addressed me.

Thirty years later, at Crossroads in Dallas, I asked Eric Clapton if that had been him all those years ago. "Yes," he admitted. There is, interestingly, no guitar solo on the song.

Nervous, disjointed organ solo and all, "Slim Jenkins' Place" found its place on the *And Now* LP by Booker T. & the MGs. Like "Green Onions," Mrs. Axton had stepped in and exhorted, "You can't name a song 'Slim Jenkins' Joint'!" with the same finality she had years ago with our first record's title, but the name originated from a real place on McLemore Avenue, very near Stax Records.

MEMPHIS—Summer 1967— ♪ 4

Stax was a home away from home for many people. But its greatest omission, or defect, was that it didn't have a bar. Or worse, it wasn't close to a restaurant. Whites had always been free to use any black institution or establishment. So, enter the Four-Way Grill, Slim Jenkins' Joint, and the Lorraine Motel. I don't know if you can have a great studio without having a great bar and restaurant nearby.

Even better if the restaurant serves soul food and is part of a sixteen-room *Green Book*–listed establishment that welcomed whites, like the Lorraine. The only inconvenience was that every guest had to pick up a key at the front desk. If you were checking in or going to your room, you could see the front desk.

It all illuminated how curious and interesting it was that Stax's white males boasted of their trysts with white girlfriends to us black coworkers but kept their indiscretions with black women to themselves. But we saw the goings-on. There's no more revealing a place in town than the check-in counter of a hotel or motel.

Slim Jenkins' Joint was located in the last unit of our building, on the other side of the radio parts store. We sat in the large dark booths near the back, with one eye on an exit, as you did in Memphis's honky tonks, especially if you had white counterparts like we did. Out the front window, we could see Packy Axton and his father, Everett, perpetual figures, standing or sitting on the sidewalk, a case of Bud within reach. Our trips to Slim's were brief. Back to the studio as soon as possible so as not to get into a rift with one of the locals.

One block north and two blocks west on Mississippi at the corner of Walker was located the Four-Way Grill. The Four-Way was the only eatery my mother would go to for Sunday dinner. It was a nice restaurant in back, a bar and grill in front. Good, famous soul food. There was a great-sounding jukebox with lots of Bill Doggett and Jimmie Smith hot organ records on it.

The Lorraine, meanwhile, was the only hotel for blacks in town. Stax staff meetings were held there over lunch at midday, then an afternoon swim before heading back to McLemore Avenue. On any night, you might find Eddie Floyd and Steve Cropper holed up in their favorite corner room, laboring over a new groove. Albert King loved to surprise me with a room key, which I would use to open the door where a beautiful girl awaited. Such was Albert's love for me.

When I wasn't luxuriating at the Lorraine at Albert's expense, I played every conceivable musical instrument at Stax Studios. I was the cleanup man. From tuba to trombone to sax to tambourine, I tried to contribute whatever was needed or asked for. The "pop" with the snare on the backbeats of "Soul Man" is me, hitting a tambourine with a stick. All the mikes and inputs on the session were used, so I had to jump on the drum platform and play into the hi-hat mike, standing next to Al.

We hadn't been that physically close during a performance since the club days. This time, I didn't miss a beat. I wasn't "little young motherf—er" anymore.

In June 1967, I had just moved my new family from Gary, Indiana, to a house in Memphis next door to my parents. I was two-timing my wife with a beautiful girl who was lead singer in a girl group with great prospects. We would meet at the Lorraine Motel for lunch, lovemaking, and a swim.

Things were going so well. We had recently completed a sold-out tour of Europe and had been treated like headliners at the Monterey Pop Festival. Otis Redding had become a superstar in Europe and had killed it at Monterey. We had played for over fifty thousand people that night. Sales and moods were up. People were excited about the prospect that Otis might soon become a major rock star.

Near the end of the summer of 1967, though, something was amiss. Otis Redding was missing from the Stax scene in Memphis. He was quietly absent—for an extended period of time. I thought he was taking some well-deserved time off at his ranch in Macon. As it turned out, Otis hadn't gone home after our Monterey performance. He had ventured alone to Sausalito, California, and spent some time on a houseboat. I flew back to Memphis, completing the Europe/Monterey tour, not realizing anything was wrong.

At night, I would frequent a new downtown club, the Hippodrome, which was owned by my friends Al Jackson and Al Bell, where the Bar-Kays played nightly. The place gave them somewhere to dress up and hang out and audition new talent. Sometimes Otis would stop in because he loved sitting in with Carl Cunningham (Al's protégé) and the rest of the Bar-Kays. One night a good friend of Otis told me that Otis was going to have an operation on his throat. This friend wasn't very specific about the details but confided that it was not a joke.

Fear paralyzed me at the table. I didn't talk or move. I had never considered the absence of Otis and his singing. He had become the energy center of the entire operation. He was spending more and more time in Memphis. I had taken him for granted. If he couldn't sing, what would this mean to us, to Otis, to his fans? Why couldn't I have a positive attitude about the outcome of Otis's operation?

My mother had recently suffered throat surgery and regrettably had to quit the choir at church. She never sang again. She had been Mt. Olive's featured soloist for years, doing cantatas and arias. We could not afford to lose Otis. What was really going on with our newly created rock star—my quiet friend, who said so much with only a well-timed glance?

I was unavailable to Otis. So much was going on in my life with my new family and my marriage in turmoil. I was emotionally headed to California myself, with growing uncertainty about my future. I wish I had been there for him after the show in Monterey. He would have said, "Book, I want to talk."

Otis and I had a quiet understanding. A silent communication. Neither of us was a man of many words; all it took was a look or a gesture. In the studio, Otis was comfortable with my piano accompaniment, having come from a similar gospel background. There was an intuitive flow between us—I related to his passion when he sang, which transferred to my playing. There was an ease and comfort, a certain joy in our musical relationship—it didn't seem to matter if I was playing piano, organ, or guitar, we were musical kin.

Suddenly, the roadie who was begging to sing had people begging him to sing. That fateful twist put Otis in a position of not being able to give enough or do enough for anybody. Otis's inner nature became disquieted, and—not used to these types of pulls from so many sources—he had no experience, no place to turn for advice.

Otherwise, from the outside looking in, the growing Stax family was a happy one. And for all intents and purposes, it was. People loved what they were doing and wouldn't have given it up for anything. Otis Redding (like some others) was evolving as an artist. In England, he had hung out with and listened to music with British rock stars who had been influenced by the same blues artists as him. His horizons and options expanded as his star rose, and he began thinking for himself. By the time Otis rented that Sausalito houseboat, he was searching for the meaning of his new level of stardom.

Soon, everyone knew about the operation, but no one would discuss it. I never knew the nature of the procedure and hated not understanding the details. I kept on with my activities and commitments with a deep sense of regret that Otis would have to go through the surgery and the resulting uncertainty about his voice and future.

MEMPHIS—Fall 1967— ♪ 2

One day late in the fall, I noticed Steve Cropper's mood was up. What was going on? Otis had fully recovered from the operation, and he was singing! What? Otis was singing, man—really singing! As a matter of fact, Cropper said that we would be going into the studio soon—for an extended session. He had been writing new stuff.

There could be no better news. I had begun taking a salary at

Stax—enough to purchase the house I was renting from my dad. Otis was back. Life was good.

I thought "extended sessions" meant going a little longer than usual—maybe starting a little earlier than ten, quitting at midnight instead of eleven. No, we were about to be ensconced at 926 McLemore and taken over by a man possessed. Otis was consumed not only by music but by some supernatural premonition of his fate and destiny.

At Otis's behest, meals became takeout affairs consumed over desks in the private offices. Everyone started calling home to assure wives and families that "everything is OK, just staying at the studio a little longer tonight." Just like last night and the night before. Some, including me, slept on the floor. We had been engulfed in a marathon of songs and music surrounding Otis Redding.

People don't question kings. Not real kings. They just try to do what's expected of them. Ron Capone stepped in as the most capable engineer we ever had. Steve Cropper was amazing as Otis's producer. His stamina and sense of purpose set a steady pace for the whole novel, slightly illogical marathon we had slipped into. Steve had been the Stax A&R man for years—but this week he took all his cues from Otis Redding, ubiquitous, who sent energy in every direction and to every person. We may have become stupefied by the music; we were so insulated. Song after song after song was recorded. I don't remember the sequence.

There was no place in the room Otis wasn't—sitting next to me at the piano, in the booth barking horn lines at the horn players, in the control room looking over Ronnie's shoulder, in the vocal booth with his arms flailing, pounding one foot after another into the carpet along with the rhythm—his face torn with emotion. We could see him through the small, rectangular glass in the tall gunny-sack baffle that kept his voice from ripping into our microphones.

Otis was out on the street during the day—talking to kids and people passing by, who couldn't believe they were meeting and talking to Otis Redding. Pretty soon, Otis was in our heads too. His voice was in my head when I hit the low, midrange piano circle of fourth chords on "Dock of the Bay," my fingers finding the notes to emulate the nautical, seagoing tone I envisioned. No problem. Stuff like that just happens when you follow people who know where they want to go. I had experienced it before with Prince Conley, Mahalia Jackson, Bobby Darin, William Bell, Albert King, and others.

Looking back, the throat problems were not the main problem. The lyrics of "Dock of the Bay" tell the story. How could it be that this jovial, tremendously popular star was deeply troubled by a lack of being understood and by crippling loneliness? How had we let our beloved star escape to a place where he thought he couldn't confide in one of us? Sadly, this was the case with Otis Redding in the fall of 1967.

The playback, however, was amazing. Cropper was at the top of his game. My memory is of him sitting at the console with a long piece of quarter-inch tape draped about his neck, adjusting a couple of faders, and in the next two and a half minutes experiencing something that had never happened before in that room! The most unlikely music you could expect from Stax's most unlikely artist, an anomaly for sure. An uncompromising tone poem of the simplest chordal structure created the setting for Otis's most heartfelt plea for love and understanding. The song took us on a journey together right there in the control room and washed us clean. For a minute, we were one.

The silence after the playback said everything. No one wanted to make the first attempt to comment on how "(Sittin' on) The Dock of the Bay" had made us feel, but we were all happy and proud to be where we were right there in that moment. Otis was both depleted and energized. He was still ready to go.

After that, my memory escapes me, but most likely someone said, "Well, back to work!" or something to that effect, after which we piled out and, in the most professional manner, started to learn the chords to the next song.

It was a song Otis Redding and I wrote together and may be his most suggestive. "Let Me Come on Home" appears as an album cut on his *Dock of the Bay* LP. Written after our trip to Europe, *Days and nights feeling so blue, Lord, I just don't know what I'm gonna do,* the collaboration marks my return to the acoustic guitar as a staple and reflected both our leanings toward rock music. Neither Otis nor I, however, could part completely with our past habits, so the song starts with a characteristic Otis horn line, and I am playing piano triplets, even though I wrote the tune on a Gibson J-45 acoustic. Indeed, old habits die hard.

The only reminder that we are a blues band comes from Steve Cropper's soulful fills and Otis's inescapable pleadings, singing

Crying my eyes out over you
I don't know nothing in the world that I'm gonna do

Typical for me, the tune veers from blues changes at bar 9, going to an E minor chord instead of the traditional blues D chord change, but makes a token attempt to get *back in line* by going to the D chord for the resolution in the last two bars of the phrase. Unconventionally, there is a short, gripping interlude after Steve's solo on the D chord. It's a build that incorporates syncopated drums, horns, and rhythm. A false climax, if you will, that allows Otis to moan into the final verse. With that, we are on our way home, but not before revisiting the compelling interlude briefly, to let Otis plead once again and Steve twang once more, before we play the resolving chords into the fade-out.

To my knowledge, there has been no singer in the Western world who pleaded with the earnestness of Otis Redding. It wasn't fake. His tempestuous inner self was full of apprehension, yearning, and love for everything he touched.

Otis milked Eddie Floyd's lyric for every note it was worth in his rendition of "More Than Words Can Say." Eddie and I wrote it expressly for Otis, knowing this would be the outcome. He needed the song to complete his album *Dock of the Bay*, as he didn't have time to write everything himself.

Standard structure found me once again playing triplet piano arpeggios—a sad 6/8-time ballad, à la Jerry Butler. The painful verse, which Eddie crafted for Otis like a skilled tailor, leaned on the seventh chord in the melody. As Otis sang the word *please,* you couldn't imagine him in any other posture but on his knees. By the time the song floated to the second verse and Otis crooned halfway through: *"I was tempted to call it a day,"* one is reminded of the vocal renditions of Percy Mayfield and Ray Charles, or Billie Holiday, which implied love was more important than life.

There I am, nearly pinching myself, goose bumps on my arm, unbelieving of my participation in such moving music, trying to focus and concentrate on my part.

Otis was made for singing heartbreaking songs, and I was made for writing unrelentingly unconventional verse and bridge changes. Such was the case with "More Than Words Can Say." What song moves from the major one chord to the major two after two bars? Somehow it works. There are only five chords in the whole song. The simplicity makes way for Otis's soulful melismas and Eddie's painful words.

"(Sittin' on) The Dock of the Bay" became a huge hit—not because it was a musical side trip by Otis but because its theme touched the hearts of a million people who recognized the lament either in themselves or someone they were close to—or they just simply felt for the fella singing the song.

DECEMBER 10, 1967— ♪ 6

In a Cincinnati, Ohio, airport bar with Steve and Al, Duck was teasing me: "You just wastin' that drink; why did you order it?" We were marking time, waiting for a connecting flight to Memphis. A page came over the loudspeaker for Al Jackson. It was his wife, Barbara, on the phone with news that Otis's plane had crashed in Wisconsin. I finished my drink. So did the others.

I was twenty-three years old. The Bar-Kays were onboard that plane. Not that long ago, we were in the studio recording the Bar-Kays singles, rubbing shoulders, and playing music together. It was the first shock of that kind in my life. The Cunningham family was like my own family. Leander and Luther (Carl's older brothers). They filled out the drum line next to Maurice White at Booker Washington High School and were like brothers to me. Carl was the youngest in the line of drummer brothers. His mother would be devastated.

It was unthinkable news. My mind went blank. All I can remember are the details of the airport bar. The shape of the counter, the bright light of the morning, the glasses on the counter, the bottles behind the bartender. The conversation escapes me, as do the details of the flight we took back to Memphis and much of the next few days in general.

Barbara had few, if any, details for Al. Just the crash. My mind raced. Phalon Jones was the tenor sax player in the Bar-Kays. His mother, Willa, was one of the comely waitresses at the Harlem House, a hamburger restaurant right next to BTW High School. I stopped by there every day after school, and I was one of her favorites. Willa would be beside herself with grief.

Then there were Ronnie Caldwell, organ, and Jimmie King, guitar, my favorite. The candidate to take Steve's place. We weren't told that Ben Cauley (trumpet) survived or that James Alexander (bass) wasn't on the plane.

My next distinct memory is sitting at the organ in Macon, Georgia, playing music for the funeral, and before that, being squeezed in the back seat of a limo between Jerry Wexler and Ahmet Ertegun after having waited an eternity for Jerry's plane from New York to land because they refused to fly together. It was company policy to ensure one of the Atlantic executives survived a crash. I remember thinking, *But they will ride in a limo together?*

The funeral was unbearably sad; once again the details escape, just an inescapable reluctance to look at Otis's widow, Zelma, and no glances at his children at all. It was all I could do to focus on playing the organ without falling apart. I was a different man in those days, full of the southern edicts that a man is not supposed to cry. If I had to do it again, I would let the tears flow, I'd let it all out without reservation instead of keeping it all in. But it was 1967, in Macon, Georgia...so the crying was mostly done by the women and children.

I had played "Jesus Keep Me Near the Cross" a thousand times at Mt. Olive—for the men's Bible class and in Sunday school since I was a boy. Joe Simon was to sing this song, and I had agreed to provide the organ accompaniment. But this morning, at Macon's City Auditorium, the song, the melody, all, became lost on me. It left my mind, and I didn't know where to start. My professionalism vanished. Joe, down at the podium, waited for me to start. An endless, uncomfortable interim. Fortunately, I brought the music, fumbled frantically to place it on the stand under the light at the huge pipe organ, and began to play. The hymn always brought tears at Mt. Olive during regular church services, and when Zelma Redding heard Joe Simon's mournful strains, she fell apart. I could hear her stomping the floor from where I sat at the organ. My heart sank lower. Where did I find the strength to keep playing? Why did the job fall to me? I was a mourner too. It was the saddest funeral I had ever been to.

The pain and disbelief were felt by all. The church was full; the day was surreal. Otis was gone. He was a good friend to me... didn't talk too much, always straight to the point. He was just quietly there, keeping company in the old southern way.

CHAPTER 12
Time Is Tight

MEMPHIS—1972— ♪ 4

In 1972, someone set fire to the Cossitt Library Negro Branch on Vance Avenue in Memphis, Tennessee, and it burned to the ground. The system was desegregated in 1960. Until then, the Vance branch was the only public library available to black Memphians.

For a boy growing up in Memphis, the Cossitt Library was so much more than just a library. Until I made the band, it was my destination after school. In second grade, I learned to use the card catalogue. The large two-story building was a refuge for hundreds of my classmates as well. There I learned of the Dahomey man of Africa and saw photos of Siamese women in Indonesia and cobra snakes in India. At the library, I was able to see photos of African men that resembled me to my eye. My father would take me there on Saturday mornings.

I can still place myself in the building with its tall windowpanes and its imposing front lawn stretching out from formidable steps leading up from the street. My father often dropped me off at the back entrance, where I could quickly skip in from the small rear parking lot.

The Cossitt Library was Memphis's only depository of titles by and about black authors, save a few shelves in the small libraries of the seven black high schools. The Cossitt was where the black history books lived alongside European and world literature. It was the treasure chest of Memphis's African American written word.

I had left Memphis and moved to California when I learned of the burning of the Cossitt. Of all the acts committed in the battle to keep blacks down, this seemed the most vicious and desperate.

In keeping with my family's custom, those early trips to Cossitt whetted my appetite, and I never lost the craving for learning, even beyond my college years.

Universities exist to fight poverty...poverty of thought. Life, and progress in life, as well as sustainability, are all constructed of ideas, which are born of thought.

If there are no ideas, there will eventually be no life. To feed the body and not the mind is nearly an exercise in futility. Can affluence of mind be attained if it is never perceived?

MEMPHIS—April 4, 1968— ♪ 6

Dr. Martin Luther King Jr. was a man who believed in education. He understood that racism was an encumbrance on the entire human race. He came to Memphis to help the troubled garbage workers with their strike because he was disturbed by the lack of progress.

Then, on April 4, 1968, Dr. Martin Luther King Jr. was assassinated at the Lorraine Motel.

Because our studio at Stax Records was a made-over movie theater, without so much as a conference room large enough to seat the staff, we convened at the Lorraine's dining room, often during lunch. There was no lounge at Stax. We hung out in the small foyer, in the hall, or on the street. The Lorraine provided the only suitable location where black and white could congregate without intervention.

When Dr. King was shot there, it was as if the act had been carried out on our own turf—a dreadful mockery of the harmonious racial mixing that went on at the Lorraine, and of our espousing of the motel.

A man of inordinate strength and sensitivity, Dr. King has survived through his four children. There were very few African American preachers who had fewer than seven children in my day. It was a mark of pride and intelligence to be able to recite the names of your pastor's children without hesitation, like being able to spell Mississippi or know the capital cities of the states.

Martin Luther King Jr. Boulevard. There is one in every city. You won't find it in the white neighborhoods. More often than not, it will take you to the airport. I've tried this; if you're lost and need to catch a flight, just get directions to Dr. Martin Luther King Jr. Boulevard.

His name drives my mind to the garbage workers of the world. My daddy used to always tell me, "Make sure to go back to the alley and say hello to Mr. Fletcher; the garbagemen are coming today." Their fight was our fight, and they had no chance of winning against Mayor Henry Loeb or Mr. Crump's long-implanted system of city government.

That's why Dr. King came to Memphis. He was their only hope. He was our only hope. There could be no mistake. No backing down from this one. No violence, no fear, no wavering. The time had come. When I'm driving to the airport, I think about it before every flight.

I was struck by the same force that killed Dr. King. The shot killed him, but it impelled a new part of me to come alive. Now, I live with as much joy and humility as I can.

Thank God, thank God, for my brown, African American skin and all that came with it. How can I tell you the pride I feel—the good fortune to come from the place I do? And as a result, to be who I am. All the oppression, the racial prejudice, the inequalities and inequities, the lack of privilege and opportunity—the lashes my forebearers endured on their backs, the rapes my grandmothers endured, even the fears my children suppressed, don't dampen the feeling of privilege I harbor as a person of my race.

I am a fighter, but I am not bitter. I know the value of love and forgiveness. I hold tight to the power of my conviction and faith in the ultimate victory of love. There is no doubt in my mind that the human race will succeed. It is no accident that we have not already destroyed ourselves. Even our own ignorance and stupidity are not strong enough to overcome the life force that brought us here. We may not come together of our own accord; however, our own genetic code will override somatic differences to the point where one's race will not be discernible. It is just a matter of time.

Dr. King's spilled blood on the balcony at the Lorraine Motel in 1968 produced a resolute sense of purpose in me. As a result, I have always led with my heart, often violating long-standing rules in the process.

MEMPHIS, Stax—1968— ♪ 5

My band was the "face" of racial harmony, literally and figuratively, from as far back as 1962. That has placed an inordinate amount of pressure on me to reassure the constituencies that it was indeed the case and confirm that the conception is accurate.

What family is not dysfunctional to some degree? Am I supposed to believe I was not referred to in derogatory racial terms behind my back? Should I believe I was defended during racist dinner discussions in East Memphis? If so, I was never told.

African Americans have long been aware of the terms racist whites used to refer to them, and only the strongest white protesters had the courage and gumption to stand up to their families regarding this. I would be surprised if any of my cohorts were included in that group. To be fair, there was no shortage of derogatory terms used to refer to whites in the general black community.

We started out with a true and genuine love and respect for each other and the music. You don't make music as glorious and original as we did without some kind of inspired purpose from all involved. The MGs did love each other. You don't have white and black working closely together every day in close collaboration without developing some kind of family unit. That unit became an example of how the races could escape the plantation mentality, and with that also came a sense of comfort that failed to evolve into a sense of caring beyond the boundaries of our work space. As we were held up more and more as an example to the world of how integration could work, it became more and more a veneer.

I began to feel a responsibility for voicing the needs of my people and the struggle we were involved in. It came to where the social issues demanded us to identify our allegiances. I wanted my bandmates to champion civil rights, not just be willing to play with blacks.

It wasn't easy. Dr. King's murder exposed the fact that our group dynamics were more complicated than I realized.

After Dr. King was shot and killed at the Lorraine Motel, Steve made these remarks to an interviewer:

> You know, Memphis was a refuge for black people, it really was. Blacks were blacks and whites were whites, and everybody was cool. We all loved each other. The black people were perfectly happy with what was going on. I don't think anywhere in the universe was as racially cool as Memphis was until Martin Luther King showed up. That just set it off for the world, basically. What a shame. There must be something political about that. Let's go to the one place in the South where everybody is getting along and blow that fuse. That's the only way I can see it.

I just happened to be reading Charles Hughes's *Country Soul* when I saw this. It hit me hard. This was the guitar player in my band speaking! How could I continue to knowingly collaborate with anyone who supported the mind-set that made Dr. King's murder possible?

In my opinion, all forward-thinking whites needed to play a significant role in the fight for racial progress—especially the whites in my band, whom I'd spoken up for in the face of black radicals.

ATLANTA, GA—1968—♪4

Once, I was sitting with friends in the open-air lobby of the Peachtree Plaza Hotel. Three black men with large Afros approached our table. They were wearing the long wide-legged jeans and bright-colored shirts with exaggerated collars characteristic of the times. My friends, Dick "Cane" Cole and Joan "Golden Girl"

Golden, both of WLOK in Memphis, were intimidated by the glowering presence of the men. I looked each of them in the eye; they glared back.

It would be my guess that under their vests all three men were packing. This would be the second time this group had let it be known to me their disapproval of my playing with white musicians. Similar to Fillmore Street in San Francisco, just before a performance at the Fillmore Ballroom, a man expressing his displeasure with my choice of bandmates had engaged me. He told me it was not their nature to love me.

The San Francisco man may have been accurate in that respect, but I had a right to choose who was not going to love me—and the menacing demeanor of his Atlanta comrades was not oozing with sweetness. I don't know the identity of the San Francisco man, but the conference in Atlanta took on a siege mentality when the Oakland cadre made its grand entrance.

I was an early target because I was the most visible. Booker T. & the MGs were the first interracial band on the black music scene. Other whites were involved in less conspicuous ownership and management roles. In general, they did not attend the conferences. The meeting at my table was the last of its kind, and it ended on a contentious note at best, when my new "friends" simply walked away.

MEMPHIS—1968—♪ 5

Injustice, such as having to work in dangerous, life-threatening conditions, were a very real fact in the world I inhabited and grew up in. People who lived in privilege and plenty knew nothing of the resolve needed just to subsist under those conditions, much less the courage required to fight for any betterment. Every knowledgeable, able-bodied person needed to make his or her case for equality in any way they could, else more life or limb was lost. Additionally, as black garbagemen were not being paid the same as their white coworkers, identical injustices in the economic sphere existed at my own work.

The fact that I, as a principle songwriter at Stax, was not invited, or permitted, to participate in the publishing of my own music contributed to my need to turn away.

The only band member allowed to participate, Steve Cropper, advanced unabashedly in the company, and knowledge of his holdings and interests in publishing the music was withheld. Had those kinds of facts been declared or revealed, a feeling of trust would have prevailed. My own intuition was the only indication that something was amiss.

Just that gut feeling that as writers we were the rightful owners of our songs. However, no one wanted to rock the boat. Even so, we were chagrined, and there was an underlying sense of humiliation that none of us would cop to, as is necessary when a large working group is subjected to this kind of concealed theft.

And, of course, there was anger in the ranks, abated on a daily basis by the joy of being involved with such awesome music. The amazing music came about as a result of the work of writing the songs and developing them. Magic doesn't happen by accident. And so, fortunately, the anger never grew into rage.

The unsung hero of Stax was its resourceful neighborhood that kept it supplied with talent born right under its nose. Regrettably, that same resource provided thuggish, pugnacious figures that were anxious to use coercion and take charge of the street after Martin Luther King Jr.'s death.

B. W. "Chicken" Bowen harassed me from my early days in the band at Booker T. Washington High School. A baritone horn player, he was a tall, thin boy with a large Adam's apple and teeth and facial and body features that made him resemble a tall chicken.

When he showed up on the corner of College and McLemore, it was the dread of seeing an old adversary that you hoped was in your past, but it was surely just your luck that he would find you once you had found some measure of fame, fortune, or security. So Chicken gave me a friendly greeting and promptly offered to sell me an old rickety handgun, which I was obliged to purchase from him.

The gun was useless as a weapon. Even at my tender age, I knew firearms. I had been trained in their use and nomenclature for years at the armory under the stadium at BTW. I was the National Defense Cadet Corps–appointed leader—battle group commander— having been promoted from corporal to lieutenant to captain to colonel and finally to the top rank a student could hold. I passed the exam of breaking down and reassembling an M1 rifle (as used against the Vietcong) blindfolded in the allotted time period.

In high school, Captains Powell and Johnson taught us handguns and the tactics of insurgency—as though we would be officers. In reality, with our dark skin, we would enter combat areas as second lieutenants, commissioned ranks but with less authority on the battlefield than an experienced sergeant.

As fate would have it, while I was at Indiana University with a scholastic deferment studying music, my second-in-command was sent to Vietnam. I can't count the times I have seen his face in my mind since I got word in Indiana that he had been killed in active duty. No doubt I would have been at his side.

Since tenth grade, guns had been commonplace in my life, most usually the five-pound M1 carbine I carried during the cadet drills at school. That gun dwarfed the one I was forced to buy from Chicken. I began to scoff at the little pistols the corner gangsters brandished.

I put the shell of Chicken's gun in a drawer and continued to walk past him and into Stax every day, no longer intimidated. I had stood up to street thugs before and gotten beat up, but I always felt better, even though I had bruises. In most cases the thugs would later come and try to befriend me. Sometimes even years later as adults.

Before I left Memphis in 1968, I heard stories of Stax family members being beaten and threatened by Johnny and Dino at the behest of a prominent artist on the label. What had Stax come to? What had I given my all to help create? Where was the feeling of ease? Where was the future?

Both inside and outside the company, there seemed no bounds to the upheaval and disorder.

MEMPHIS, Lauderdale and Wellington—1968— ♪ 5

"Send five thousand dollars if you value your son's life," the caller said to my parents. The drop-off location was designated as the corner of Lauderdale and Wellington, seven blocks away. At two o'clock, Dad was to come alone and leave the money on the sidewalk in a paper bag below the storefront window at Waltham's Grocery. The call rattled my folks beyond belief. Who would do something like this? I was their only son, barely twenty-four years old. My parents called the police.

I knew the location well. It was the east boundary of my paper route, right in the middle of a route I had turned down because of the Wellington Street gangs. Above Waltham's Grocery was also where my girlfriend Marie stayed in her friend's apartment when she lied to me about being in Nashville in the summer of 1962.

A plan was devised to pay the money and deliver it to the drop-off point while I would be safely ensconced in my living room as police cars surrounded the house on side streets.

Dad went to the bank.

The bank provided Dad $5,000, which he carried in a brown paper bag.

I took a chair in my living room by the door. My mother sat on the couch. We waited. My wife, Gigi, came in and sat down on another chair. She was nicely dressed, with high heels and makeup. Dad's car pulled out of the driveway, and we waited, looking through the curtains at the street.

While we were waiting, Mama informed me that the police had advised the money be paid in marked bills. I hadn't known that previously. Mama also told me that unmarked police cars were waiting, hidden, near the drop-off point. Not long after, Gigi went into the bedroom and made a phone call.

After an excruciatingly long time, Dad's Buick pulled into the driveway. He left the bag at the corner and saw no one. We were just glad he got back safely. I was surprised and gratified by the help and cooperation of the Memphis Police Department. My mother went home to wait with my father.

Finally, the phone rang. It was the police. No one ever turned up to pick up the money. The brown sack remained on the sidewalk on the street. It was 6:00 p.m. We had waited four hours. The officers confiscated the bag and called off the watch.

I was rattled at the core but kept my composure. I didn't want to lose my young life, but the event was so odd, I couldn't imagine where the threat had come from. During the whole episode, Gigi sat quietly in a pleasant mood. She listened and observed but offered no comfort to me. The night and the following days passed without incident.

STAX, New Order—1968— ♪ *4*

Meanwhile, a New York parking lot attendant was working hard and setting a course that would intersect our lives. His name was

Charles Bludhorn. He saved and borrowed enough to buy the parking lot and dozens of others in New York.

I never met Charles Bludhorn. Never spoke with him. No direct correspondence. Ever. But we communicated as clearly as two people ever have. The Austrian-born New Yorker exerted his strong will and authority as far as Hollywood and Memphis before the Securities and Exchange Commission finally caught up with him and his vast conglomerate, Gulf & Western Industries. But not before he bought Paramount Pictures, which bought Stax Records, which owned me.

Described as volatile, Napoleonic, and ruthless, Mr. Bludhorn's company began sending memos directly to the staff at 926 East McLemore.

One advised us we were to have three shifts of sessions—3:00 p.m.–11:00 p.m., 11:00 p.m.–7:00 a.m., and 7:00 a.m.–3:00 p.m.—in order to up our music production. Under Al Bell's direction, the directive was activated, and I was forced onto the 3:00 p.m.–11:00 p.m. shift. The old Capital Theater recording studio became a 45-record/song-production conveyor belt, quite different from the little studio of years before where I carried my baritone sax and haphazardly played an intro to a twelve-bar blues by Rufus and Carla Thomas.

MEMPHIS—1968— ♪ 7

A few weeks into the new configuration, just after we showed up for our shift, Al Jackson pulled me up to the record shop. He wanted me to listen to something and stood there while the song played, assessing my reaction. The music was different from anything I'd ever heard. The instruments—a steel drum, marimbas, and guitars—danced to a gentle, persistent conga rhythm that brought swaying palm trees to mind. Immediately I connected to it emotionally.

Soon after listening to the island songs, Al was the impetus for the creation of "Soul Limbo." He came up with the unique idea of starting the phrase with a tom-tom on beat 1, and I wrote the organ melody and bass line to his rhythm. Duck covered the organ bass line, Steve played a calypso rhythm, and we had a happy, refreshing lilt—different from, but inspired by, Jamaican beats.

Featuring the jazzy piano and guitar, "Over Easy" is Booker T. & the MGs uptown, with a touch of Latin conga for tang. It's me and my cohorts at our most pretentious. Despite our efforts to relax when we were recording, "Over Easy" came off as an upscale, ritzy tune, marked with, and enduring, an underlying tension.

The offering from my Ramsey Lewis–, Young-Holt Trio–, freedom-fighter–tinged period, "Over Easy" purports to be the type that might be appreciated by a hip, educated, cautiously religious, intellectual, sophisticated wine lover. The song is so un-Memphis-like, so un-MGs-like. It sounds as if it was recorded at some swank Chicago nightclub on the south side, mere steps away from the church, and the gents wore the same suit to either.

LOS ANGELES—1968— ♪ 5

After "Soul Limbo" became popular, a Latin theme took hold of the day, and instrumental groups from Chicago, New Orleans, and New York gravitated toward California. Herbie Hancock recorded "Watermelon Man" in New York, then moved to LA. Los Angeles was "the happening place."

On one of my first trips to California as a young musician, I had the unfortunate experience of having my right leg fall out from under me during a photo shoot for the album *Soul Limbo*. We had been playing football at Venice Beach in the warm spring California sun, and suddenly, my right knee collapsed. "Get up, Jones, you missed that pass!" Al Jackson barked as I lay writhing in the hot, dry sand. I would not "get up" for another four months, and I would not walk on that leg for another year.

It turns out that the previous eight years of playing the Hammond B-3 organ had been an occupational hazard. The wooden bar just below the keyboard had deteriorated the bone just below my right knee from all my physical abandon when I was sitting there playing the instrument.

I ended up in the Cedars of Lebanon Hospital in East Hollywood because Mark Lindsay, a new friend I made on the set of *Shindig,* the TV show, had heard about my unfortunate dilemma and called his family physician, Dr. Gerald Leve, who quickly gathered a team of doctors for a meeting and initiated the early-morning surgery for me. Bone was to be taken from my hip, pulverized, and implanted in my leg.

Mark Lindsay, who founded the group Paul Revere and the Raiders, is one of those special people who take care of other people without being asked. I will be forever grateful to Mark. He dealt with everything by phone from the set of the TV show and never asked for any thanks.

The surgery, though innovative for its time, was successful, and the young surgeon came to pay me a visit early in my recovery. He lit a cigarette as he greeted me with a smile, and when I asked for one, he advised me against smoking during and after my recovery, saying, "Do as I say, not as I do." Of course, I proceeded to smoke cigarettes for another ten years.

Only a day before, they shot enough photos before I became crippled to get the timeless cover for the *Soul Limbo* LP, which shows the four of us flirting with a pretty girl.

HOLLYWOOD—1968—♪7

In 1960, the Academy Award for Best Song went to "Never on Sunday," also nominated for five other awards, including Best Writer and Director. The handsome, charming, smiling, happy-go-lucky Greek sailor in *Never on Sunday*, the guy who got the girl (Melina Mercouri) in the movie, also in real life, was Jules Dassin. He was also the successful Hollywood producer and director who walked into my hospital room to offer me my dream job: composing the score for a major Hollywood feature film.

"Hello, Booker T. I'm Jules. Jules Dassin."

"I know who you are."

"I'm here to tell you I'd like you to do the score for my new film, *Uptight*. It's starring Ruby Dee and Frank Silvera, and we have a wonderful rising young star, Julian Mayfield." He took my head in his hands.

I was won over, but I said, "Mr. Dassin—"

"Call me Jules."

"Jules, look at me! I don't—"

He put his finger over my lips.

"When do I start?"

"Right away. I've arranged an office for you on a lot in Culver City, near your sister's house. You can start as soon as you start to feel better." Smiles all around.

This, even though I was fully incapacitated, was the express intention of one, Jules, who not only insisted I was the right person for the job but who also pledged all manner of personal assistance, wheelchairs, limousines, offices, and the like to my disposal in order to complete the score. And then, having said his bit, he said nothing, just standing there with his staff and smiling at me.

What was I to say? "Sorry, Mr. Dassin, I have only been waiting for this moment since I was a young boy, but now because I'm hurt

I must turn you down?" The film was Paramount Pictures' *Uptight*, and in the opinion of some, the first of Hollywood's "Blaxploitation" movies, but to my mind it was the film swan song of black America's underground resistance movement.

My sister, Gwen, gave me the back bedroom at her Crenshaw District duplex for my recovery. Paramount sent over a Moviola and reels of film and reams of soundtrack that I had to manipulate from my wheelchair. She brought the piano from the living room to the back bedroom for me to write on. Quincy Jones sent over a large click book that reconciled music beats per minutes with film frames per second so I would know how to sync the score.

CULVER CITY—1968— ♪ 5

The lot at Culver City was a behemoth. It was a whole city unto itself, with streets and neighborhoods within its perimeters replicating various cities of the world. The movie company sent a car for me, but Gwen's husband, Floyd, insisted on driving me. "Yes, but I know how to get there!" And he did that every day while I worked in Culver City. Floyd was familiar with LA because he had been all over the city as a photographer. He knew how to slip around Jefferson Boulevard to National, and he dropped me off right at my door on the side street, Ince Boulevard, on the east side of the Culver City lot, avoiding traffic while the limo sat in front of Floyd's duplex.

At the Ince Boulevard entrance, carpenters had installed a ramp so I could get into my wheelchair on the street and "drive" myself directly up into my office. It was a small bungalow with dark green wooden siding, an older building, quite comfortable, with ivy growing up the walls. A small sitting room with a couch and a window, a bathroom, a workroom with a window, a piano, and a

Moviola, my reels of film—I was home. From the window, I could see Ince Boulevard with its rows of cars and buckled sidewalks with no pedestrians.

No sooner had I settled in than a meeting was called, summoning everyone to come to the production office. The night before, Melina had gone on *The Tonight Show Starring Johnny Carson*. Melina told the world that her uncle—the mayor of Athens, Greece—had been deposed by a military junta. His assigns—including her father, minister of the interior—had been forced, at gunpoint, to leave their offices all over the city. Her citizenship and property were taken as well. Greece was occupied!

Melina, Jules's wife, was a high-profile movie star. The heartbroken actress innocently conveyed the tragic news to Carson's large US TV audience. In so doing, she became a prime target for the aggressive military faction, along with her coworkers and loved ones. Protection was in order, and France was a country we could disappear in, not so visible as Hollywood. The small, quaint town of Quai Carnot was the last place the violent junta would look for a movie postproduction company such as ours.

Everything changed. My breathing became faster...I noticed Bob, my friend, the editor, fidgeting and jiggling his keys. There were suited guards at our gates. They just stood and looked blank-faced at us. We had to move. Quickly. The company had already relocated once, from Cleveland to Hollywood, before I came aboard. Now everyone and everything had to be packed up and moved overseas, to France—Paris—a city Jules knew well and was comfortable in, and a city that knew him well also. We moved into a vacant, nondescript building on the west bank of the River Seine.

FRANCE—1968— ♪ 1

I fell in love with Paris on that trip. During those weeks, I learned to drink Beaujolais, order chateaubriand avec frites, and argue in French—the people seemed enamored of short, quick fights and prompt makeups. Many times on the side streets, I saw Frenchmen break off into fistfights only to walk off together seconds later as if nothing had happened. My chauffeur had a habit of borrowing a few francs from me when he picked me up in the morning with the promise of paying me back that evening, all in French of course. Naturally, the first word of French I learned was *maintenant* (now) in an attempt to get Claude to pay me back. He was always able to persuade me to loan him more money and of course never paid me back. Not one franc. Every day Claude showed up faithfully and drove me with my great casted leg out of Paris to the neighborhood called Quai Carnot across the river. I found the patience to walk up and down steps on my crutches and to navigate cobblestone side-walks even as the rubber tips on the ends slid into cracks between the rocks.

In Quai Carnot, I would walk down to the river and lunch on one of the boats, and every day Claude picked me up to drive me through the traffic back to Paris. Claude was even available in the evenings for my roustabouts until all hours of the morning.

Paris grew on me. Something in the art, in the wine, in the language. The architecture, the excess, the passion. Something made the artist in me feel comfortable. Statues of African American jazz artists in the parks. Restaurants refusing to charge my lunch to my credit card—a message from the chef: "Booker T. Jones doesn't pay here." I was walking the streets of the city Europe patterned itself after. It all spoke to me.

At the Madeleine Palace, I savored chateaubriand avec frites. French steak and potatoes, with wine—and a certain chambermaid named Pierette. Tall, with dark hair, and very French, Pierette was the epitome of courtesy and beauty, serving *petit dejuner* and many other aspects of my suite's requirements.

Jules was father to the famous and handsome French singer Joe Dassin. Joe and I became friends. Joe's sisters, Julie and Rickie, were two of Paris's most enticing and striking young women. The beauty of Jules's daughter Rickie was not lost on me.

One evening, even though my right leg was cast from my foot to my hip, I had Claude take me to Rickie's home, knowing full well the impropriety. Rickie was still living with her mother, Jules's ex-wife.

Next morning, at work, Jules took my face in the palms of his two hands and smiled broadly. He gave me a smack as he recalled the young man he had once been. We continued work on the film, and I never saw Rickie again.

And then there was Melina, who savored the role of a prostitute and nearly won an Oscar in the process. Best Actress at Cannes the year I was born. I sensed her presence behind me as I sat in her husband's director's chair.

Because she believed it would bring good luck to run one's hands through a black man's hair, Melina would slip up behind me. I would feel her long fingers running through my hair and smell her perfume. Melina Mercouri, the famous Greek actress, was massaging my scalp. A seductress, she was attractive with her dark, low voice, and she called me darling. The boss's wife!

All of Melina's charms couldn't keep Jules's eyes off a certain French film editor, smitten as he was with Melina. You would think he would have had more sympathy for my inability to resist his daughter.

Even on my days off, I had Pierre pick me up and take me to Quai Carnot, in St. Cloud, because I loved it there so much. I loved to walk up to the ornate house, built years ago by a rich family from Lyon, and walk past the garden on the street.

One Sunday, on our trip back to Paris, there was more traffic than usual, and then French soldiers appeared just before we approached the Sorbonne University. It appeared there was a big uprising at the school, and I was stuck in town and didn't get to go back to work for a week or so. Back home, Stephen Stills, under the influence of outrage and Joni Mitchell, wrote and sang "For What It's Worth," and the French, as well as much of the world, turned their backs. Now it had reverberated around the world to the exact spot where I was. The French students revolted! They closed the Champs-Élysées! We couldn't get back across the bridge to St. Cloud for days.

During our time off, Jules took me around Paris like I was his son. He introduced me to this important director and showed me that famous studio with that infamous smile and a great sense of comfort and pride. We ate at his favorite restaurants and visited his children. I pretended to know all the important people and their films, and all was good.

Being there in the old European city was having a profound effect on me. All the French composers I had studied while underneath the music building at Indiana and all the theories and lectures about long musical motifs and themes began to take root and make sense as I soaked in the foreign yet not so foreign culture.

Jules was powerfully attached to the central character of his film, Tank, and his attachment translated to me as well as the rest of the crew. The film became our life. Soon, Tank must die, and I must write music to accompany that transition from life to death. At some point, the theme came. But it was not an ode to death but one of life, clearly a melody that allowed death to take place in all its sorrow and tragedy but in the context of life and hope. The music seemed to give eternity its due importance and yet reconcile the loss with the gain of equality (racial equality) that was sure to be one of the payoffs.

In the parlance of late sixties' black hip culture, a man could call another man "baby" or say "I love you" to him without sexual implications or overtones.

"Johnny, I Love You" is a song of affection and betrayal between two militant revolutionary brothers in the black resistance movement in Cleveland. Although I wrote it in France, it was recorded in Hollywood with A-team musicians Herb Ellis on guitar, the inimitable Ray Brown on upright bass, and Fats Domino's drummer, Earl Palmer. There was no risk of having to split songwriter credits if I recorded in Hollywood on Paramount's dime instead of Memphis, and since Paramount was willing to cough up the money, I went for it.

I took the liberty to both sing and use the best available session musicians as if I would never get the chance to do either again.

The tune started with regular blues changes, and I took my usual liberty of defecting away from traditional changes at bar five or nine, by going to the flatted five chord (F flat), and walked the changes back down chromatically to the tonic, twice, ending on B flat. The turnaround used the traditional two chord to the five chord to get back to the chorus.

Lyrically, Cleveland was depicted as a city that was socially and morally broken because of its racial intolerances, and that disrepair was the reason Tank and Johnny needed to arm the brothers. Tank guarantees Johnny he "has his back" in the heat of battle and will be his support when times get rough. Based on *The Informer*, the song makes no reference to Tank's weakness, being mainly a paean to the dissidents' loyalty to each other.

The sound was warm and bluesy, in the comfortable key of B flat. Ray's bass filled up the studio with warmth, there were smiles all around, and the session was a joy. I was thrilled to have recorded my first vocal track.

QUAI CARNOT, FRANCE—1968— ♪ 2

The contrast between the well-appointed, acoustically sophisticated LA recording studio and the rickety narrow steps leading up to my third-floor work space in France was stark.

In that small room in Quai Carnot on the River Seine in St. Cloud, not far from Paris, I laid the theme for "Time Is Tight" into the temp track for the movie *Uptight*.

I used the old piano in an upstairs room in the quaint French town. "Time Is Tight" was the culmination of my composition studies at Indiana University converging with the cultivation of the musical exploits in Memphis that became the Stax sound, including my explorations into jazz and blues and my gospel roots.

When the melody to "Time Is Tight" came to me, I knew nothing of the concept of the golden ratio. However, the phrase is an example of the golden mean; its pattern is an eight-bar phrase followed by a fourteen-bar phrase, a representation of the golden ratio—a reflection of the divine in its unique properties of proportion. Other examples include a rose, a sunflower, spirals, galaxies, and paintings by Leonardo da Vinci and other Renaissance artists.

The melody is the simplest I have ever composed. I hold the first G six whole beats. A whole note for four beats and a half note for two more beats into the next bar before I move up to C and B in eighth notes, right back to G again for four more beats. A child could easily play it. The pattern is repeated in a shorter form starting with a C note, which is held for a full eight beats at the end of the phrase. At its core "Time Is Tight" is the essence of simplicity, only three notes. However, while holding those notes, I try to exude the character of my heart each time I play the song, and much is left to the imagination of the listener.

"Time Is Tight" encapsulated an era of struggle and exploration, a period of my life in a piece of music.

Tank's death scene at the bridge, when time was truly tight and Tank was most weak, was the vessel for the musical tome of my life and career.

Tiringly, with the power to change the world, Hollywood abstained in the sixties, leaving only director Gordon Parks to keep the token black producer chair warm.

It took a white man to take this film to Hollywood, and Hollywood spit it out, as well as the man, as it tends to do. Hollywood, however, not to mention its conservative bent, could not also kill my melody, and it still lives, reminding us of the tenacity of the human spirit and what any man can set out to accomplish, whether large or small, white or black, strong or weak.

For that opportunity, I will always be grateful to Jules Dassin, who passed away in 2008 in Athens. It was a sad day for me. He was a man of the world. As sophisticated and uncompromising as he was, you would have thought he was born in Paris or Greece, but he was a child of New York City. Like Ahmet Ertegun, Dick Clark, or Harry Belafonte, he knew where to be, what to wear, what to say, and how to carry himself. For his influence and his contribution to my career and welfare, I am profoundly grateful.

MEMPHIS—1968— ♪ 3

When the soundtrack album came out with my name listed as sole songwriter, I noted that as a first. The MGs had come over to Paris and played on the song with me for the recording at an old dark and cavernous soundstage in Paris for inclusion in the film. The high-ceilinged property with its ornate windows and vast floor had a prestigious air, as though it was a bastion of the French film industry. The old stage was likely used to score many vintage French films, but the recording equipment and the acoustics were antiquated.

The sound on that version, recorded onto 33-mm film, was of lesser quality than our previous recordings in Memphis, and it was decided to rerecord the song back in Memphis at the Stax studios.

The Stax studio version appears on the single 45, and the Paris soundstage recording appears on the album. Much to my dismay, these later releases listed three additional songwriters in the credits.

By this time, I was numbed to the ways of the record business and show business. I was truly serving a different master—that of my creative muse.

After being in California and France with Jules and his family, meeting the big film producers, and working on the huge old soundstages in Paris, the trip back to Memphis for the "Private Number" session was more like an afterthought. The sound and smell of the surf was still in my ears and nose, and the taste of French wine was still in my mouth.

With the purchase of our new Scully eight-track recorder, the hits began to come.

Eddie Floyd migrated from Montgomery, Alabama, to Detroit and became the third wheel along with Mack Rice and Wilson Pickett, of the Falcons, whose hits included "I Found a Love." When the Falcons moved to DC, they met Al Bell, who brought them to Memphis.

By the time I wrote the arrangement for Eddie Floyd's "Never Found a Girl," I had transcribed a Bach fugue for orchestra at Indiana and, for the first time, really understood how to write for strings. More specifically, I learned the mark for pizzicato. Why couldn't the technique be used in soul music? I used it to have the strings answer my guitar line in the solo.

Writing songs with Eddie Floyd was a straightforward process. He was a lyricist who knew what he wanted once he discovered, or stumbled on, what that was. Usually, the first words to come out of his mouth ended up being a lyric that made it into the song or was the general idea of the song. And invariably, he sat quietly until I played a chord or some notes that sparked his interest. So our writing sessions started with me strumming a guitar or playing a chord sequence on piano, which morphed very quickly into a finished, or nearly finished, tune.

Very often, Eddie used our physical location at the time of writing or some incident in his recent life experience as a starting point for the subject of the song.

Hearing recordings made by Andrés Segovia affected my life and psyche so much that I would have loved to have been born in southern Spain myself. It appears Chicago guitarist Curtis Mayfield was struck with Segovia's magic wand.

William Bell and Judy Clay's "Private Number" finds me once again playing my Curtis Mayfield–influenced Spanish-style guitar. By this time, I had figured out how to write glissandos in harmony for strings. With a good-sized string session, and horns for the long, contrasting legato lines, the glissandos—which we put before each section—were like colorful flowers complementing the vocal events.

The soundtrack needed to be tied in with current events, namely, the assassination of Dr. King, by a moving rendition of "Children, Don't Get Weary." There was only one voice capable of handling the task—the third voice of the Drinkard Singers, along with Cissy Houston and Dionne Warwick—Judy Clay. When I called she gave me a resounding yes!

I was in love with Judy Clay's voice. She had flown over to Paris when I was scoring *Uptight* and sang "Children, Don't Get Weary," bringing the small studio audience nearly to tears with her purposeful, emotional delivery. She, too, had reminded me of my experience with Mahalia Jackson when I was a boy. Al had brought her down from Washington, and there was extra time after her session. William and I quickly revamped an idea we had for him to include a female point of view, and we tacked William onto Judy's session to record the duet.

MEMPHIS—1968— ♪ 4

On my return to Memphis from Paris, doing something he had never, ever done before, Al Jackson told me I should go out to a club or to a studio and check out this leggy white blonde singer, so I did.

Priscilla seemed shy and withdrawn, and Rita was outgoing and friendly. I couldn't have guessed there was a rivalry between them because they sang so well together, like one voice. These were (white) sisters who would have done anything to make it in the music business. And they would have done anything for each other, or to each other, to make it happen.

Sam Samudio of Sam the Sham and the Pharaohs didn't like me seeing his girl but kept his contagious smile whenever he was around me. Priscilla had been his for a long time, and they had been a notorious couple around Memphis, riding around on his big bike. But Sam wasn't a staff producer at Stax Records, so I got Priscilla.

Nobody, though, wanted me to marry Priscilla. I had people taking me for rides, trying to talk some sense into me. My first divorce attorney (Seymour Rosenberg) took the case only if I promised not to get married. Al Jackson accompanied Priscilla and me on a trip to LA, and every time she turned her back, he said, "Jones, you don't know what you're doing."

My mother stopped speaking to me for a time. A friend of Priscilla's had been calling my mother, giving my mom the blow-by-blow on our relationship, unbeknownst to me, and my mother was getting sicker with each phone call. My wife, who had accepted my philandering until now, called my hotel room in New York, where I was staying with Priscilla, and said, "This is your wife calling, and you'd better come home now!"

Mickey Gregory, a trumpet player friend from downtown at the Flamingo Room, said, "Well, I see Priscilla finally found a way out."

I replied, "A way out of what?"

"Poverty," Mickey answered, looking into my eyes.

The only person who related to what I was doing was Isaac Hayes. He was as crazy as I was in those days. We were wearing long coats and boots and couldn't get our fill of women. In '67 we ran into Priscilla and her sister, Rita, at the Rosewood on Trigg one night in South Memphis, and he just looked at me and said, "Man, man, man," and shook his head. At the time Isaac was divorcing his first wife, living with his fiancée, and going with about six women that I knew of, and I know he didn't tell me everything. Two of the women he was going with were roommates.

Priscilla, however, was irresistible to me. She was such a beautiful person in so many ways, searching, looking for love and trying to find herself, trying to find others...and at the same time devouring people like oysters, large and small. Now I know she herself was afraid of being devoured, but it was also what she wanted most. She steered her own ship, just didn't know where to direct it.

During those years, my problem was that I was afraid to steer my own ship. I was so innocent that I needed someone to hold on to. When I met Priscilla, I was just a boy. Still a boy. She would say, "I can't believe how innocent you are." And I was like, *Innocent? What is she talking about, innocent? What does she mean by innocent?*

I had spent my entire childhood and adolescence learning about music—and I knew nothing of life. Priscilla appeared to know everything about it. She had a copy of Kahlil Gibran's *The Prophet*, which I picked up and glanced at. It was my first exposure to anything metaphysical, and it opened the door to questions about human existence. The essays sparked a rebirth of my awareness, and I became a spiritual infant determined to grow.

In the summer of '68, Gigi took T back to Bloomington for a week's visit with our neighbor across the hall during my senior year at Indiana, Becky. Becky and her husband had separated. In the house alone while they were gone, I came to terms with myself. I was miserable in my domestic life—lying to my wife and myself. Denying truths that were staring me in the face. I married her out of duty as a southern gentleman because she was pregnant and I considered it the honorable thing to do, which was fine, but I was not in love with her, and I didn't think she was in love with me.

MEMPHIS, Holiday Inn—1968— ♪ 4

In the fall of 1968, I packed my belongings into my Oldsmobile and moved from my house with Gigi at 670 Edith Avenue into a room at the Holiday Inn at the Memphis Airport. After a few days, I leased an apartment at the Lowenstein Towers apartment building on Main Street.

In a short time, Gigi served me with divorce papers at the Lowenstein Towers, having engaged William B. Ingram, former mayor of Memphis and the mastermind of the devastating situation facing the city's sanitation workers that caused Dr. King to come to Memphis.

Mayor Ingram's power in the city of Memphis was unchallenged and undisputed. To represent myself, I chose the only attorney I knew, Seymour Rosenberg, who was the in-house counsel for Stax Records and was a local trumpet player known as Sy Rosenberg. He was no match for the ex-mayor, who had inherited the power-rich endowment of the E. H. Crump dynasty in Memphis.

There was no judge in the Mid-South that the mayor didn't have in his pocket. This certified racist bureaucrat reveled in taking Willette's case. I can only imagine the look on his face when she came to his office and told him I had left her for a white woman. In the city so graphically depicted in the movie *The Blind Side*, my goose was cooked. I was young, brash, outspoken, defiant, and financially done for. Gigi repeated over and over that she would "take me to the cleaners," and she did.

Priscilla was furious because I paid Gigi $900 a month, in addition to the house note, the car notes, and other incidentals, with no court order. Willette was uninterested in royalties, not believing in my future as a musician. She declined royalties and opted for a cash settlement of $50,000 plus all the property we owned, which was the Edith Street house, a duplex on Regent Street, and a six-unit apartment building on Crump Boulevard in Memphis.

When the settlement was due, I could only pay half—$25,000—and the rest had to be made in monthly installments until I was able to borrow the rest. Screaming at me every time I went to pick up my son, Willette would yell, "I want my motherf—ing money!" She never had to work a single day and was never homeless or hungry. She never lacked a car or adequate clothing or spending money as a result of my support.

Gwen would say, "Don't marry Priscilla 'cause she know so much more than you," and I would think, *What is she talking about?*

With illusion, one can make anything happen—a relationship seems to be love, or a myriad of other situations appear tolerant or beautiful.

MEMPHIS, Stax—1968— ♪ 7

With all the disruptions, changes, challenges, and turmoil in my private personal life, my work was the only constant—dependable and comforting. My muse played hide-and-seek with me, forcing me to hone my skills for recognizing musical possibilities in random places. "Hang 'Em High" didn't take much searching.

It came in a white package in the mail, addressed to me on McLemore Avenue from Dominic Frontiere in Los Angeles. The box of cassette tapes had begun to get fuller and fuller since the company began having hits, and the custom was to ignore unsolicited tapes. People from all over wanted our artists to record their songs or to become an artist on our label. Our staff began to view the box as a waste of time since it seemed no one ever got a hit out of it, but I opened this one and popped it into the cassette player on my desk. Dominic's demo had the logo of a movie company on it, and the music immediately struck me as serious business.

The opening chords were ominous enough, but when I heard the first low guitar lick—answering nothing but a portent of impending doom—I couldn't hit the stop button. I kept the guitar lick in the MGs' song, but the rest of the arrangement came to me right there, sitting at the desk after hearing Dominic's demo. The tension, the buildup, would come via successive modulations of one half step at a time. Halfway through, I would halve the melodic line to make it twice as long, but in a new key. The tension would build so much that even with no lyrics, you would know something grave was about to take place.

The ominous, somber music produced a picture in my mind of a man standing on the gallows between two others who would soon lose their lives. His tousled hair hung off the front of his bowed head, and he slumped at his knees. The progression would be from E minor to F minor to F sharp minor and finally to G minor. At

G minor, the rope would snap; a body would fall. People watching would condone the tragedy. The music would verify the fact. And then it would happen again. The rope would snap; another body would fall limp. By the time we reached G minor at the end, as many as six men would have been hung. The music would fade, and you would feel strangely exhilarated by the drama.

I couldn't wait. I wanted to record it immediately. Before I forgot the arrangement. Maybe we made phone calls and got everyone to the studio right away. I was caught up in the moment.

LOS ANGELES—1969— ♪ 9

Memphis had no freeways. Los Angeles had nothing but freeways. I had a knack for going fast on them—west on the Santa Monica Freeway to get to Hollywood when I should have headed east, or south on the 405 to get to the valley when I should have headed north. The drive to Devonshire Downs took forever. How could we still be driving and be in the same city? It was a freeway I would get to know well, although I had no idea of that then. I was still a neophyte at this rock festival thing. It seemed the people were a little jaded and tired. What I hadn't realized was that this was the third day, and they'd already seen Hendrix, Taj Mahal, Joe Cocker, Albert King, Creedence, Jethro Tull, and others. They were nearly burned out. We got there in time to catch the Chambers Brothers set, psychedelic as all get-out. Newport '69 at Devonshire was my first glimpse of a rock festival performance.

I was blown away. The big amps. The big sound. I stood in the crowd for "Time Has Come Today." The esoteric references in the music. *In the lyrics and the music. Had pop music been narrow in perspective before now?*

I had plenty to think about on the drive back. I had played a few of these festivals and begun to wonder about the hippy movement. There had been one in Atlanta, then one in Detroit, and finally Monterey Pop. What was this new philosophy? Need I be affected by it? Did it challenge my strong spiritual background?

At Stax, I was handed a persona that was limiting—that of an instrumentalist and music arranger exclusively. Day to day, I presented that persona and allowed the singer-songwriter side of me to be overlooked, ignored, in line with the designs of Stax's people in power.

Traveling to places outside the confines of Memphis's narrow social, intellectual environment exposed me to talent and concepts that sparked self-exploration and personal growth. These changes showed in the lyrics I started to write.

MEMPHIS—June 1969— ♪ 12

I was excited about having finished the mix on a new song, "Ole Man Trouble," and couldn't wait to play it for Al Bell.

It was late one night when I left the studio. I got out of the car and walked around back of it, to the dark path leading to the steps to Al Bell's house. I shouldn't have been there at that hour. Many times before, the four of us had hung out, and Al and Lydia had invited Gigi and me over for dinner. But this time was special. I walked up the dark steps and knocked on the door. Al was still up.

A frown, then a smile, a warm welcome. It seemed he was alone in the house. Inscrutable, Al was an enigma to me. I never figured him out. He appeared strong, but his nature seemed delicate. Maybe he was both.

"Hey, Booker! Man, come on in! What's goin' on? Is everything all right? How's Gigi?"

"Yeah, man," I answered. "Everything's great!" Masking my excitement, I said, "Matter of fact, I just left the studio. We had a session, and I recorded this song!"

In the preceding days and weeks, I had undergone a complete rebirth. A full-blown spiritual metamorphosis through self-examination and a desire for self-discovery and to find the truth in all things as a way out of the mental and physical bondage I was born into.

I handed Al the quarter-inch rough mix of "Ole Man Trouble," and we sat down in his den to listen to it.

Ronnie Capone and Al Jackson had stayed late with me at the studio. Ronnie worked the board, Al played drums, and I played guitar, piano, and bass on the track as well as performing the vocal. I went to great expense to hire a large horn section, as I had license to do in those days, and paid for a late-night, double-overtime session.

All six feet, four inches of Al overflowed his favorite chair, and he turned the volume up a little, as if to hear a treat, even though it was late. Lydia, I suppose, was still awake. I positioned myself at the end of the couch.

As with certain soul songs like Sam Cooke's "A Change Is Gonna Come," a delicate, light, ethereal calm encompasses the room just before the song moves from its spiritual expression into the material world. Feeling this force, Al closed his eyes. But unlike Sam's song, "Ole Man Trouble" started in a minor key, not a major, and Al reached for his already loosened tie.

There's a man, O called Trouble,
And he follows me, everywhere I go

In this lyric, I was talking about self-denial and negative thoughts. I knew this was a pervasive tendency of mine and in the African American culture.

Well now, Ole Man Trouble,
You can't get me, now I know

Here I'm talking about conquering and letting go of fear.

By the time Al's eyes opened, he had sat up in his chair, turned to one side, and crossed his legs.

The song continued.

Mister Charlie, you know I work hard for you,
And you're mean to me, just as mean as you can be

This lyric is a metaphor for institutions of human oppression of all types.

As a black man and a Stax executive, Al was on both sides of this issue.

Well, now, you and Ole Man Trouble
You can't get me, 'cause my mind is free

This is about my realization of the unlimited scope of my own inner powers, which are able to overcome the tangible confines of racism.

Al clasped his hands between his legs, put his head down, closed his eyes. Introspective and compassionate, he may have been torn between his business obligations and his social responsibilities as an African American.

Well, I get what I need, and I need what I get
And I ain't had no need, for nothin' I couldn't get yet

These words were confirming my appreciation and thankfulness for the life I've had.

So, Ole Man Trouble, I'm gonna live like I want to
And do as I damn well please
'Cause my heart is in my song
And my song is blowin' in the breeze

The lyric is affirmation of my acceptance of a new way of life, asserting my new attitude of confidence, freedom, and inner security.

Stopping the tape, Al said, "Booker, songs like these scare me. I-I don't know what to say; there's just something about them that just...I-I-I don't know man, it just—"

Some blacks, even some in my own company, were afraid to stand up and speak out. In a split second, I realized that Al and I supported different approaches to the problem of racial oppression. Al's hands were tied due to his position at Stax.

I felt the meeting and especially hearing the song were really hard for Al because in so many ways we were surely partners. The truth was, he chose neither to confront nor engage me on our differences that night. At least not at that time. And in 1969, with Dr. King's body in the ground, timing was everything.

Before Al could pull his large frame from the chair, I was at the door.

His face said everything.

"No problem, Al. I understand. I really do. Sorry to disturb your evening. I'll get going."

"Oh, no! Really, Booker! I've spent a lot of time mulling over this issue. I just don't know if this is the time for Stax to...You know, man, songs like this...they, they have a way of...I don't want you to think..."

In that moment, surprised, disappointed, and heartbroken, my past came to an unforeseen, abrupt, disruptive halt—destiny took the reins. Determined to heed my inner voice, I mounted a different steed. Our paths may cross again, but Al

Bell and I were on different roads, even if we looked to the same destination.

I opened the door and stepped onto the porch. I thought, *Time is tight.* Then, slowly and carefully, I placed each foot down on one of the concrete steps, holding on to the tape of "Ole Man Trouble." I didn't look back to see the inevitable compassion on Al's face. I knew he felt my pain. But he too knew, at that moment, that time was tight. It was time for me to go.

I rolled down the passenger-side window. "I'll talk to you, man. I'll talk to you."

I took Union Extended to McLemore Avenue, came in the back door, and entered Stax for the last time. I found the panel and turned the control room lights on, casting a shadow into the dark studio. I had never erased anything before, and I had to think a minute. There was no erase button, only the record button. I put the twenty-four-track tape on the Scully deck, selected the vocal track, and pressed record. Then I put the quarter inch that I played for Al on the two track and pressed record. The two machines erased together.

I walked down the control room steps in the dark, since in my haste I had neglected to turn on the studio lights. I went home to pack.

CHAPTER 13
Melting Pot

LOS ANGELES—Summer 1969—♪ 1

I left all my possessions in Memphis and had my '68 Olds
Toronado driven out to California. There was no promise of gold
for me in California. No promise of anything at all. However, after word got out that I was in town, I started getting calls to play
sessions. Only a few at first, then finally as a song arranger and
keyboard man.

When I first arrived out west, however, I had no vehicle and had
to ride with someone absolutely everywhere. I was crammed into a
tiny BMW with two friends of Rita's. Leon Russell drove me to his
house after a session to show me his studio. The studio was great.
The drive there wasn't. We went fast up Laurel Canyon Boulevard,
which was the only way to get to the San Fernando Valley without going all the way to Hollywood or to Westwood. I never met a
more generous guy, though. "If you ever need a studio or a place to
stay, it's yours," Leon told me. His offer wasn't lost on me.

Regardless, being without a car in Los Angeles was like crossing the Sahara without water, so I used a company called LA Driveaway to have my Toronado driven from Memphis. It was supposed to take five days. When the driver finally showed up eight days later, he took forever just to get out from behind the steering wheel and didn't seem to want to release it to me. I was never so glad to see a car.

MEMPHIS—1968— ♪ 9

I met Leon through my really good friend Mabon "Teenie" Hodges in Memphis in 1968. Teenie and I were still best friends even though he had taken my girlfriend (Evelyn Jones) and, on occasion, my drummer (Al Jackson Jr.).

Usually, Teenie left his car at my house and we went out together to see new acts and shows at clubs, but this windy, wintry night he didn't answer his phone. Ike and Tina Turner were at the Rosewood, a few blocks from my house, so I dressed and went alone. They gave me a small table near the front that I shared with a couple I didn't know. I looked over the room. Standing against the wall was this very light-skinned woman with an enormous Afro wig, larger than any I'd ever seen. And next to her was my friend Teenie—smiling at me as though he was aware of me all the while.

The woman was white. Teenie had brought a white woman to the Rosewood. Was he out of his mind? No one else in the club seemed to notice, or to mind. Their attention was on the amazing Tina Turner and her dancers.

Where Teenie went, people stared at him. The way he dressed. His demeanor. They took a table, and I joined them. The woman was Rita Coolidge. Teenie was cheating on my girlfriend with Rita. He flashed that smile and poured me a drink out of his bottle. That smile seemed to get Teenie anywhere he wanted to go. An audition with Willie Mitchell. Tina Turner's dressing room. He had one of those *magnetic* personalities.

At that time, Rita was hanging out with a guy named Don Nix, who played baritone sax in Steve and Duck's band, The Mar-Keys. Don had been to LA and was crazy about a band he'd met, Delaney & Bonnie, and the musicians in their band. He took them to Stax, and they signed with the company. Rita met Delaney & Bonnie through Don, and they invited her to sing with them.

Soon after, Teenie and Rita took me to a small rehearsal studio in Memphis—the first time I met Leon Russell. He was the keyboard player in Bonnie and Delanie Bramlett's band. It was the first time I was in a room of hippies after Monterey. Slowly I realized my friend Teenie was one of *them.* They greeted me so warmly and enthusiastically, a small part of me secretly fantasized I was one of *them.* However, that could never be. They all looked so different. Leon—with eye makeup, long hair, a carnival hat, and a nose ring and outrageously dressed in tie-dye, skins, and high boots—was nondescript in the room, which included Carl Radle, Bobby Whitlock, Jerry McGee, Bobby Keys, and probably Chuck Blackwell on drums.

LOS ANGELES—1969— ♪ 7

With Stax in my past, Providence located me in sunny Southern California, leading the unorthodox hippie life and feeling magnificent about the new arrangement.

Of all the people at Stax I tried to persuade to come to California, Eddie Floyd was my only taker. No sooner had I rented my house in Beverly Hills than he had a room at the Hyatt on Sunset. Like me, Eddie had been searching. With his natural affinity for creativity, Eddie didn't hesitate or think twice about offending Stax by following me to California. After all, the injustices had affected him too. Eddie had always been quick to deal with his conflicts. Sometimes too quick. He and Wilson Pickett had gotten into fistfights as members of the Falcons in Detroit. Again, like me, Eddie came from the Deep South, and the inherent beauty of California spoke to him.

I took my Gibson J-45 that Duck had given me to Eddie's room, and in no time, we had written "California Girl." A couple of days later, we had "Never Found a Girl."

Eddie hung in Hollywood with me. Mornings in the California sun were intoxicating, and with the pretty girls parading Sunset Boulevard below Eddie's balcony, Eddie and I were living our dream. Two southern boys, free in Hollywood. Instinctively, we wanted to write a love song. It could be about a girl we fell in love with in this magical place. (Years later I got my California girl.) I started strumming a happy little C chord rhythm on my acoustic guitar. Eddie walked over to the balcony. *California girl, you're living in a different world*—in his best, most romantic baritone. I went down to the F chord when he got to the word *world*. We were doing it. (I repeated the C chord to F chord sequence.) Before Eddie said another word, I played an A minor chord. Another A minor. An A minor suspension. A long D suspension, resolving to a G suspended. A normal G seventh. *Till the day I die.* Back to the C chord that I began with. We had done it! Without so much as a word to one another. Such was the writing rapport I had with Eddie Floyd. No one would have believed it happened like that. But it did!

I called a drummer, and we went down into Leon's studio that night and cut the track for "California Girl" with me playing everything but drums. We didn't even call anyone at Stax.

The only problem was, all of Leon's effusive generosity couldn't offset the fact that he had a monkey loose in the house (a real monkey!), and the monkey was crazy. Everyone knew it. When Leon wasn't around, the monkey bared his teeth at me and made me feel certain he would kill me if I ever came back. It might have been the reason Rita finally left Leon. True to his word, though, Leon never asked for a dime. I had Stax send him the equivalent payment for studio time.

Eddie and I did our songwriting work at his hotel room or at Leon's house. We couldn't write at my house in Beverly Hills. It was a madhouse. Rita, who had been living with Leon, moved in with nine cats. Nine cats. The house was always full of her friends. Good people. Just so many of them. Clydie King. Venetta Fields. Claudia Lennear. David Anderle. Marc Benno. Herb Alpert. Jerry Moss. Donna Weiss. Our house was right there off Wilshire and Fairfax. Everybody visited. And used the piano in the living room. Except me.

I needed at least a modicum of privacy. In Memphis, my proclivity for kicking people out of the room who weren't directly involved in the writing earned me a reputation. Moreover, I savored solitude, which was nearly impossible to come by there.

Joe Cocker, broke and homeless after his Mad Dogs & Englishmen tour of the world, spent a few days recuperating on the floor of Rita's upstairs bedroom. Stephen Stills asked me to play organ on "Love the One You're With," but I lay passed out on the couch after too much indulgence, and Stephen had to play the organ solo himself. Graham Nash, dropping in at the session while staying at Stephen's house, hit on Stephen's girl, Rita.

BEVERLY HILLS, CA—1969— ♪ 5

With so much energy swirling around, something was certain to give. Our swimming pool was constantly blanketed with large brown fronds whipped off neighbors' palm trees. The violent winter winds plagued our stay in Beverly Hills, and regularly flung debris from the high-rise construction sites a block away on Wilshire Boulevard. It seemed an omen when a huge block of steel crashed through the french doors of our bedroom one night not long after we moved in.

Priscilla's state of mind, volatile at best, became unhinged when I balked at marriage. An ambulance pulled up in front of 6132 Warner Drive in Beverly Hills. It was an unfamiliar destination for them because the home's owner, Rabbi Max Vorspan, a peace-loving man, was away on sabbatical. He was the least likely Beverly Hills resident to call emergency.

But the home had different occupants now. I had rented it and was living there with Priscilla, her two children, and her sister, Rita. On this occasion, Priscilla had slashed both her wrists, and Rita and I were wrapping them up with bathroom towels, both scared to death. For months Priscilla had been asking me, grilling me, as to whether I was committed to her. Even before we left Memphis, if there was any hesitation or unsureness from me, a battle ensued, lasting sometimes for days.

"No, I want to know if you are committed to me, not if you care for me or if you just want to keep seeing me! Why do you need time?" Priscilla screamed.

The second time Priscilla cut her wrists, the doctor had her admitted again, to the same psychiatric ward as before. I visited her nightly and tried to console her. I took care of Priscilla's kids, Paul and Laura, on my own, taking them back and forth to their grammar school and supervising their homework. I was doing the shopping, managing the meals, and trying to make a living playing sessions to keep us above water.

I ignored my inner voice. My will disappeared.

In no time, it was like Priscilla's mouth gaped open wide enough, and she swallowed me whole. Body and soul. The light of the sun disappeared. All I could see or feel were the dark, cold, moist walls in the gut of her soul as she washed me down. Instead of a proud eagle flying in the sky, I became a spineless gray lizard, caught in the coil of a charming, relentless, hungry python.

Nevertheless, wedding invitations went out within days of Priscilla's release from the hospital.

The first to respond was San Francisco's Scott McKenzie, who drove over from his home in Joshua Tree, California. At the wedding, all the women wore flowers in their hair out of compliance with Scott's song, "Be Sure to Wear Some Flowers in Your Hair." The ceremony was performed on July 16, 1970, by Priscilla's father, Reverend R. M. Coolidge, in Beverly Hills, at the home we were renting, and attended by her mother, Charlotte, her sister, Rita, along with Stephen Stills, and my parents, Lurline and Booker T. Jones Sr.

In attendance was a small cadre of Hollywood locals, mostly friends and associates of Rita's, including Annie and Terry Rodgers, David and Cheryl Anderle, Marc and Fran Benno, and the ubiquitous Hollywood socialite Bobby Neuwirth. Not in attendance was my sister, Gwen, nor my brother, Maurice.

I wore a brown suit, Priscilla wore a white dress, and Rita caught the bouquet.

After our wedding, Priscilla and I rode around the back hills of Southern California in my Olds Toronado, looking for a ranch to buy. Once, I found myself lost in Agoura Hills...trapped in a nest of Hells Angels in a back-mountain valley. I just hastily turned around and backed out—as they glared.

HOLLYWOOD, Paramount Pictures—1969— ♪ *7*

With all that driving around, I was beginning to get a sense of the layout of the massive Los Angeles region, and I discovered that my Beverly Hills house was not too far from Paramount over on Melrose. I visited the lot so much working on *Uptight*, the guard knew my name. Although they owned Stax, Paramount tried their own hands at the music business, initiating Paramount Records in 1969. Walking past the president's office early in 1970, I heard my name called. I turned back and stepped in. They had been turned down by the Beatles, the man confessed. Not everyone had a price in Hollywood.

I already had so much respect for the group, but this information increased my appreciation of the band. We had recorded "Lady Madonna," and now the Beatles' LP *Abbey Road* had been released to rave critical reviews. The Beatles had fame. All the accolades. They could have stopped and rested on their laurels, but they didn't. They kept reaching, for the sake of creativity and the love of music.

I decided someone should make a statement of gratitude and appreciation.

"You want to do what?"

"A tribute to the Beatles' *Abbey Road* LP."

"Why? You're an R & B band. It won't sell."

Even though Steve had a previous commitment for sessions in LA, I flew to Memphis to record with Duck and Al. I couldn't wait. My head was full of the melodies from "Mr. Mustard Seed," "Because the World Is Round," and "She Came in Through the Bathroom Window." I was rearranging everything to fit the MGs' four-piece format. I forgot about the cold Memphis weather and froze walking to and from the studio. To make matters worse, my rental car was gone—stolen. I had parked it over on College Street because there were no spaces on McLemore. Outside, I blew warm air on my hands. There was no time to buy a coat.

We started the sessions with only three pieces, leaving room for guitar parts and leads. I memorized Steve's parts and immediately flew back out to LA and walked him through his overdubs. It wasn't "I Want to Hold Your Hand." There were suspensions, seventh chords, uneven bar lengths, and other surprises and aberrations. The Beatles had grown up musically, and I wanted to document it.

It was so much fun to play musically advanced rock and roll instrumentals.

HOLLYWOOD, Wally Heider Studio—1969— ♪ 5

A few months later, I remember walking out onto Cahuenga Boulevard, out of the Booker T. & the MGs session. There had been laughter and happiness inside; the band was jovial. On the sidewalk, I lit a Salem and noted a strange sensation that I seemed to be on the wrong side of the street.

Everybody was happy but me. I had left Memphis, and Stax Records, but I hadn't quit the MGs. Now I wanted to leave the MGs.

All the new original material we tried to come up with that day, and for every session before that for as long as I could remember, sounded like a lame imitation of one of our previous hits. "Green Onions," "Hip Hug-Her," or whatever. Nobody seemed to notice that. Not Steve. Not even Al. Everybody was flush with success and money.

This part of town had been my good luck charm. The grim realization was settling in that it wasn't the location; it was the inspiration and the material that was the missing four-leaf clover.

"What's wrong, Jones?" Al Jackson startled me, walking up behind me. Duck's loud cackle came through the studio door.

"Oh, nothing, man; just stepping outside for a little break."

"What's wrong, Jones?"

Al knew me. He opened the door to the studio, and we went back inside for the start of a long, heartfelt discussion of the band's musical arc, and I confessed how I had been feeling "unartistic" and "unoriginal" in all our musical undertakings. I was just plain unhappy. Why were we settling for less?

The guys decided to call the session off, go back to Memphis, and regroup. Those words hit me in the chest. Had I been too demanding? Was this the end of the road for this band? I couldn't take back what'd I'd said, and it was the truth, but I'd presented it clumsily. The session ended abruptly, and our parting was awkward.

NEW YORK, A&R Studio—1969— ♪ 9

Sometime later, I got a call from one of the guys. They had booked a great studio in New York. Get on a plane.

It was A&R studios. Bill Halverson, my go-to engineer, was nowhere to be found. I asked no questions, hung my coat up, and walked over to the B-3. There was new energy. I could see it on the faces of Al and Duck. Al got that little twist in the corner of his mouth when he smiled that indicated a Max Roach–like intensity in his playing, and he started hitting the cross stick with his left shoulder sunk down to the side. His head was looking away as if he was in a trance. Steve started a funky rhythm like a precursor to "Chic." Something Nile Rodgers might have struck up. Duck chimed in, using his first and third fingers to pull the strings hard, his lips poking out like they did when he was on a mission.

They were playing the beat to "Melting Pot." What could I do? A few bars went by while I was just digging on the rhythm. Finally, it came to me that I might sneak in by hitting a chord while the reverb was turned all the way up, but with the volume pedal all the way down, so the chord sounded like it was coming from nowhere.

It worked. I did it again on another chord. Then another. I had made a Hammond organ sound eerie. The guys were plugging unmercifully away at the rhythm. I had to make some attempt at a solo.

I pulled out my normal first four stops, with a soft percussion setting. Time was slipping by. Who was I? What was I going to say? Where was I going to start? Down low. Way down low. I crossed my right arm over my left to the swell manual. We were on our way. I sensed a sigh of relief from the guys when I finally played something. I made a statement. An exposition. I had jumped off a cliff. Now I had to fly.

I closed my eyes. It was time for reckless abandon. I would have to play some wrong notes to get to the right ones. Who cared? I built my solo up like I was flying through space—hitting unseen objects and getting knocked around—leaving the key, coming back. Soaring, soaring to a place of no sound, no boundaries, I turned my engines off and let the music take me. Finally, I opened my eyes. I needed to return to reality. I played a turn, and the band turned with me, like a big ol' heavy semitruck, down to a big, deep F chord. We had created a turnaround. I played the notes to indicate we should do it again. We did. And then I went right back out into space.

After what seemed an eternity, there was no chance this would ever be a normal record, it made sense to go to a bridge—one that was reassuring and traditional—with normal major chords and a solid, positive attitude. So we morphed into the big C major pattern, which soared and arced like a real suspension bridge over a river would, and it dropped us into safe territory—a rewarding G chord. From there we hopped to a more suspenseful D minor and gave in to the urge to get back on that high C bridge one more time, just so we could land in G again. But on this go-around, we tippy-toed on stepping-stones back to the apprehensive A minor of

"Melting Pot" that we started with, and Steve took off on a journey all his own.

Steve's journey led us up a mountain. A one-chord mountain that tested our musical bravery. I stepped back and started hitting A minor stabs on the great keyboard for his accompaniment. Steve had room to take giant steps. He did.

We re-created the whole musical pattern again, just like real veteran music creators, and by the end of Steve's solo, we had a song.

However, I hadn't had quite enough. I stepped in one more time. One last time. I wanted the final say. I played an epilogue. And then, just before the song ended, Steve played the same A minor rhythm, exactly the same as he had at the start of the song. Of course, it was perfect. At the very end, Al leaned his left shoulder in and tapped out the cross-stick rhythm the whole business had started with.

"It's too jazzy." That was Jim's reaction, leaning over on the console, looking around at us, with one hand on his hip, pulling his coat back.

After a moment Jim mused, "Well, I guess we could put it out with some other stuff we haven't released yet."

Jim continued. "It's too long. Can we cut it down to four minutes?"

Rather than cut new stuff for the album, Jim Stewart gathered songs recorded in Memphis he hadn't wanted to release previously because they were too "jazzy."

MALIBU—1969— ♪ 8

The next time I boarded a jet it was bound for the West Coast, where my mind was set on finding a new home.

When Billie Nichols drove me and Priscilla out to Lana Turner's old ranch on Winding Way in Malibu, she may not have been aware of one key fact: blacks were not allowed to own land in Malibu. Not that it would have stopped me from living on a horse ranch. The smell of horses either attracts or repels a person. I found myself surprisingly drawn to the scent.

Almost suddenly, through the influence of people like Stephen Stills, Marc Benno, Ray Stinnett, and Glyn Turman, I was a different person. The suits and dress-up clothes I wore in Memphis were replaced with Frye boots and dungarees. I melded into the California lifestyle—I started smoking marijuana, and working with some jazz artists and rock musicians, I had more musical freedom with the studio I built in Malibu. I was spending more time outside and began to spend days at the beach and on horses. I was much more physically active, more informal. My lifestyle changed, and I got dirt on my hands.

The problem of self-respect aside, I began to make a life in Malibu. I took up with an Egyptian man named Mina E. Mina. His first love was music, and he became my best friend. Mina tolerated my dope smoking and provided an escape from the ranch.

He introduced me to the music of Uma Kalthoum. She was an icon in Egypt, bigger in comparison than even Elvis Presley. Her songs and concerts were akin to a religious experience. Music you must hear to understand. Mina used Um's music as a bridge to establish our friendship. There were times I'd be at his house for hours. One song alone could last up to forty-five minutes given the time Ms. Kalthoum took to use her vocal abilities to emphasize an emotion and, using an Arabic scale, to bring that emotion to such intensity that her audience became ecstatic. Even though I didn't speak the language, I felt I understood Mina better after I listened to her music. Just to hear Um's scale in my mind, which we Westerners call a "double harmonic," gives me goose bumps. I love it so much. It makes me feel I'm a gypsy at heart. To me, it seems to reflect a great truth that will stand the test of time, despite my unfamiliarity with Arab culture. I could only hope that my music might bring people together in a like manner. Mina kept a quiet counsel with me and let his home and family be my escape.

Why'd I need a refuge? Because there was a nonstop party going on, twenty-four hours a day at my house. Priscilla's parties were famous for the "treats" she provided—on her dresser, Priscilla kept a small scale, the purpose of which escaped me, which she carried in her purse. I should have guessed, as often as she went into the bathroom with strangers at parties, the parties often ending with banquets at the Malibu Pier with its long tables into the night. I didn't push Priscilla about her bathroom visits, because I didn't really want to know the truth about it.

My parents, in Memphis, shouldering the embarrassment in the black community for my lifestyle choices—marrying a white woman—found it too much, and they decided to move to California, into the twenty-by-forty I had constructed for a recording studio.

They adapted so well to the new lifestyle on the ranch. So much so that I was awakened by a chopping sound coming through my bedroom window. It was my sixty-five-year-old father, protected with gloves, feverishly delivering sharp blows, one after the other, with a garden hoe, to the rattlesnakes in the nest under the window, plant debris and snake parts flying high into the bright sun.

At my Malibu ranch, Paul Satterfield and I sat alone in my living room. He hadn't seen his kids, Paul Jr. and Laura, in over two years. A fireman in Nashville, he had saved enough money for the trip to California as well as enough money to buy a small dirt bike for Paul. Priscilla hadn't pressed him for alimony or child support, but she objected to the dirt bike.

I had sided with Paul on the bike issue. We lived in the Malibu hills, and other boys Paul's age had small ones. On his fireman's salary, Paul couldn't afford to fly his children to Tennessee or come to California on a regular basis. He was heartbroken. He loved his kids and wanted to see them, and here I had moved his family far away. I felt for him. We sat there in silence for a long time.

During the discussion, Priscilla walked into the room, glared at the two of us, and walked out. I saw a man who just needed to be with his kids. And there he was two thousand miles away from his home in Nashville, sitting in my living room in Malibu, a tall, southern white man with a black man, me. Complete opposites, but somehow I was on his side. Not a word said.

It was hard for me. Both seeing him come and seeing him leave. He was simply a good man who loved his kids and wanted to see them. I related to Paul's dilemma because Gigi, T's mom, kept the time and number of my visits with him to a minimum to hurt me. The uncertainty of when I would next see my son and the knowledge that Paul Sr. had this same worry created an inner turmoil in me. Added to this was an almost frantic need by the adults in Malibu to gather.

There were so many parties, the memory is a blur. Every night someone gave directions over the phone that detailed how to get through the winding hills to someone else's house, where at least thirty people were gathered.

I met Ramblin' Jack Elliott at Roger McGuinn's house one night. Ramblin' Jack's name reminded me of some blues great from Mississippi. Peg-Leg Slim, or Ironing Board Sam. But he was a normal-looking white man. He didn't even have a handicap. He looked me in the eye and paid special attention to me that evening. The winter wind howled in the early mornings in the Malibu houses high on the hills. Loud bursts rattled windows and doorways in the early mornings when the conversations turned away from the groups and people focused on each other. I returned Ramblin' Jack's attention because of his age, thinking he must have something to offer, and the deference everyone paid to him. I don't remember what we talked about, just that we appreciated each other's company.

The hills of Malibu could be every bit as lonely as a cell-like room in Manhattan. At night, the hills became quiet and seemed to close in so tight on you that you'd swear you were going crazy. Just like the noise in New York. Especially if you were alone, or with the wrong person.

The locals, however, were unique and unlike anywhere else on earth. There was a girl working the checkout register at the Pt. Dume supermarket in Malibu. I couldn't help looking at her a certain way, even though I was too shy to ever say anything to her.

One day, she said to me, "You can have anything you want. All you have to do is stop smoking." But for the life of me, I couldn't do it. I would drive back to the ranch, look at Priscilla or one of her family members, and light up another one.

The protracted breakup with Stax didn't help either and felt like a dream where I couldn't get my feet to move. Consequently, I suffered an abundance of emotional fallout as well as sharp criticism from fans and interviewers.

Standing up to the ownership of Stax Records, I demanded to be treated fairly, like a human being. I refused to be a slave on a plantation.

When they discovered that I had escaped and one of their workers had left the farm, they started throwing money at the remaining workers and began pleading with me, begging me to return.

Jim Stewart called me every day at my ranch in Malibu, saying he was sorry. They never saw me as an artist, only as a slave worker. They took the benefits of my creations in the form of ridiculously low royalty rates and the entirety of my publishing.

While giving me the opportunity to record, they did not treat me fairly in turn, like a subservient worker and not a creative artist.

The parties, meanwhile, continued nonstop. Often, they were at my house. By the time James Taylor appeared in my living room one morning, it was anyone's guess who was more startled. I came out of the bedroom to find him sitting alone in a chair in the foyer. I was pretty sure he didn't know where he was, what time it was, or who I was.

At the same time, I was becoming overwhelmed with demands for my time: Evie Sands wanted a songwriting partner. Jackie De-Shannon wanted to hang out and make friends. Bob Dylan wanted feedback and confirmation that his stuff was good. Bill Withers wanted someone to listen to his songs. Alan Sides wanted my Neumann microphones. Chris Etheridge and Bruce Langhorne wanted to jam. Kris Kristofferson wanted Rita Coolidge. They were an insular pack. Nobody wanted to drive into Hollywood or Beverly Hills. After dark, the Pacific Coast Highway was a completely different road. Lonely, desolate, and treacherous. You could find yourself smacked into a musty hillside or nose-down off a cliff into the Pacific with one glance at the dashboard. Malibu was a haven for creative types—actors, directors, and so forth. It seemed to me that I was always running into musicians and musical groups.

LOS ANGELES, 405 Freeway—1965— ♪ 7

Bob Dylan complained that people always stole his bands. Well, I wonder why? Maybe it was because he attracted sensitive, nuanced musicians like a magnet. I wanted to steal one of Bob's bands. They were called the Band. It turned out they lived right down the road from me in Malibu.

I was driving down the 405 South toward Santa Monica in hard rain when "Like a Rolling Stone" came on the radio. First thing I noticed was the piano. *What is this? An ensemble for a traveling circus?* The group was on a mission from the first note. Then, when I heard the lead character's voice—a man who seemed to have no regard for all the conventions society had set in place, no reverence at all, I nearly ran off the road. I swear, I felt an affinity for every person playing on that record. But then, I had recently been reborn, reimagined, myself.

Rainwater beat down on my windshield, and I turned the volume way up. It was a moment I will never forget. Akin to hearing your own record on the radio for the first time. Music magic.

MALIBU, Shangri-La—1969—♪ 10

So when I finally walked into Shangri-La, years later, it was like walking into, well, Shangri-La. There was mastermind Robbie Robertson, twins Rick "Man, I just want to break even" Danko and Richard Manuel, maestro Garth Hudson, and mastermind Levon Helm, looking at me like I was the second coming or something. They showed me around their home, and I wondered how such amazing music could have come from such an unassuming space. I tried to imagine Bob Dylan with this nonchalant crew.

I walked over to Garth's organ. I'd been around organs all my life; however, I didn't recognize a thing. He'd rebuilt everything. He wasn't there, but his energy, so strong, poked out at me. The guys smiled.

Out in the yard, the view of the Pacific was outstanding. You could see from Catalina to the Channel Islands, and I took in deep breaths, enjoying the company of my new friends. The three who gravitated toward me were Rick, Richard, and Levon. I stayed with

Levon for a while at his house in Woodstock, and we formed a band, the RCO All-Stars, with Dr. John (Mac Rebennack) and Steve Cropper.

Mac, who was also staying at the house, and I hit it off, and I started riding in his limo. We started writing songs together, and he told me stories about Professor Longhair and other New Orleans legends. Mac kept tons of voodoo stuff with him (which I ignored). I was surprised to find out what a sense of humor he had and what a prankster he was. He always found a way to stay close to me; his body always spilled over onto mine. Early one morning, on a train to Washington, DC, Mac was sitting in the seat behind me. He rapped me on the head with his voodoo cane, waking me out of a sound sleep.

"Hey, Boogah, let's call up some mu-fugh-as out in Cal-fonia an' wak 'em up!" (He wanted me to be the culprit, to do the calling.) I smiled and went back to sleep. Another time, in his thick Cajun dialect, Mac said, "May'n, I was in Europe, and I say, 'I see Boogah playin' downtown tonight, Um 'on go down ayr an see 'im.' May'n, I went down ayr, I say, *'Dat ain't nunna no Boogah T!* Um'a tell Boogah!'"

The folks back on Edith Street in Memphis would have been aghast to see me hanging out with a character like Mac, but my horizons had broadened, and all things New Orleans and Creole had crept into my life. Our Winding Way ranch was cluttered with hanging baskets and items from Pier One Imports.

MALIBU, Winding Way Ranch—1971— ♪ 2

Priscilla had let her candles and macramé get out of hand and burned the speakers on my old Craig tape recorder. They sounded all messed up and distorted. Bob plugged his guitar into the input, and he thought they sounded great.

One day, outside in the horse ring, Bob sang me a song, "Forever Young." We stepped outside my twenty-by-forty makeshift studio into the yard and walked down toward the tack house. Bob carried my Gibson J-45 under his arm. The horses were close, just hanging in the ring. As usual, we didn't say much of anything to each other. We sat down on a bench under the big oak in my backyard, and he started to strum and sing, as if to ask, "What about this one?"

That day, alone with Bob Dylan on a hill in the bright California sunshine, I felt that by virtue of the words of "Forever Young" being sung directly to me, I was being christened and blessed by the premier guru of '60s rock culture. It was like having a private audience with Woody Guthrie incarnate. I was sure to have a privileged life from that point on. It didn't hurt that I'd had a few hits on a joint of fine California Gold.

He could make rhyme and compose melody at the drop of a hat.

Who can say what the true powers of music and words are?

Bob wanted to know if I thought the stuff was any good.

"That sounds great, Bob! You should record it," I told him.

He did. The record sounded nothing like what he sang for me that day. Not even close. Only the lyric "forever young" was the same. The bridge chords were completely different, except on the demo version he released.

BURBANK, CA—1973— ♪ 7

A few months later, Bob knocked on the door shortly after midnight. He knew I was a bass player.

"Hey, Booker, you know we're doing a movie over in Burbank

with Jason Robards and Sam Peckinpah"—name dropping—"why don't you grab your bass and meet me over there?"

"Aw, naw, Bob, I'm not going out to Burbank at this hour."

I grabbed my bass, went out to Burbank, walked into the studio, and there was Kris Kristofferson up on the screen.

Bob walked over to the microphone. *Mama come take this badge from me. I can't wear it anymore.*

Turns out I played bass for one of the most charismatic scenes in a motion picture, "Knockin' on Heaven's Door."

Gradually, I became a session man. Starting with Bobby Darin in the midsixties, I started to get more calls as a sideman on Hammond B-3 and piano. Living at my ranch, I played on music by Richie Havens, Barbra Streisand, Joe Tex, Rita Coolidge, Stephen Stills, Bill Withers, Willie Nelson, Marc Benno, Bob Dylan, and Kris Kristofferson.

MALIBU, Winding Way Ranch—1970—♪3

Meanwhile, businessman Clarence Avant was busy selling Stax Records to Paramount Pictures for millions of dollars. Al Bell made sure I knew who he was. Every time I talked to Al, it was "Clarence this, Clarence that." Then, in the summer of 1970, my phone rang.

"Booker, this is Clarence. There's a guy out here in Inglewood building airplane toilets who writes songs. I think you ought to hear him."

"All right, man. Send him out."

I hung up the phone. I didn't know Clarence Avant that well, but he was a friend of Al Bell's, and he had just arranged the sale of Stax to Gulf & Western Industries, quite a feat for a black man in the seventies.

I looked out the window, and up walked a man who looked like he had everything but his lunch pail with him. Big brogan shoes and overalls, with a smile and a short Afro. He brought his guitar and had a big, thick, worn notebook.

After the perfunctory introductions, he sat down on the couch, guitar on his lap, and even before hitting a chord, Bill patted his foot on the carpet for the beat and sang:

Ain't no sunshine when she's gone—It's not warm when she's away.

Bill had hardly gone into the second verse before I got up and went into the next room, my studio, and started making phone calls.

Still listening to Bill sing out in the living room, I called Heider's. The studio was unavailable for an extended period.

I put in a call to Al Jackson in Memphis. Phone was busy. Finally, I got Duck on the phone.

Bill stopped singing and meandered into the room, his face a question mark.

"Oh, I'm sorry, man; I had to make some calls. Let me hear something else."

Priscilla wandered in from the bedroom, smiled, and took a chair to listen.

Grandma's hands used to issue out a warning.

I got Cropper on the phone. "I'm producing a session. Sorry, Booker; I can't make it."

I found Stephen Stills's number in my book.

By the time Bill got to the song "Harlem," I had put together a band and had Conway studio on hold.

I could get into Conway Studio without paperwork, and as soon

Marrying my sweetie
(Artist Collection)

My Livvy and me,
November 1986
(Artist Collection)

At the mouth of the mine in Yosemite with my new blended family.
From left: Lonnie, Nan, Olivia, Brian, Michael, Matthew, and me
(Artist Collection)

Rock and Roll Hall of Fame Awards, 1992. From left: Steve, Duck, me, Rufus, Isaac, and Carla *(Artist Collection)*

My twins, Cicely and Teddy, Paris, 1993 *(Artist Collection)*

With Neil, the band, and the crew at the end of the 1993 tour *(Pegi Young Photography)*

The triumvirate in
Buffalo, New York:
me, Steve, Duck
*(Andrea Zucker
Photography)*

Playing the Conn trombone
for my twins' preschool
(Artist Collection)

Presenting letters to President Clinton
from Olivia's third-grade class
(Official White House Photograph)

My mountain girl and me *(Artist Collection)*

Nan and the boys. From left:
Michael, Nan, Brian, and Matthew
(Artist Collection)

The fam celebrating my sixtieth. From top left: Booker T. IV, Olivia, Jade, Cicely, Teddy, Lonn
D'Laynie, Booker T. III, Nijel, Brian, Matthew, and Michael *(Lorin Schneider Photography)*

On the Cal Berkeley
soccer field with Teddy
(Artist Collection)

Backstage at Antone's during SXSW. From left: Duck, Isaac,
William, me, and Steve *(Rick Diamond / Getty Images)*

Onstage in San
Antonio with the great
B.B. King *(Darren
Abate Photography)*

My favorite Austin club,
Antone's, with Teddy
(Suzanne Pressman)

Playing with Gary
Clark Jr. at the fiftieth
anniversary of the
Monterey Pop Festival
(Greg Chow)

Early lobbying for the
Music Modernization Act.
From left: Cory Booker,
me, Patrick Leahy, and
Dionne Warwick
(Leigh Vogel / Getty Images)

Booker T. — Thanks for a wonderful evening!

Michelle Obama

performance at the White House, 2013.
om left: Olivia, Cicely, Teddy, President
rack Obama, First Lady Michelle Obama,
an, me, Janine, and David Slucter *(Courtesy of
e Barack Obama Presidential Library)*

At the Hollywood Bowl with Carlos
and Teddy *(Artist Collection)*

Addressing the class of 2012 and
receiving an honorary doctorate
(Courtesy of Indiana University)

Leon takes over "Green Onions" *(Artist Collection)*

Olivia earns an MBA from UCLA. From left, Nan, me, Olivia, D'Shalen, Cicely, and Teddy *(Artist Collection)*

as everyone confirmed, the session was booked for Clarence Avant's Sussex Records.

Al Jackson and Duck Dunn flew in from Memphis, and I picked them up at the Hyatt on Sunset on my drive from Malibu. Once again, I used Bill Halverson at the board. Filling in for Steve Cropper was Stephen Stills, who I've long considered to be the tastiest, highest-caliber rock guitarist.

Already there when I arrived, Bill showed up for the recording session in the same clothing he wore to the ranch—he was a carpenter at heart.

Bill poked his head in the control room door. "Who's going to sing these songs, Booker?"

"You are, Bill."

And he obediently walked back out into the studio and up to the microphone.

Once Bill started singing, his habit of slamming his foot down on the floor made an annoying sound, leaking into the mike, indistinguishable from the drums. Al suggested we mike the sound of Bill's foot instead of trying to mask it. Bill Halverson went out back to the alley behind Heider's and found an old wooden crate. He stood it up right under Bill's knee and stuck a mike in front of it.

When we got to the breakdown, Bill just started to repeat "*I know, I know, I know,*" over and over again. He said he couldn't think of any more words and wanted to edit that part out.

"Leave it in!" I insisted, and I had Halverson turn up the volume of Bill's foot stomping on the crate during that part. It sounded like a good hook to me.

I hadn't paid much consideration to the budget, and Clarence balked when I told him I had written strings for the song. I flew to Memphis and recorded a low-budget string session with Noel Gilbert at Ardent with Terry Manning engineering.

I still had no savvy about the music business. Naively assuming I could do as I wished, unaware of the possible legal consequences of leaving Stax, I had no attorney for advice.

MALIBU—1971— ♪ 4

On my birthday in 1971, my contract with Stax Records was suspended. I didn't learn of the suspension until months after. Maybe there was a legal situation that required them to take action. I don't know. With that action, the life of Booker T. & the MGs came to a formal, if inconspicuous, end.

Priscilla was anxious to record some of the songs we had written together, and I hastily signed a recording agreement with A&M Records to record the two of us as a duet, "Booker T. and Priscilla." We played a few shows and met with some moderate success.

I had strangers tell me they were inspired by the relationship I had with Priscilla and by the music I recorded with her. They saw us as a couple not unlike Minnie Riperton and Richard Rudolph, or Bruce Sudano and Donna Summer—interracial, fairy-tale, musical love-marriages in the Age of Aquarius, blazing a new trail. Our relationship bore no resemblance to the love songs we sang.

In 1970, I produced Priscilla's first album, *Gypsy Queen*. Over the next three years, we recorded three albums together: *Booker T. & Priscilla* in 1971, *Home Grown* in 1972, and *Chronicles* in 1973. I also produced Priscilla's solo album, *Flying*, in 1979.

Money was funneled from my accounts at A&M for Priscilla's solo projects. I had objected to paying for her session from my A&M funds. A&M Records were my champions and benefactors when I came to Hollywood. They pulled out all the stops when it came to getting me out of my obligations to Stax. The owners, Herb Alpert of the Tijuana Brass and Jerry Moss, a promotion man from New York, had faith in my creative abilities. Herb and Jerry, along with Gil Friesen, the president of A&M, embraced an expanded view of me that included collaborating with their writers and producers as well as my recording as a featured vocalist. I was entrusted with unlimited free range to explore my artistic possibilities, unrestricted to soul music, and surprising shifts and changes in my musical direction were regarded with a positive attitude. To boot, they put me front and center among producers being presented to Hollywood's top-notch talent. I was living the California dream.

Little did I know, but as injustice and inequality chased me out of Memphis, so would the incessant Santa Ana winds chase me out of Malibu.

I never made friends with the Santa Ana. It didn't seem to be the same entity I loved when I was out at sea on a fishing boat. It was a strange, cruel wind that drove the fire down the hill and burned my hay and my fencing.

Fred May, the de facto mayor of Malibu, befriended me. "True Malibuites don't leave, Booker; we stick it out."

CHAPTER 14

Stardust

Remote Northern California Road—February 1974— ♪ 5

Priscilla may have been flattered by being mistaken for a woman who was thirteen years younger. Not much was more important to her than her looks.

Numerous highway patrol cars and sheriff's deputies surrounded me and my Caucasian wife.

The authorities seemed convinced the woman in my truck was Patricia Hearst, heiress and daughter of publishing magnate Randolph Hearst, who was the subject of a nationwide manhunt at the time. The highway patrol had allowed me to drive more than seven miles inland off California Highway 1 before they pulled up behind, turned on the lights, and drew their weapons.

Guns were everywhere. The forest was lit up like searchlights at a movie opening.

Knowing better than to be out of the car alone, I refused to leave my vehicle but did show my license. I survived, but not without spending anxious moments sitting still in my truck waiting to have my license plates, my life, and my future verified.

Finally convinced of my identity, they allowed us to continue to our ranch on top of a mountain of old-growth redwood.

The old-growth trees were the main attraction to the area and to the property. They were held in reverence by a number of my friends because of their age and the fact that they seemed to have an eerie presence about them—like an awareness of *your* presence.

COMPTCHE, CA—1972— ♪ 1

My friend who spoke of the old-growth redwoods was a lanky, long-haired, slow-talking bass player from Meridian, Mississippi, named Chris Ethridge. He was a great player and played on my demo for "Higher and Higher." His child, Necia, was the first baby I ever witnessed born into this world. At a session one day, Chris asked, "Booker, how'd you like to be the owner of a thousand acres of redwoods in Mendocino?"

"What? I'd love that, Chris!" My newfound mentality embraced a love of the outdoors and gardening.

Chris had a friend who was onto a deal to buy some acreage. The road to the house site was treacherous. Overgrown, not maintained for years. Lumber trucks had traversed it in years past, but there had been no ditching, graveling, or grading since I don't know when. Still, I wanted that land more than anything.

Kris Kristofferson and Rita came to visit and see the land. They had just gotten together—all touchy-feely and intoxicated with one another. I took them on hair-raising rides up and down steep hills in my trusty 4x4, but they never really took their eyes off one another.

Other partners started to buy into the land deal. John Barbata of the Turtles and the Hollies bought in for 160 acres. Then Chris Ethridge and Joel Scott Hill bought in. Finally, Tyrone Hill, Joel's cousin, bought a prime piece of land at the bottom of the hill. I ended up with a 238-acre parcel with old-growth redwood on it and, after a period of time in Malibu, made the move to Comptche, the rural Northern California community near Mendocino.

As it turned out, Malibu, with its coyotes and rattlesnakes, was tame compared to this new territory. Ranchers kept shotguns near the doors to keep the mountain lions away from their chickens and sheep. The cats were smaller, leaner, and fiercer than I had expected.

Regardless, I drew plans for a geodesic dome for our dwelling. I thought building a simple, uncomplicated dome would be a trouble-free, elementary process with few difficulties because it's basically only a series of intersecting triangles. A piece of cake. I purchased connector plates for the two-by-four frame lumber at a company on Melrose Avenue in LA. I stacked over two hundred steel plates (each about the size of a large hubcap) into the bed of my Chevy three-quarter-ton pickup and hauled them six hundred miles to the Northern California Comptche building site. Altogether, gathering the materials was a sizable, costly undertaking that I sunk a lot of effort into.

I submitted my plans and applied for a permit to the Mendocino County Department Planning and Building Services. After waiting six weeks, my permit was denied. The reason given was that the building was unsafe. The plans were noncompliant with county code—a geodesic dome lacked "structural integrity."

Ruefully, my gaze fixed on the heap of rusting steel plates on the red dirt. Abandoned, fading, rejected, discarded, and wasting in a humongous lonely stack near the shed, their heads poked out, looking like so many uncrowned stars and landfill. I realized my nonconforming dream was not to be. The planning department would determine the anatomy of my new home.

We pulled our old camping trailer onto the property and rented a three-bedroom farmhouse on a property known as the South Forty for the Coolidges, my in-laws. I was keen to build my "mountain house," so I drew a traditional blueprint with a sixteen-hundred-square-foot plan, consisting of three bedrooms, two baths, and a loft. The building department issued a permit almost immediately.

I opened an account at Rossi's Building Supply in Fort Bragg, bought some gloves, a shovel, a Stihl chain saw, and a new four-wheel-drive Chevy truck. I ordered a propane gas tank and a 5-kW Briggs and Stratton generator to build the house with. Also, since I had paid for, watched, and helped Reverend Coolidge build his house on the hill in Malibu, I figured his carpentry skills could be helpful in putting my house in the mountains together.

A cold drizzle greeted us the morning we started building the forms. I wanted to try to get in the house before fall, so we started excavating right after Christmas. I chose a site high on a hill to catch the panoramic views for miles to the south and east. I hired Bill Shandel, the tall Russian whose family we bought the land from, and his brother Norm to cut out the pad. I figured they knew the lay of the land best since they had owned it, and their equipment was closest by. They rolled their big Cats up the hill and cut a new road.

While my only skill was knowing how to drive a nail, I was so excited to build my own house on my own land that nothing could stop me from helping out. We built forms and laid a concrete pad for the propane tank about fifty yards from the house site. Then we constructed another pad for the generator about twenty yards from the house site. The tank came first, looking like a white missile being towed up the hill through the trees. The generator was shipped, and I brought it from Fort Bragg on my truck. Once propane was fed to the generator, we had power, and the real work could begin.

There was a community of hippies in the area, and I made a lot of new friends. During the grading process for cutting out the pad for our house on the hill, I had the tractors level a nearby acre on the hill in anticipation of planting a garden. All the locals were garden savvy. I visited a large number of gardens and got tips from everyone.

I went crazy. I had cantaloupe, tomatoes, corn, carrots, green onions. I used a hoe and planted everything from seed in hills and rows. All around the garden's perimeter were my sunflowers, which grew to eleven feet tall and were the crowning glory of the whole group, glistening yellow in the morning and afternoon light. And I had five marijuana plants—two tall males and three short females.

Before all that, however, I had to finish the house. I ordered three-inch nails, two-by-fours, plywood, concrete blocks, and braces for the foundation. Then I got two-by-sixes and brackets for the floor joists.

By the time we poured concrete, the short, cold, wet winter days had given way to the fresh sunshine of spring, and my body took on the shape of a carpenter.

SAN FRANCISCO—Fall 1974—♪ 12

That fall, Gigi called and insisted I meet her in San Francisco to take our son. She refused to give a reason why—insisting I send him back to her after one year. I consented, drove down, and picked him up.

"Oh, by the way, I noticed a bottle of birth control pills in your bathroom in Malibu when I was out there last," Gigi said. "Just thought you might like to know."

I didn't answer.

In Comptche, at the South Forty, you would have thought my ten-year-old boy had died and gone to heaven. Every day he was down at the stream catching frogs, playing with polliwogs, or running breakneck through the field. The school Paul, Laura, and T attended was a one-room country schoolhouse down the road. The kids walked. It was the first time in years I didn't have to get up in the morning and drive them.

However, after we moved into the new mountain house, the children started going to school in Mendocino on the coast, and it was my job to get Paul and Laura to the school bus, as it had been in Beverly Hills and Malibu. If we missed the bus, I drove them the eighteen miles into Mendocino. Most nights dinner was at Priscilla's parents' house, just a short drive down the road on our own property, consisting of canned corn, white bread, applesauce, and canned peas.

Having resources for houses and cars made us an anomaly in a subculture. Most of our land-group partners, save John Barbata, who was busy drumming with Crosby, Stills, Nash & Young, and most of my friends eked out a meager living off the land, eating from huge gardens. We were land poor. My income sources dried up. I received no money from Stax, which was in bankruptcy. Having left LA, I was no longer in demand for session work.

Desperate, I called Quincy Jones. "I'm sorry, man; I don't have anything for you."

With two families to support, and a $4,600 annual mortgage to pay, I needed to work. Also, busy as I was with building the mountain home, I still had a burning in my chest to make new music.

EVERGREEN ALBUM—1974—♪2

Fortunately, in Mill Valley, a small town in Marin County, California, I ran into George Daly, who discovered the Cars and who had a connection with Ron Alexenberg of Epic Records in New York. After asking to manage me and Priscilla, he was able to convince Epic to give me a $75,000 fund to record a new solo LP.

The closest good studio was the Record Plant in Sausalito, but the vocals for "Jamaica Song" were recorded at San Francisco's Columbia Studio on Howard. The album cover was shot by photographer Jim Marshall, who became a friend and confidant in the process. Jim and photographer Joel Bernstein became regulars, dropping by the studio and the house to snap pictures at all hours.

You could say the album was performed by my version of LA's Wrecking Crew. I was a big fan of Bobby Hall's percussion playing and used her on nearly all my productions. Jim Keltner was my go-to drummer even when John Robinson was available. David T. Walker was hands down LA's tastiest session guitarist. Sammy Creason's drums and Mike Utley's keyboards were warm, familiar touches from Kris and Rita's band, like family. Bob Glaub did Duck Dunn better than Duck Dunn on bass. It took some convincing to get the children, Paul, Laura, and T, to make the trip to a studio in San Francisco to sing on "Jamaica Song." Still, the childlike innocence of their voices lent the cut a unique quality. Tender, precious, and inimitable.

That's me playing the mandolin on "Mama Stewart." Paying respect to my childhood influences from listening to John R. Richbourg on Nashville's WLAC when I was a toddler. A white man speaking in the black vernacular, you would have thought he was a black man playing country music. It was my first exposure to Chet Atkins and his guitar picking.

Evergreen was no more a soul album than a mule is a horse, but they came out of the same stable. Regardless, it's an accurate representation of my musical palate at the time. It's roots music with a touch of folk and reggae. Calling it folk funk wouldn't be wrong either.

SAN FRANCISCO AIRPORT—Fall 1975— ♪ 6

The first year went quickly, and I was unprepared when I got the call from T's mom that she wanted him returned to her immediately. Just when my son had assimilated into our family, when I was used to having him near, it was all upended. Everything was turned upside down. Having to let him go wounded both of us.

At the airport in San Francisco, walking T to the gate, I ran into Buddy Miles, who just happened to be flying to LA. I explained why we were there.

"No problem, man! I'll watch after him on the flight down!"

I let go of T's hand, and Buddy took his other hand.

So T took off—under the watchful eyes of none other than the great Buddy Miles.

There was no more soulful drummer in that period than Buddy. Hendrix hired him—and Buddy had his own band as well. I'm surprised he and my son didn't record and mix a track on the flight down.

COMPTCHE, CA—Winter 1975— ♪ 4

My relationship with Priscilla continued on shaky ground. One morning in Comptche, after Priscilla had stayed out all night and came home wearing a miniskirt that exposed her, Reverend Coolidge said to me, "She's not my wife; I can't slap her."

I was so surprised to hear this kind of talk come from the minister. As if there were a street-thug type hidden under the self-righteous mask.

"You need to hit my daughter!" is what he was basically saying. "So she'll behave, and your marriage will stay intact."

But why would he go this far? Possibly he was concerned that the gravy train of money he was receiving from me every month would halt if my marriage to his daughter fell apart.

George Daly was managing both of us, but he had only obtained a solo record deal for me. Not one for Priscilla nor a joint deal for both of us. Maybe the last straw was the "boing" sound made by the strings of my Gibson J-45 hitting the door behind me when I left the house that morning. Priscilla had thrown it.

Within six months, I was spending more days away from the house. My usual destination was the bench outside the Comptche Store, where I sat for hours smoking cigarettes.

Once, a man with a bright smile sat down next to me.

"You can have anything I got. All you have to do is ask for it."

I asked for, and got, an honest friend. Everything from advice on which hands to hire to which direction my house should face came from my new friend, Bob Evans. It got so that I could stroll into his front door without knocking, and vice versa.

"You know, Booker, you can't keep on walking around like this," Bob declared one day as we sat on the bench outside the store.

"Like what, Bob?"

"With your face down in the dirt all the time."

"What are you talking about?"

"Life's too short, man."

"Too short for what?"

"Not to feel good every day."

There is no way to calculate the value of an honest friend.

His job with me done, Bob got up and ambled over to his truck. A cowboy with not a care in the world. I, on the other hand, had some hard choices ahead. I hadn't noticed how much my down mood was affecting people around me.

Emotionally, I was constantly upended. Like a ship at sea in a storm that never ended. A series of visits with friends kept me afloat.

LOS ANGELES—September 1975— ♪ *5*

The meeting took place at Lee Housekeeper's house in the Holly-wood Hills. Lee was Steve Cropper's friend and manager and had been instrumental in trying to get the MGs back together. It was a festive dinner, and Al had decided to seriously consider moving to the West Coast. He would go back to Memphis and talk to Barbara (his wife) about it. Just as we were leaving, I told him I loved him, and he took me out to the balcony. "I want to show you something, Jones." He always called me Jones.

On the balcony, Al opened his shirt and exposed a bullet wound in his upper-right abdomen. I had never seen a bullet wound before. The sight of it shocked and scared me. It had healed quite a bit, but it looked horrible. We just stared at each other. His wife, Barbara, had shot him. I wondered what was in the future if he returned to Memphis. He buttoned up his shirt. We hugged and went back inside. I understood he was determined to start over, both with the MGs and with Barbara.

NEW YORK—October 1975— ♪ *11*

Reunited, the MGs made their debut at New York's Bottom Line Club, where Stevie Wonder was sitting at the bar. It was hard not to recognize Stevie's familiar form. I wandered over at the break to say hello. We had been periodic telephone buddies since the late sixties, and he had sent a tape of his song "The Thought of Loving You" when I was still at Stax. As I was walking away to go back on-stage, he said, "Keep your spirits up!"

That same night, I had somehow managed to get my first synthe-sizer, a Maxi-Korg 800 DV, on the stage. Sitting side stage unseen to my left, it didn't get used the whole set until the very end, when we closed with "Time Is Tight." When we got to the coda, which I had written to extend the song, the key suddenly changed to F. That's when I reached over with one finger of my left hand and hit a very low F on the Korg. The thing was duo phonic—the second voice entered the sound after my hand had left the keyboard.

The sound was very deep and strong and dramatic.

The band was so shocked that they just held the F chord and let the Korg do its thing, and its big sound progressed through the envelope and it billowed from a dark low tone all the way through the high brilliant overtones that only a powerful synth can create. I just sat there while the sound enveloped the stage and the entire room. Steve Cropper looked around and smiled...I had graduated from the Hammond B-3 with Stevie Wonder in the audience.

LOS ANGELES—October 1, 1975— ♪ 6

The next time I heard anything about Al was a few weeks later when walking up to the porch of my dad's house in LA. As we approached, I saw my name flash on the TV through the screen door. It was the evening news. "Booker T. & the MGs band member shot and killed in Memphis." I went inside and watched in disbelief with my mom and dad.

We were all in shock. My mind raced. Had Barbara shot him again? What were the circumstances? What were the details? My mother was scared to death. She was afraid that if I went back to Memphis to attend Al's funeral, something bad would happen to me there. After all, there had already been the ransom situation before we left Memphis.

Mama begged me not to go back to Memphis for the funeral, and I didn't. We knew of all the guns at Stax Records.

I learned from Duck Dunn that Al had taken eight bullets in the back. Shot multiple times in the back and with a big, different gun.

One of the tragedies that marred my early childhood was the 1958 shooting of Dr. J. E. Walker, who lived ten houses away from me on the corner of Edith and Mississippi Avenues. This crime, along with the killing of Emmett Till in 1958 in Mississippi, terrified our neighborhood.

When I was growing up, if a report that a white man was shot came in to the police station in downtown Memphis, they would launch an investigation. If a black man shot a black man, they would just go out for more coffee.

It's an outrage that the murder was never solved. No investment made. No further investigation. It remains a travesty and a charade of police work. Another black male life determined insignificant, not worthy of public concern. Case closed. But I, for one, will never let go of this.

This act robbed the world of its most talented drummer. Someone who spent hours being the creative genius at Stax from 11:00 a.m. to 6:00 p.m., had dinner, and then went on to write and play on some of the world's best R & B at Hi Records with Al Green and Willie Mitchell.

This was on a daily basis.

The murder robbed his children of their father. Robbed me of my old roommate. He wasn't perfect, but a lot of people loved him. Otis Redding loved him. Duck Dunn loved him. Women loved him. Jim Stewart loved him. I loved him. He was my best friend, even though we broke up over my departure from Stax Records, which he took personally.

I spoke at his class reunion in LA a few years after his death. Both surprising and painful was how few of Al's classmates were aware of the huge contribution he had made to the world of music. Aspiring drummers the world over were trying to emulate his style.

Years later, Steve Cropper took up the campaign with me and started to sing praises about Al's musical prowess.

But now he was gone. Al's death was a big shock. A hard blow to the chest. Other deaths, like my grandparents', were expected. Now I had to look the unpredictability of life in the face.

Unfairly, I compare all other drummers to Al Jackson. To me, he is still the king.

I didn't do much music for a while after Al's death; however, Priscilla was busy pursuing her solo career with an independent producer in Nashville.

NASHVILLE—JANUARY 1976—♪9

"There's a baby at the hospital in Willits," Priscilla told me one night after her session. "I'm flying back to San Francisco to get the child early in the morning. You can take a later flight."

"Oh, really? I didn't know we were considering adoption," I said.

"I meant to talk to you about it."

"You knew all this while?" I asked, my mouth wide open. The news had come as a shock. I was astonished Priscilla would make such an important decision without so much as mentioning it to me. It was a bolt of lightning. I was appalled.

"I need to get some sleep," Priscilla said from the bathroom, taking her makeup off. "There was only room for one on the flight. I'll see you at home."

I got very tired. I felt numb, deprived of the power to control my life. I didn't sleep.

A few hours later, Priscilla hopped into a cab for the Nashville airport and left me a number to call her producer and cancel the day's session. I got a much later flight but made it to Comptche in time to be there when she got home late that night with the baby. The tiny little newborn girl slept on my stomach. She was a beautiful, placid little thing. Priscilla named her Lonnie, after her maternal grandfather.

MALIBU, CA—1976— ♪ 1

Early one morning in 1976, I stepped out onto the deck of my beachfront Malibu condo to get some fresh air and watch the waves crash onto the sand. A man with long red hair was running on the beach down below. I said to myself, "That looks like Willie Nelson." He glanced up, smiled, and waved as he ran past. I waved back.

It was Willie Nelson. He had rented the condo just below mine. Introductions were made, and in no time Willie and I were spending time sitting on his deck or mine, guitars in hand, having fun going over old standards we both had loved and played in the past.

TUCSON, AZ—1976— ♪ 9

In 1976, Kris Kristofferson contacted me about playing in his band in a movie with Barbra Streisand, and off I went to Tucson to appear in and play on the soundtrack for the Barbra Streisand film *A Star Is Born*.

Barbra had the voice. But that meant nothing without the material. And for that, she went to the source: Paul Williams. She wanted the best of everything and knew how to get it. She was the first one at the studio and the last to leave. Because of her working harder than everyone else, no one said no to her, except Kris Kristofferson. And not because of Rita. Kris was not acting the part; he had become John Norman Howard, and he was my brother-in-law at the time.

Kris came to my dressing room when he was sober. We talked about all the times and ways we had messed our lives up. He talked about Fran (his ex) and the kids, and I talked about Gigi and T. Riding in my truck with me, Kris pulled out a royalty check for $70,000. He laughed. "What the heck am I going to do with this?" Kris had never received that much money before. Then, Jon Peters, producer of *A Star Is Born,* gave him $800,000, and he was really lost. He wouldn't even buy a ride.

"Kris, you can afford a nice car," I told him, but he continued to drive a rented Chevy Impala. He never turned it in.

Priscilla had a key to their house, and the relationship became strained as more and more, Rita recognized her clothes in Priscilla's closet. Kris also began to get drunk before he came home. I couldn't drink with Kris. Couldn't keep up with him. None of us could. Not Donnie Fritts or Mike Utley or Sammy Creason, not even Willie. Kris worshipped the ground Willie Nelson walked on and tended to behave around him.

Kris and I kept a good, respectful relationship, but around Rita and Priscilla, there was always a scene.

By the fall of 1976, Priscilla's dad began complaining to me privately about Kris. "Doesn't seem like much of a man to me. You?"

Kris had more courage than me. He left first.

BEVERLY HILLS—December 1977— ♪ 7

I don't know how they got the thing up the hill to Emmylou Harris's house in the eastern part of Beverly Hills. It was a humongous steel animal, like you would find following circus trucks down the highway, filled with sensitive, temperamental, fragile recording equipment and couches. It rolled like it was filled with lead, weighing way more tons than the California DMV would allow.

However, there it sat in Brian Ahern's and Emmylou's front yard, blocking the entrance to the front door—the Enactron Truck. Brian, Emmylou's husband, was the owner of the mobile recording truck. If a truck could cause a divorce, this one would. The thing was that imposing.

It was Brian's baby. The reason I used the Enactron Truck was because it housed an old Stephens twenty-four-track tape recorder and more vintage mikes than you could shake a stick at. A machine built to uncompromising standards, the Stephens was quiet without noise reduction, but the tape was always falling off the transport.

During playback, we would be listening, and the sound would stop. I'd look over, and our valuable tape would be reeling down off the machine onto the floor. The transport was operated by an old delicate servo with a take-up motor that would quit. Then Bradley, the engineer, would say over talkback, "Uh, could you guys do that again?"

He'd then hurry over, wrap the two-inch tape around his neck, rethread it onto the transport, and we'd continue like nothing happened.

I could tell by the notes Willie sang and played that he had a rare, innate, and effortless understanding of music. Like some people who just know what colors go together. All that belied his apparent nature, that of a happy-go-lucky guy out to have fun at any cost. Willie didn't take music too seriously, but music took him seriously. Given those attributes, the two of us fit like a glove. I laughed at all the jokes he threw at me. Seriously.

When we were socializing, I let Willie take the lead. Which wasn't so easy for me. The reason was I knew Willie knew how to play cards. Even when he was losing, he was playing to win. And win he did, in the most unconventional of ways.

Every one of Willie's characters was there for a purpose. Each one had his place in the pecking order. It was amazing because none of this was arranged with words. Just silence, looks, laughs, and entrances to and from rooms. In every rock and roll retinue, there exists a pecking order—necessary for the survival of the group. A structure among the employees: musicians, managers, roadies, and so forth. An outside producer must find and make his place in that structure in order to produce a successful album. I didn't understand the order at first, so I made missteps on a daily basis, which drew guffaws from the retinue. For one, I took too many hits on the joints. So much so that I regularly lost my place. As in, I really lost it. "Aw, that's just Booker stoned." I never correctly judged the potency of the grass.

On the warm Malibu nights, Willie would come up to visit, bringing his guitar, and we sat outside on my deck looking out at the waves. Just inside the door sat my electric piano, and sometimes I'd duck inside to hit a chord or two on it while Willie sat outside singing and playing. After a jam on "Moonlight in Vermont," Willie said, "Booker, why don't you do an arrangement of this for my band, and let's just go into the studio and cut it?"

"Sure, Willie, let's do it!"

After a couple more jams on the porch, he said, "Why don't you just do a whole album of these, and let's pick out a few more."

Our favorites turned out to be the same. Tunes we both had played in the clubs years ago when we first started in music. "Stardust," "Georgia on My Mind," "Blue Skies," and others. On December 3, 1977, we went out to Emmylou Harris's house in Beverly Hills and met Willie's band. Her husband had his recording truck situated in the front parking area, a convenient, ideal arrangement for recording instruments located in the different rooms in the house.

Brian and Bradley took care of everything. I didn't make a call or lift a finger. When I got there, my Hammond was sitting in the living room right in front of Willie's mike, and a grand piano was just on the other side, both in Willie's line of sight.

Paul English (drums) was just to Willie's right, and Bee Spears (bass) was behind me. Chris Ethridge (bass) had his own room, as did Rex Ludwick (drums) and Jody Payne (guitar). The only room not to have a musician was the kitchen. I believe Mickey Raphael (harmonica) was in the bathroom.

In the studio, Willie followed my lead. Mostly. He intuitively knew when I was leaving things out—leaving room for something. His greatest gift was his faith in my vision. And his henchmen made sure I didn't go too far from Willie's vision—which I was capable of doing. Brad Hartman exhibited the patience of Job with me while I sat for hours in a trance listening to the takes. I was absorbed with the music, and it took eons to get objective on small practical issues.

Everybody thinks the *Stardust* album was done in ten days. That was just the recording. The mixing took a short lifetime. Donivan Cowart, the second engineer, was the glue that held me and Brad together in a tiny trailer. Just the three of us.

Sometimes I wonder why I spend the lonely nights dreaming of a song. When I listened to Willie sing those words through the headphones, it was reminiscent of when I heard Albert King play the first few notes on the guitar for "Born Under a Bad Sign." Those notes belonged to a song that determined my destiny due to the fact that they were written by Hoagy Carmichael, who was schooled at the Indiana University School of Music. When I graduated from high school, I rushed to Bloomington to walk the same steps as Hoagy and literally stand on the same ground. I used what I learned there to write the charts for Willie's *Stardust* album. The moment Willie sang the song "Stardust" is crystallized in my memory because the words, the melody, and the chords were sung and played so naturally, with just the right blend of dissonance, tension, and release, with no hint of effort, that I would never forget it.

Of all the renditions of "Stardust," this one is my favorite. To get to play on one of your favorite records is one of life's gifts that money can't buy. In this way, I have become wealthy.

Willie has been a lifelong smoker and wanted to enjoy his pastime with his friends. Willie rolled joints for all his friends and everybody who worked for him, which was a considerable number of people. Cleve (Dupin), Rex (Ludwick), Jody (Payne), Chris (Ethridge), Paul (English), Bee (Spears), and Mickey (Raphael), and I sat in the easy chairs in Willie's office while he sat at his desk and did the honors.

SPICEWOOD, TX—1978— ♪ 5

Willie loved the finer things. He didn't mind if I rented a Thunderbird or Mercedes at his expense. When I visited, he always provided a full house with a daily housekeeper in case I needed food or had visitors.

He provided free golf and tennis for his friends and musicians. I wish I had been a golfer back then. Willie's greens were some of the finest I'd ever seen. The problem was getting him off the golf course and into the studio. Many days I waited while they played till dusk.

Mixing the *Stardust* LP took meticulous attention because of the many quiet passages. Mixing engineer Bradley Hartmann applied a scrupulous, painstaking effort, resulting in a recording so silent you could hear a pin drop.

Meanwhile, I had the hardest time getting contracts out of Mark Rothbaum, Willie's manager. Willie would just laugh. "Aw, Mark, he's all right!" But I had to keep an eye on him. I finally got a good contract, which Columbia honored, but they wouldn't press any records at first.

Rick Blackburn called his staff together to listen to *Stardust*, and they loved it, so I flew back to California, only to find out they had pressed just five hundred copies. I called Bonnie Garner, and she confirmed everybody loved it. I flew back to Nashville to fight for the album. The music was too good to go without promotion, cast aside because Willie had forced country music's first black producer on Columbia.

He really was an outlaw.

Finally, in April 1978, they released the *Stardust* LP. It went straight to number one on the *Billboard* country album chart. The singles "Blue Skies" and "All of Me" also went to number one on the Hot Country Songs charts. Willie went on the road to promote the album and won a Grammy for Best Country Male Vocal for "Georgia on My Mind."

Then, the album became a worldwide success. Columbia sent me a triple-platinum LP to go with my gold LP. A few years later, they sent me a platinum LP representing sales of six million copies.

My checks were huge. I always knew when CBS was sending me a big one because it went to the wrong address and my lawyer had to track it down.

PEDERNALES, TX—1983— ♪ 8

For the recording of the follow-up album to *Stardust, Without a Song*, I went to Willie's studio on his golf course in the Briarcliff area of Texas near Lake Travis. When I got to Pedernales Ranch in Texas's Hill Country, Willie stopped the car in front of a beautiful corner home and handed me the key. I said, "What's this?"

He said, "It's your house," with that classic smile.

Life at Pedernales was idyllic except for the sometimes-oppressive heat. The humidity kept me in light clothing. The pace of life slowed, and everyone took their cues from Willie, who was so respected as to be godlike in the area. Life came alive in the evening, and during the day we went our own ways. There were swimming pools, tennis courts, and an eighteen-hole golf course. I played tennis every day when I wasn't riding horses or hopping over sidewinder snakes.

I don't know how long I stayed there. Months for sure. I never paid rent. I met my wife Nan while I was living there. I kept a small apartment in Westwood, but most of my time was spent in "Perd'nales," as the Texans called it.

Willie played golf by day, and we went to his studio at night. When he was on the road, I hung out in Austin's nightclubs, mostly Antone's on Congress. Clifford Antone made sure I had a good table, and I enjoyed listening to the blues. Sometimes I would go down to Sixth Street, where I could always find Eric Johnson playing somewhere.

Willie not only had a sauna underneath the pool at his ranch at Pedernales but also kept the golf course fully manned, and the sauna was always turned on. I was the only one to go down there, so I was always in there alone. My paranoia was so strong from all the grass I was smoking with Willie that I could never stay in very long, afraid the Texas Rangers would come lock the door, leave me to rot, and arrest Willie for hanging out with a black man.

LOS ANGELES—1977— ♪ 2

I was involved with one more motion picture in an unusual role.

I was paid an advance to do orchestral transcriptions of Bo Harwood's music for John Cassavetes's new film, *Opening Night.* He loved people passionately and was always surrounded by friends who seemed to love him for all the right reasons: his wit and intelligence. Such an unlikely candidate for a relationship with the mob, I thought. For some reason, they made sure there was distance between me and him.

"You look nervous, Booker; is everything all right?" asked one of John's bodyguards when I came to the office on my second visit.

"Yes, I'm OK. Everything's all right," I answered.

The man continued to eye me. What did they think? That I was going to shoot John or something? For God's sake.

It continued. With body language and gestures of the eyes, John's men forced me to keep my distance. With his permission, I presume. It didn't jibe because John himself was always warm to me. However, his makeup seemed to be a curious mixture of warmth, humor, and coldness.

I remember walking into a private room at a restaurant, full of people, sixteen or so, strangely silent. John Cassavetes, an eloquent, kindhearted, honest man, saw no reason for being diplomatic. One of John's henchmen, noticing me walking into the scene, whispered, "Booker, you'd better not ruin this beautiful moment."

It was a prolonged kiss, with a woman who wasn't his wife. Executed without shame in front of intimate company at a business dinner table. I stopped dead in my tracks before I reached my seat. John Cassavetes, a consummate showman, was leaning forward from the standing position and keeping his tongue in a woman's mouth for at least ten minutes or more while the room hushed.

When the kiss ended, people began talking and socializing again.

The recording session was one of the most glorious experiences of my career. John spared no expense, and I hired a meticulous contractor, Jules Chaiken. Subsequently, I stood in front as conductor of one of Hollywood's finest orchestras. John used the music to promote the film on TV.

LOS ANGELES, CA, Universal Language—1977— ♪ 6

Time passes slowly when you face the loss of a friend and band-mate. You expect to hear them call your name or play the perfect rhythm for a song, but it's not to be—not ever again. After more than a year of staring at the finality of Al's death, the MGs decided to record an album without him.

Al Jackson's death hung over the band like a dirge. The *Universal Language* LP was the MGs' attempt to turn that dirge into an elegy. We had all cared so much for Al, even Willie Hall, the drummer we chose for his replacement. Willie was second in line as Al's ap-prentice successors, behind Carl Cunningham, drummer for the Bar-Kays, who had died in 1968 in Otis Redding's plane crash. It was very hard emotionally for Willie to step into Al's shoes under these circumstances. Tom Dowd offered to produce, and Asylum Records offered us a contract.

We decided the album would be dedicated to Al Jackson. While Willie Hall played great, and despite our best intentions, the pro-ject served to illuminate what a necessary component Al's drum-ming was to the MG sound.

Almost every day my father would tell me mama was in pain. Her pancreatic cancer made my dad and me afraid for her life. After consulting with her doctors, it became clear she needed almost daily medical attention.

Mama's condition worsened, and my parents moved to Los An-geles, closer to medical care and to my sister, Gwen.

LOS ANGELES—September 30, 1977— ♪ 6

What have we done? She hadn't spoken in hours, and I was startled that she spoke and undone by the import of what she said. My mother lay dying on the bed next to me in the hospice, and she was asking me if we had done anything of significance in her lifetime.

I had a very close relationship with my mother and never found myself at a loss for words until now, when the minutes and seconds were so important—what should I say?

If I could have had these years that have passed to reflect, I would have spoken more of the huge contribution she made to people's lives and the musical knowledge I received from her.

Or I would have said something about the sheer sacredness and pleasure of the moments spent in her presence, experienced by myself and anyone else who knew her.

I stumbled. And in the seconds that I had to respond, she wondered if we had done anything on this earth that mattered. I regret the generalizations that I made in answer to her query. The undeniable reality was that we were in a hospice. People spoke quietly and walked softly with a slight condescending smile on their faces and alluded to the unavoidable truth. Death was imminent. And very close.

I went to the bathroom located in the room next door. While I was there, I felt her leave. When I returned to her bedside, her mouth was open, and she wasn't breathing.

Now I understand that's the way life goes. It is a song sung between the verses, a game played during the time-outs. To grasp it you let it slip through your fingers.

CHAPTER 15
Don't Stop Your Love

22660 PACIFIC COAST HIGHWAY, MALIBU,
CA—1976— ♪ 9

I gazed lovingly and intently at the Pacific, aware of that body of water's propensity for catching people unaware and consuming them. Taken with its beauty, I knew I had to turn my fear into a healthy respect in order to fully enjoy the ocean. Who would have believed it? I ended up with a surfboard on my deck and a hunger for the taste of salt water in my mouth. I had built up enough shoulder strength to catch a wave from building the mountain house, and I became a beach bum.

The Malibu days were often warm in February, not unlike the hot July days. I loved the way the air felt; I snuggled into the warm breezes. The smell of ocean air etched and colored those precious days.

Like most Malibu residents, I was there for the ocean and the sand. To be able to fall asleep to the constant sound of waves crashing, the assurance that another wave would come, brought me peace.

From the time I first moved to the Winding Way Ranch, I loved taking the half- and full-day rock cod boats off the pier at Paradise Cove. Everything was provided for you—bait, tack, buckets. All you had to do was drop your line when they found where the fish were. The only catch was, I didn't like eating cod. I only went out because I loved spending the days at sea.

As enchanting as the salt water was, though, it could be treacherous. One afternoon, a good way out from the pier at Oxnard, I was suddenly at the top of a gargantuan, forty-foot wave. I had seen it coming but had no idea of the size of it. There was nothing to do but grab the sides of the little nineteen-foot boat and hold on for dear life during the ride down the crest. The little boat didn't capsize. Fortunately, there were no other waves like that. Old time seamen at the pier told me we had caught a rare event, a rogue wave. I thought it might have been the end for me.

19100 PACIFIC COAST HIGHWAY, MALIBU, CA—1977— ♪ 5

The big storm had been brewing out on the ocean since 4:00 p.m. It was now two in the morning. I was under the house trying to assess the water damage. The ocean waves had been so strong that by about four in the afternoon, the fireplace in the living room developed a huge crack right down the middle. Earlier that day, we had friends over for a patio barbeque, and when they came inside and saw the fireplace separating, they quickly left. It was an unexpected rough sea, and we knew the ocean's potential. My heart went up into my throat, and I put on high boots to go under the house and look at the piers and floor joists. A blinding light appeared from the street side. "Is this Booker T. Jones's house?" The cameras were running, and the reporter was standing a few feet away from the cameraman, whose feet were in the water. I discovered you are famous when you least want to be, and the price can be exacting to an unbearable extent. They wanted to televise my house being pulled out to sea, and I couldn't stop them. I was so put out I couldn't speak. I went silently past them, up the stairs, and into the house, uttering not a single word. Then I grabbed the yellow pages and called an emergency moving company.

31627 BROAD BEACH ROAD, MALIBU, CA—1977— ♪ 4

Lesson learned. My third house in Malibu, in less than two years, was a home that was positioned across the road from the beach.

By the time we moved from the "house that went to sea" to Broad Beach Road, I realized my marriage to Priscilla was doomed. I had known numerous times my marriage was deeply troubled. Now it became apparent there was no hope for our relationship. She was spending long days and nights in LA, or Hollywood, and I was there with the three children. She didn't bother to even make an excuse for her absence, even though Hollywood to Malibu was a short drive. I didn't have the belief in our marriage to even question where she was. I began to express my condition in song. The Eagles' "Try and Love Again" was one I played over and over on the piano. I decided to record it.

There was no lyric that spoke more to me at the time. I was alone, and I was searching, even though I had been twice married. Searching for myself, and searching for someone. I was out there on my own. That's what it all came down to.

The sentiment spawned my *Try and Love Again* album, not a commercial one but one true to my current frame of mind. All the money in the world couldn't point me toward my true self or someone to love me. Success and fame meant nothing without another person to hold. I found myself spending more and more time alone, taking care of our one-year-old, questioning my musical approach, my approach to life. I was trying to find an anchor inside. A voice to let me know I was doing things the right way.

Tom Snow, who wrote "He's So Shy" for the Pointer Sisters and "Love Sneakin' Up on You" for Bonnie Raitt, came out to the house, and we turned out one original song, "I'll Put Some Love Back in Your Life." Working with Tom brought my spirits up; however, I couldn't help thinking this lyric somehow applied to me. Still, it was great being around such a positive person. Tom wrote a million hits for other people after our session. The only other original song on the *Try and Love Again* album was "We Could Fly" by Dennis Linde (he wrote "Burning Love" for Elvis) and Thomas Cain. The rest of the songs on the album were cover songs. I was really happy to do one of Thomas's songs because he had been so good to me at BMI in Nashville. Thomas was Nashville's only black music executive in the seventies. He was well liked for being generous with advances against royalties. My friend Jay Graydon played fabulous guitar as he had on my other productions.

I was troubled and disillusioned, and the Eagles flew into my life with their songs about the vagaries of love. Others had told me that my music helped them through hard times, and now the Eagles were helping me.

The Eagles were a pretty slick group with lots of hits, but Randy Meisner's songs kept them rooted to earth—simple songs about our daily struggles rather than more metaphoric ones. It was the start of an Eagles period for me. The music ushered me through a period of depression. Days and nights alone in the house, taking care of our daughter, I listened to their music over and over.

I was as cold inside as the coming fire was hot outside.

The huge fire destroyed every single home except mine and my next-door neighbor's, a Malibu fire department captain. He had to save my house to save his own. This fire was fiercer than the 1971 Malibu fire that destroyed part of my ranch on Winding Way. In the '71 fire, I lost thirty tons of hay, my barn burned down, and I lost all my fencing. This new fire appeared in the early-morning hours, and I walked outside and saw the flames at the crest of the mountain on the east. The fire devoured the hill with speed and force. The flames raced down the slope and hopped over the highway, replacing daylight with blackness. People were running everywhere. I went into the bathroom and wet a bath towel to put over my face. The roar was so loud it sounded like the boiler room I accidentally wandered into in the basement at Porter school when I was seven. We threw a few things into two cars and made it to a hotel in Oxnard after sitting in a long line of cars on the PCH, nearly the last ones out of town.

I was never able to get over that fire. We only escaped because we lived so far north. When we returned, I walked down the street among the hot timbers; I couldn't take my eyes off the house across the street. I had just sat in front of their fireplace—which had disappeared.

After the inferno, our house was not the same. Black soot was everywhere. The lease was up anyway, so I rented an undamaged house in Trancas Canyon on Manzano Drive, where I began to recover from all the disruption and trauma by listening to the Eagles' new album, *Hotel California*.

"Try and Love Again" was an attempt to put my life and career back together. Deep down, I dreamed I would find love. At this point I was caught in a sorrowful relationship with Priscilla.

HOLLYWOOD—1978— ♪7

Then Earl Klugh came into my life, and it couldn't have happened at a better time. Kris Kristofferson's manager, Bert Block, called and asked if he could give Earl my number. I said sure. And Earl came with his buddy Scottie Edwards, a bass player if I ever saw one. Earl had the tunes too, along with as much energy and freshness a young jazz player could be endowed with. He was one of the nicest, most respectful young men I've ever worked with, as well as being one of the most accomplished musicians I've recorded. Earl's style was rooted in the Spanish guitar influence that I loved so much. At a time when synthesizers were threatening to take over, Earl held true to his nylon-string acoustic. His fingers were strong enough to make that box sing.

In the studio, he gave himself to me, submitting most creative decisions to my discretion. The album, entitled *Magic in Your Eyes*, was Earl's fourth studio project and featured his hero, Chet Atkins, on one song, "Goodtime Charlie's Got the Blues."

For the recording, we went to my familiar haunt. Hollywood Sound on Selma, right behind Wally Heider's Studio, had always been a good room for me. I hired Greg Phillinganes for the keyboard chores. Those sessions were a joy. After organizing the project and doing the string charts, I sat back in the control room next to engineer Jim Nipar and let the music take me. My only real chore was selecting the takes and deciding whether to do another one or not. It was the first time I was a control-room producer. *Magic in Your Eyes* surged to number four on the *Billboard* jazz chart.

MALIBU—1978—♪ 4

I tried to lose myself in my work, which was becoming increasingly difficult. I got no encouragement from looking at my past and was reluctant to ponder my future.

Priscilla's late nights out turned into no-shows. She was spending nights out away from home. I assumed she was staying at a hotel with Phil Walden, her label exec, working on her new album, *Flying*. I was wrong. She called from New York.

"Let me talk to Lonnie."

Our two-year-old was beside herself with tears and missing her mother.

"I'll be home in a few days."

When Priscilla came back to "La-La Land," as she called it, three of her friends and her sister, Rita, staged an intervention with her at a posh restaurant in Malibu. She couldn't, just couldn't, keep leaving Lonnie the way she did, one of her friends reported to me after the lunch. Priscilla ignored her friends and her sister.

That day, Priscilla described an unnamed New York man, a meticulous dresser, a man about town, as someone she was seeing. Everyone in the house knew. She pulled some suitcases out of the closet and flew back.

The darkest point came in the fall of 1978 when I realized I'd spent a decade of my life with Priscilla. On her last stay in our Malibu house, the days and nights were filled with contempt and anger. I would never be able to make up for having made her sister, Rita, a star while those same efforts had not paid off for Priscilla. On the other side, Priscilla would never be the woman I dreamed of. It was very late one night after she loaded her bags into a limo headed for a flight to New York to continue her affair with Ed Bradley.

"You won't fight for me," Priscilla protested. Then she was gone. I silently allowed the limo to back out of the driveway and watched the taillights disappear into the black Malibu night. I stood out in the driveway for quite a while—conflicted between feelings of disgust that I had let myself remain in a toxic, destructive relationship for so long and a sense of relief that I might finally begin a new, realistic, maybe even happy life.

Inside the house slept our two-year-old, Lonnie; Priscilla's fifteen-year-old daughter, Laura; and her seventeen-year-old son, Paul, with his girlfriend, Alex. Paul was home from his freshman year at college, an expense I couldn't afford. Did I still like myself? Why hadn't I had the courage to end the relationship earlier? Breathing deep in the night air, I stood alone in the dark, exhilarated that I might now begin to really live but dubious about my treatment of my own self.

At long last, I went inside, sat at the kitchen table, and decided to learn to cook Japanese food. Finding myself alone, I gradually set out on a self-improvement regimen, starting with eating lighter food. I drove with Lonnie all the way into West LA at least three nights a week to Aki, the closest Japanese restaurant. The entire staff called us by name.

After a few weeks, I started to get late-night phone calls. Priscilla was in bed with Ed, while he slept next to her, talking in her soft, breathy voice. She wasn't sure. She wanted to see me. Maybe spend some time in the house. She wanted to hear my voice.

She did, in fact, come back, staying with a friend of hers in Malibu. A change, however, had taken place in me. Her key didn't work. I'd had the locks changed. I'd had enough. I was done.

MALIBU—1979— ♪4

As soon as I became single, people began to set me up with women. Rita slipped me Penny Marshall's phone number. Another friend arranged a sushi dinner with one of her girlfriends.

Ironically, the minute Priscilla walked out the door, I began to make serious money. The hit records on Willie Nelson and Rita Coolidge passed into their first royalty payment periods at the same time, and large deposits were made into the joint account I held with Priscilla at Security Pacific Bank in Malibu. The account was accessible by phone. She took large sums and left none for taxes.

Back in Memphis, everybody paid taxes once a year. I sat in the back seat of my dad's car while he waited in line on April 14 to drop the return into the post office box before midnight. I didn't know the government wanted their money quarterly.

There was a letter from the Internal Revenue Service. I should have been making quarterly income tax payments for my new tax bracket. An IRS agent came to visit. A very kind, personal man who preferred to drive to Malibu rather than have me come to his Westwood office. It was the beginning of a long relationship and friendship whereby I would make him tea, and he would deliver the bad news: taxes were mounting. I was filing annually, and big checks had come in with nothing put away to pay state or federal taxes. At least half of the money Priscilla had drawn from our account should have been placed in a trust account or deposited in a federal tax account.

I was in serious trouble. I replaced my accountant and hired a new attorney. Too late, still, but better late than never.

MALIBU—1980— ♪ 5

Raising Lonnie as a single dad was the hardest thing I ever did in my life. For nights on end, she cried until morning for her mother. Futile attempts to get Priscilla on the phone made things worse. I began to lose my connections in Hollywood, unable to make sessions on time, unable to get babysitters. In public, women, strangers, took Lonnie to the bathroom. At Trancas market, I ran into Donna Summer, and her husband, Bruce, who stopped us in the aisle. Donna just went crazy over Lonnie. Thought she was the "most beautiful baby" she'd ever seen!

Meanwhile, money started disappearing from my checking account. There were all these withdrawals. The bank told me there was nothing I could do since California law regarded Priscilla as half owner of the account. She made the withdrawals long distance by phone. I needed to move, get a new address, and change my accounts, fast.

I discovered someone was drawing cash at the Trancas market counter, drawing cash from my account and sending it to Priscilla in New York. I closed the account at the market, but how could I move? I had a houseful of people. I needed to get Paul and Laura out and on their own so I could move with Lonnie.

Laura reluctantly moved in with Rita, then spent some time with her grandparents in Mendocino. Paul started spending more time in Walla Walla, Washington, where he went to school. Paul's girlfriend, Alex, didn't want to leave. She was driving Priscilla's Audi, all expenses paid, living the life. I felt like I was untangling the arms of an octopus all around me. I'd get one off, another would wrap around.

When Alex finally gave me the keys and moved out, I found myself with two new Audis and a Volvo. I kept the Volvo and one Audi and traded the other Audi in on a new truck for my son T. I found a nice house up on Skyline View Drive in Malibu, headed for a new life. The day before I moved, there was a knock on the door.

A pitiful-looking man identified himself as the owner of Malibu Jewelry, in the shopping center downtown. He said that for years they'd had a policy of lending jewelry to stars for parties and TV shows and never had a problem until now. I let him in.

In the living room, he broke down. There was a grown man crying in my living room.

Priscilla had accumulated so much of his stuff that he was now in trouble, worried about making his payments this month. Was she there?

"God, Tim, she's in New York, man. I had no idea."

"You have no idea," he repeated. "Is there any chance of getting anything back?" His voice trailed off.

"How much stuff does she have?"

"You don't want to know. I trusted her for years. She's your wife. Nobody in Malibu does this, Booker."

Within two weeks of our meeting, everything I owned went into receivership, including the royalties from Willie's *Stardust* album and Rita's *Anytime, Anywhere* album. Even Epic Records garnished my wages, and suddenly there was not enough to pay the third month's rent on my new house or my car payments.

I called Mark Rothbaum, Willie's manager.

"I'm in trouble, Mark."

"Are you kidding me? We've paid you a small fortune."

My lawyer told me to get an accountant and tax lawyer, fast.

"You know, you're never going to get out from under all this," Phil Frucht, my new CPA, said, looking over his glasses at me after assessing my situation.

Security Pacific Bank in Malibu saved my life. Saved my life. The accounts had been drained, and Priscilla wanted $3,500 to go to London to persuade Ed to marry her. They gave me the money on my signature alone. In return for the cash, Priscilla signed off on her half of my future royalties. Security Pacific cut a check. I forwarded it to New York. My brother-in-law drew the contract. Priscilla signed it and flew to London. When she came back, she was Mrs. Ed Bradley, and I was a free man. Broke. And free.

MARIN COUNTY, CA—1981— ♪ 2

After a gig in Marin County, I stayed over a few days and visited with Carlos Santana.

Carlos was unhappy with me. Again. Often, in the early days of our friendship, he was moody and dissatisfied. We had a solid relationship, or so I thought. He picked me up at my hotel in his tennis whites and talked of my moving to Marin. "See those houses over there, Booker? Nice, huh?" And he let me win some games. Mostly we just milled around tennis shops and restaurants in Marin.

Their home was in Stinson Beach, and Carlos took the curves gently in his BMW so as not to scare his friend from the Tennessee flatlands. Debbie, Carlos's wife, was beautiful and gracious, and the home was warm and happy. The eminent arrival of Carlos's son, Salvador, was not too far away, sure to displace one of the rooms full of musical equipment.

After a few dates with Kitsuan King, Carlos's sister-in-law, didn't work out, my tennis buddy disappeared. A beautiful Sunday dinner with his in-laws at Kitsaun's home in San Francisco was the last we saw of each other for years.

I returned to Malibu with the Bay Area on my mind—specifically Marin County. I envisioned myself living on an eastward-facing hill in the small town of Sausalito. I felt I could make a new life there. Shortly, a strong new musical and spiritual force would come into my life. His name was Narada Michael Walden.

In 1979, living in Malibu, I heard Narada's solo album, *Awakenings*. Although I had been meditating for some years, the music on this album spoke to me in a spiritual way. I was moved to contact Narada to thank him for the music, and he responded with a huge shipment of flowers. We have been friends ever since.

I spent a lot of time at Narada Michael Walden's home in Tiburon, which is in the Richardson Bay region and an area I fell in love with. Narada was generous with his home, his recording studio, and his resources. A small community developed around him that included Clarence Clemmons, Randy Jackson, and the disciples of Sri Chinmoy.

Narada's musical family grew to include Jeff Beck, Jaco Pastorius, Aretha Franklin, and eventually Whitney Houston.

Although I wasn't inclined to the spiritual leanings of Sri Chinmoy like Carlos and Narada, I was on my own spiritual journey, led by my private daily meditations. I was comfortable in the Marin environment.

LOS ANGELES—1981— ♪ 12

As much as I was enamored of Marin, there was not enough musical activity there to support me. Hollywood and LA were still the center, still in charge of the music business. However, my brief time in Woodstock, New York, at Albert Grossman's and Levon Helm's places reconfirmed the hippy in me. I gravitated toward Richie Havens when he came to Malibu, and we went shirt shopping together. Albert managed him and Bob Dylan as well. We seemed to have so much in common, Richie and I, and the studio recording of his "I Was Educated by Myself" only confirmed to me his spiritual awareness as I accompanied him on piano. While sinking to the depths emotionally, I had surrounded myself with great people.

By the time I was ready to record my third album for A&M, people like John Robinson (drums) and Freddy Washington (bass) were in my phone book. I had started to write with Jean Hancock (Herbie's sister) and Leon Ware. Leon was a writer and producer who coached Marvin Gaye. I had heard Chic perform "Good

Times" and followed their lead. I was off to the disco, with strings and horns by Benjamin Wright. I never knew I was so drawn to dance music. Looking back, most of the MGs' music and a lot of Stax's releases were heavy precursors to the disco sound. Big drums, heavy bass line, lilting melody on top. Still, it was a left turn for me in terms of genre.

A&M began to revamp their R & B department soon after the *I Want You* album's release. The single "Don't Stop Your Love" was released in New York and surged to number one on disco radio; however, the label declined to put nationwide promotion behind it. Soon after, promotion head Harold Childs and A&R director Michael Stokes, both African American execs, left the label. The final stroke came when Quincy Jones moved his office off the A&M lot. A&M had started as a pop company with Herb Alpert, and with the enormous successes of Supertramp, the Carpenters, Peter Frampton, the Police, Rita Coolidge, Styx, Cat Stevens, Sheryl Crow, on and on, the company was destined to finish as a pop label. I was so happy for Herb and Jerry. However, an R & B company they were not meant to be. The record business has always been fickle by nature. All the pieces have to be in place. If you get signed by an executive and that exec gets fired, you're out of luck. A fish out of water. I had to start all over again.

CHAPTER 16
The Cool Dude

GLENDALE—August 1983— ♪ *1*

At around 8:00 p.m., the phone rang. It was Bill Leopold, my manager, whose house was situated halfway up a winding canyon road in Glendale. The woman Bill and Carla had been trying to set me up with had agreed to meet.

For some reason, the date had taken so long to materialize that I thought it was some kind of hoax. At that point, Bill had been telling me about her for about a year. In fact, enough time went by that I began to think the woman was simply nonexistent. So when it turned out the delay was because she was dating someone else and that she was, at long last, ready to get acquainted, my excitement was palpable.

It was to be a tennis date, a foursome. Wanting to look my best, I went to the Topanga Mall and picked out a trendy, all-white tennis ensemble. I tried on a shirt, pants, and new shoes—everything was perfect. A smart-looking all-white tennis suit that fit me well.

I wore regular clothes to the midday meeting and took a small bag up to Bill and Carla's guest room to change before the blind date came. I changed into the outfit upstairs and timed it so I just happened to be heading to the door when the bell rang.

Halfway down the staircase, I caught sight of her. My right foot refused to go down to the next step, and I stood frozen a moment, looking at her. At the bottom of the staircase, I saw her face, and she reached out her hand. I'm sure there were introductions by our hosts. I didn't hear them and only caught her name, Nan.

When I looked into her eyes, I felt I'd known her from a long time ago. She smiled. Our eyes riveted together in a magnetic field. She stood still, hands clasped in front of her, and sucked in her breath. I braced and held her hand a little too long. Her smiling face gave instant approval of both me and the outfit. She was beautiful. For a moment, we were the only people in the room. I felt I had found a lost piece of myself. No one can be ready for a moment like this. It's when there is no past or future and all time is contained within the present. Nan has bedroom eyes. The first time she looked at me, I wanted to sleep with her that night. Maybe she could have my child.

We broke our gaze, and Nan Warhurst, the mystery girl, went off into the kitchen with my manager's wife. He sat me down in the living room and looked up at me as though to say, "You OK? You sure?"

Nan ran track in high school and ended up with three master's degrees with honors from Pitzer College in Claremont, California. Nan's family was football and sports oriented. Her father was a celebrated coach, while her mother was an accomplished artist.

The sky was clear blue, a warm, Southern California day. Nan and I both repeatedly botched the score, missed easy balls, and came to the net with annoying frequency. The entire match gave way to our constant flirting with each other to the point that Bill and Carla got tired of trying to push the game forward. Our hosts must have wondered what they had done; their gambit was on course to pay off, like it or not. Nan and I were hopelessly attracted to one another.

At dinner, after the doubles, she turned to me. "You have the same name as one of my favorite musicians!" What could I do? I followed her wherever she went. I waited a long time for a woman like her, having had my share of missteps before we met.

On the sidewalk, at our cars, Nan said, kiddingly, that she had some etchings at her house she'd like me to see.

So I went to her place, which was neat and clean. I felt comfortable there. And the "etchings" were photos of her seven-, five-, and three-year-old sons—Matthew, Brian, and Michael. Those "etchings" turned out to be some of my favorite works of art.

Three weeks after I met Nan, I went back down to Spicewood, Texas, to work with Willie Nelson. I still wasn't into golf, which was a shame since Willie had maintained his beautiful course. His greens were some of the smoothest and fastest I'd ever seen. We were working on *Without a Song*, the follow-up to his *Stardust* LP.

When I was in Texas, Nan and I regularly talked on the phone during the week.

With weekends free, I asked her to meet me in San Francisco one weekend. I was sure the population in Pedernales would be ready to hang me from the nearest tree if she showed up on my porch the next morning. I felt Texas in the early eighties was no place to flaunt an interracial relationship. They might tolerate a black man working for a powerful white like Willie, but an open display of affection might trigger a problematic situation.

I picked San Francisco's most romantic destination, the Miyako Hotel in Japantown, and reserved a suite with an ocean view. I arranged for my flight to get in before hers and picked up a new summer outfit. The weather was San Francisco's best—slightly cool mornings breaking into warm, sunny afternoons. When she came out of the Jetway, she looked perfect, as I knew she would, and we hopped into a rental car for the most marvelous weekend. We ate, we slept in late, we had dinner, and we went to movies.

This was the weekend that sealed our fate. I was so comfortable with Nan, and she with me. She even said, "We're complementary, and we dig each other."

AUSTIN, TX—1983— ♪ 10

I made a brief appearance in Willie Nelson's film *Songwriter*. Only every time director Alan Rudolph said, "Action!" I got distracted and forgot my lines because I kept taking too many drags on the joints being passed around. That was why my appearance was brief. They never got a piece of film with me saying anything coherent.

"You can't say you wrote a song you didn't write unless you really wrote it."

When I heard that line, I knew writer Bud Shrake really understood the music business. Willie loved it so much that he said it over and over, and it became a running joke on the set because it rang so true. There was a lot of laughter on the film's set. Nobody could even look at Rip Torn without breaking out laughing. It's a mystery how Sydney Pollack remained a taskmaster and got the film done with this bunch.

The picture is pretty funny, even though I'm not sure the funniest parts ever got on film. I kept it together enough to play in the band and give composer Larry Cansler a little help with the score.

LOS ANGELES—1983— ♪ *1*

Meanwhile, my relationship with Nan changed the tide of my life. We began to date, and as I got to know her, I became increasingly drawn to her natural empathy for humanity. She truly cared about people.

One of Nan's greatest passions in life was reading. She read incessantly to herself and to others. Her home was filled with books. She read to her children and to the people she loved. Nan was juggling the care of her three children plus going to graduate school—a schedule that would intimidate most people, but she thrived even under these conditions.

Nan sat across from me at my old redwood table in my kitchen, grasping a book in one hand and a cup of tea in the other.

Nan read these words to me: "My mama dead. She die screaming and cussing. She scream at me. She cuss at me. I'm big. I can't move fast enough. By time I git back from the well, the water be warm."

By the time she finished, I was hooked. I recognized the vernacular of my people. A language I listened to as a boy on the porches of my father's cousins down in the farm country of Mississippi. Nan was reading to me from *The Color Purple*, by Alice Walker. My previous favorite novels were *Old Yeller*, when I was a boy, and John Kennedy's *Profiles in Courage* when I was in high school. Now, by reading to me on a daily basis, Nan was exposing me to literature, and I was getting enthusiastic about it. She loved to read to me, and I loved having her read to me.

The next book she gave me was Chaim Potok's *The Book of Lights*. This was not simple, happy, easy reading. A strenuous book, the subject matter ultimately caused me to ask difficult questions, without which I would not be the person I am today.

When she wasn't introducing me to new worlds through literature, she and I would sit at my redwood kitchen table and talk late into the night, engaging in profound conversations about life and its meaning. As time went on, our relationship became more natural and acquired more character and depth. And she was cute too!

Even in 1983, an interracial relationship made people look twice.

Nan's three sons were young and, rightfully so, were somewhat apprehensive. I came from a family of huggers, and Brian shirked my nighttime beddy-bye hugs. Matthew, the oldest, was the wariest. He wasn't having any part of that touchy stuff. However, Michael, the youngest, jumped onto my lap anytime we were close. One day, in Matthew's room, I got down on my knees while he was playing with his rock collection and just hung out there, not saying anything. Finally, he shoved one of the rocks in my direction. I scuttled after it. After all, I had been a little boy once myself playing with my toys on the floor. He looked up at me and smiled. We started talking about different kinds of rocks. The ice was broken from then on.

To some, three stepchildren might have been too much, but I saw them as a bonus in Nan's overall package. Living in a predominantly white community, the boys would need some time to feel comfortable with my brown skin, and Nan explained to them how my skin color was simply just one way I was different. She put the boys at ease by portraying me as a loving person.

I dated Nan for nearly two years when an issue finally needed to be addressed. I was reticent and guarded. With two unsuccessful marriages under my belt, I was unsure of my ability to make a go of it.

I was afraid of getting in deep. I was afraid of getting hurt again. I was afraid of failing and having to get divorced again. To me, there were few things in life worse than divorce, and if relationships became healthy and grew, they led to marriage—not just long-term relationships.

A part of myself was not going to allow me to continue in a blissful relationship such as the one Nan and I were having. I stopped calling her. Continuing a habitual pattern that I set early in life and that was very easy for me, I disappeared. I denied myself the very thing I wanted most. Happiness. Still in trouble with myself, I thought I was unworthy.

When I pulled back, Nan was very hurt. So she moved on and started dating other men.

My phone went dead. Priscilla sent Lonnie back to LA from New York to live with me. T's mom kicked him out when he graduated from high school, and he was sleeping on my living room couch.

CANOGA PARK, CA—1985—♪ 2

I moved again, for the thirteenth time in the past sixteen years. This time, from Westwood to Canoga Park, with two children from previous marriages in tow. About a decade earlier, I began taking courses in Transcendental Meditation in Santa Monica and embarked on a quest to get to know myself through self-awareness. After ten years of soul-searching, I felt ready to choose the right mate. Thankfully, Nan and I were still on speaking terms—we hadn't given up on each other! After a while, we met for dinner. Within weeks we resumed dating, and our feelings for each other grew.

One day, I called Nan. The phone rang. No answer. I called again. No answer. The realization came over me that I wanted, really wanted, to know what was going on with her. What was she doing? Was she gardening? Was she going to class? I was always—always—thinking about her. Any time of day or night, I was thinking or wondering about Nan. Was this about me, or was it about her? Was I so bad at marriage? In my heart, I knew my failed marriages were not all my fault.

I asked her to meet me out on North Hollywood Way in Burbank. Her car pulled up behind mine, and she got into the passenger seat. There, parked in the shadows under the trees, I told her I loved her and asked her to be my wife. I have never been more certain about anything in my life. I didn't have a ring. I just wanted to be with her, married or not.

She said yes!

We got out and went into the old Japanese restaurant and held hands across the table. I told her how I wanted to move into her house in Glendale and find a small studio nearby to work in. We discussed how our families might react. Each person. We talked until the place closed, then went to the car and talked more before we kissed and said good night. We drove to our respective houses.

I called her when I got home. I wanted Nan and her boys to become family with me and T and Lonnie. I lost the sense of being fragmented, and I started to feel whole.

Reaction to our decision to wed was mixed. My dad, of course, was thrilled; he was always glad to see Nan. My sister, Gwen, was happy for me. My brother-in-law, Floyd, turned up his nose.

Nan's brothers and sisters approved, although she wasn't so sure about her parents.

When her maternal grandmother, Marguerite, found that Nan's parents weren't going to come, she said, "That's my granddaughter, and I'm going to her wedding!" She was Marguerite Spafford of "Rosie the Riveter" fame. I decided she deserved to be chauffeured to the event in a black stretch limo and ordered one immediately.

I guess Nan's parents heard Marguerite was coming in a limo and decided they couldn't be upstaged or outdone by the old matriarch, so they relented and decided to attend at the last minute. With that, any other dissenters fell in line one by one until we expected a full crowd, including my brother-in-law, Floyd. It was going to be interesting. It was.

Nan was beautiful in a light ice-pink gown, and she had that idyllic smile on her face that made me feel like a million bucks. When it came time to give her away, we needed consent from each of our five children. They sat patiently together on benches on either side of where we were taking our vows, with a modicum of fidgeting. The minister asked each one in turn if they would give their blessing to the marriage. Each politely consented until he arrived at Michael, who wasn't really sure about the whole thing. (He was only five years old.) He hesitated. The room went uncomfortably silent. The minister looked up at Michael over his spectacles and asked again, slowly, deliberately, "Do you give your blessing to this marriage?" After a deafening silence, Michael let out a loud yes, and a sigh of relief and giggles filled the room.

I looked at Nan. She gave me the most special look of love. We were going to be man and wife.

After the wedding, Arlene, Nan's mom, cornered me by the fountain and gave me a setting out I will never forget. How dare I marry her daughter! Mrs. Warhurst was horrified that one of her children had married a person of color. Overwhelmed, beside herself with disbelief and outrage, she was furious, and she let me know. The unthinkable had happened in her family, and she stood shaking, glaring into my eyes. No one noticed or knew what was going on. I was thinking, *Oh my God*. Upset as Arlene was, it was a furor I had witnessed before, so consequently I stood quietly. Nan noticed and rushed over to rescue me. She hadn't told me about this side of Arlene.

The celebration was otherwise joyous. Some were happy, I think, just because Michael had said yes. Nan and I let go and relaxed. She had worked so hard on the planning. We ate cake and drank champagne. We had done it. Against all odds.

Around this same time, early July 1985, I was selling my new home in order to move to Glendale into Nan's home. Nan came to me and said, "I want to start new. I want to live in a home where I never lived with another man." She wanted to get out of the shadow of her previous marriage.

Then, several months after the wedding, Nan and I discovered we were having a baby girl.

Nan being pregnant, however, didn't stop her from wanting to do the annual camping trip in Tuolumne Meadows in Yosemite. Nan comes from a large family of nine, and every summer of her childhood, they had spent two months there.

In 1985, on my very first hike up a treacherous hill, I heard Michael tell Nan he wanted to be in her tummy like the baby she had in there. I replied, "I know how you feel, Michael."

CANOGA PARK—Fall 1985— ♪ 8

I watched Nan over and over again taking on more than she should. It was after she had pushed herself past her limit that I felt the need to step in.

After Nan finished graduate school and received an MBA, she began work as an advertising account manager for a Los Angeles magazine.

"God, I'm so exhausted I can hardly stand up," she would say after a day's work.

After a few weeks of this, I said to her, "Nan, I'd really like you to consider quitting for a while. You can go back to work after the baby's born."

Surprisingly, she listened to me, a real triumph given her stubborn nature. I let out a sigh of relief. Our chances of having a healthy baby just got a lot better.

My love of fast cars came in handy the morning Nan told me she was beginning to have contractions. We jumped into my Lincoln Mark VII bachelor car and whipped down the 118 to Verdugo Hills hospital. In the delivery room, I held Nan's hand and breathed with her like we were taught in our natural-childbirth classes.

Not long before, I had turned the dining room of my Canoga Park house into a small studio, featuring a great-sounding Soundcraft 600 recording console. I used it to record some special music for the birthing room. The music was playing softly when Olivia came into this world. The doctor called it the "most perfect birth he had ever attended." It was December 29, 1985, a mild winter day.

Olivia Marguerite, a beautiful baby, became the personification of our love. We named her after Nan's maternal grandmother, Marguerite.

By this time, Arlene, Nan's mother, had been won over and came to the hospital to hold the baby and take pictures. She was a fool for little ones, or any newborn animal for that matter. My only regret is that my own mother, Lurline, did not live long enough to meet Olivia and Nan. My mother would have also loved my three grandchildren from my son T. Jade, my first grandchild, was born shortly before Olivia. My two grandsons from T, Booker T. IV and Nijel, were born several years after.

The care of the newborn, Olivia, was something I cherished. Nan and I were both so involved with the baby we didn't pay much attention to the outside world.

On a blissful day, enjoying our new child and family, came the news that legal proceedings had been filed to change the primary custody of Nan's three boys to their father. With their new beds barely even broken in, this was an unexpected event, however, not a derailment.

Nan went to court alone. "What kind of music does your husband play?" Nan cleverly responded, "He produced Willie Nelson's biggest album." The action was defeated, and Nan retained custody of her sons.

Not long after, a second petition was filed. However, in court a second time, Nan's attorney prevailed. The boys were still sleeping in my house.

Then the legal server came to my door. He asked for me with a pen in his hand to sign for the delivery. I was being subpoenaed. The battles you lose are the ones where the outcome is determined before the fight. You know it, and you fight to retain your dignity. The outcome may have even been decided before you were born, as was this one.

I walked into the courtroom a proud man. I wore a conservative suit and tie. They could break my wife's heart and tear apart my family. They could ignore my rights as a human being. Whatever— they couldn't touch my composure or make me bow my head. I went through the motions. The judge ruled, and the boys went into the care of a nanny in their father's Los Feliz mansion. We were devastated. We were broken.

Despite the obstacles, we maintained a close relationship with each other and with the boys, who felt isolated and abandoned. They were too young to comprehend the legal and racial complexities of the situation or how unfair it was that they had to pay the price and bear the brunt. Still, they didn't have their mother on a daily basis.

We shuttled them back and forth on the freeways. Young Olivia cried in her car seat for hours while her mother transported her stepbrothers every weekend for the three-hour drive back and forth. I finally insisted that she leave the baby with me.

YOSEMITE NATIONAL PARK—1986— ♪3

During summers, the boys were free, and the family made camping trips to Tuolumne Meadows in Yosemite National Park to hike, fish, and swim in the ice-cold Tuolumne River. Lonnie and Brian were the major packers and worked tirelessly to help Nan get ready for the trips. This had been her childhood summer home.

When I was a boy, I was fascinated with "camping." In love with my dad's stories of sleeping under the stars in Alabama and Georgia with the Boy Scouts, I made makeshift tents in my yard with towels and chairs.

My stepson Matthew was the oldest of the children and thus was the instigator of many adventures. He also is incredibly pigheaded (kinda like his mother) and sometimes would not listen to advice. Such was the case in Yosemite on our annual camping trip in 1986.

With this new blended family, Matthew was the leader of the pack, and he was always trying to establish his leadership position.

On our second trip in 1986, Matthew decided to *prove* that his first attempt to throw a pair of sneakers to the island in the middle of the river had been successful (they could only find one on inspection), and he tossed his backup pair to the island to prove his point. After much searching, Matthew had two left shoes and no right shoes. We had to drive down the hill to Bishop, two hours away, to buy new shoes for him.

Later in the week, on a day hike, the older kids took the wrong fork in the trail, and as much screaming and yelling as Nan and I did, they didn't hear us, continuing on the wrong path. Five-year-old Michael, who was with me and Nan, was known for his *very* loud voice. He yelled, and the older kids heard him and finally turned around. I picked Michael up and gave him a bear hug.

From our camping trips and my involvement in the community,

I was seeing the benefits of being involved as a parent in the day-to-day workings of our family.

I made a decision to be home with my family and cut back on travel. Being an interracial family, we instinctively knew that our strength lay in our connection to one another. Friends often commented on how close we seemed, and though there might have been some who disapproved, we stayed tight in our circle.

LAKE TAHOE, NV—1986— ♪ *2*

Despite my need to be around the family, I had to make a living. I took on the production of William Lee Golden's album *American Vagabond*. After the recording of the album in Alabama, I found myself in the back seat of a limo with William Lee, another country star on the way back to Nashville.

A few months later, the Oak Ridge Boys, with William Lee Golden, played a show at Harrah's in Lake Tahoe, Nevada. I jumped on their tour to catch a show. When the show was over, I went to the front desk to check in to my room. The clerk told me, "I'm sorry, Mr. Jones; it appears your room was mistakenly given away." (Probably to some high roller.) "However, we've arranged a car to take you to a hotel nearby." Off into the night I went—from Stateline to an unknown destination. I fell asleep in the car and woke up when we arrived at the new Hyatt at Incline Village.

Next morning, I opened the drapes and said, "My God! I've never seen anything so stunning!" It was Lake Tahoe, the northern shore. I took the elevator down from the top floor, where I was staying, and found a path directly to the lake. I was so captivated while wandering the glistening, calm lakeshore I almost missed my ride to the airport.

LOS ANGELES—December 1987— ♪6

With a nineteen-foot camping trailer behind my Ford Club Wagon, I was feeling accomplished, having made it home safely before dark. But the sight of water in front of the stoop made my heart sink. Normally, I would have stepped up onto the landing and put my key in the door, but this sight was too much. While camping with my wife, Nan, and our daughter, Olivia, our house in West Hills, California had flooded due to a broken pipe. We had been gone for two weeks. Olivia was sick, and we were anxious to give her a bath and put her to bed.

Thankfully, our neighbors realized there shouldn't be water pouring out the front door and turned the main water off. How much water had leaked? I forced my eyes to look. There was a small but wide, steady flow coming from under the sill of the front door. Worst possible news. I don't remember how I broke it to Nan, feverishly unpacking at the curb. Maybe she just saw it on my face.

The interior was worse than we imagined. Some walls had moisture five feet high. No room was spared. I rushed to the music room, the *squish-squish* of my boots in the carpet getting louder with each step. The water had come from the kitchen, next to the studio. The house had filled like a swimming pool and destroyed irreplaceable items, including photos and many master tapes I had left on the floor. They were two-inch, twenty-four-track masters I had recorded on my 3M twenty-four track; various two-track master mixes I had hauled all the way from Memphis; and my entire collection of 33-1/3" vinyl LPs. Invaluable.

We headed for a hotel. There was no point calling emergency movers this time—everything was lost. The insurance adjuster said he was glad we hadn't spent too much time inside because of health risks due to mold in the walls. No one cried.

268

It was hard to admit that the Posey Lane house was a money pit. Every day when I turned left onto my street to go home, there was water flowing at the curb a block away. No doubt the water was coming from my house. Sure enough, when I reached my driveway, the water stopped. At least I owned a home now and got off the renting merry-go-round I had been on for years. In addition to the constant repairs to the house—roof, plumbing, and so forth—I could not get work in the music business. I didn't have a record deal, and I wasn't making any money at all from the craft I loved and had worked at for years. Then, there was a godsend.

CANOGA PARK, CA—1989— ♪ 11

After several years of not recording music, I got a call from Elvis's piano player, Tony Brown, now an executive at MCA Records in Nashville, checking in, wanting to know if I was interested in recording. I had a new Roger Linn drum machine, an LM2, and Quincy gave me some old sound chips with kick and snare drum sounds he wasn't using anymore. Yamaha had just created their new DX-7, and I had one sitting in my studio alongside my Hammond M-3 organ and my trusty Soundcraft 600 console. I experimented with some new sounds and concepts. Tony was one of Nashville's forward-thinking producers, and he OK'd my demo and gave me the go-ahead and a recording budget. I cut the basic tracks at my home studio and called Rik Pekonnen to engineer.

Alan Sides, a recording equipment connoisseur in Hollywood, had my old Neumann 67 and forty-seven mikes at his Oceanway Studio on Sunset, as his brother had bought them from me. Phil Upchurch, the guy who made the hit "You Can't Sit Down" agreed to come to the studio. I recorded Phil's guitar and a horn section there and got great sound, all on those mikes. At last, I released the *Runaway* album on MCA Nashville.

The song "Cool Dude," from the *Runaway* album, is used by Midwest radio stations as their program song.

It was one of the first albums ever recorded and released with a drum machine, and one of my biggest regrets is selling that drum machine and the Soundcraft console. Nothing since sounds as fat or as good. Both are rare and expensive now.

As happens with a lot of musicians, the days turned into weeks that turned into months as our bank balance stayed at zero and our credit card balances grew. I was an unemployed musician.

When Olivia turned two, Nan announced, "I think I'm going to try my hand at real estate!" She was always happiest when busy and productive. She aced the state exams and landed a position at a Century 21 office. After moving eighteen times in the past sixteen years, I had developed an attraction to real estate myself, and I couldn't get arrested as a musician at the time, so I enrolled at a real estate school in Reseda, California, and also passed the state exam.

We became a team. We previewed property together, and we listed and sold together. From Century 21 we went to Fred Sands Real Estate in Woodland Hills. Nan was a natural. She could walk through a property once and nail the square footage within an inch. We succeeded in selling some "hard to sell" properties. That gave us real "cred" with our colleagues.

WEST HILLS, CA—1990— ♪ 2

At home, our first child, Olivia, was so delightful and beautiful that Nan and I decided to have one more child and were surprised with twins!

Cicely Camille and Theodore Russell (Teddy) were born in the middle of producing *Culture Swing*, by Tish Hinajosa, the great Texas folk singer, for Rounder Records. On a visit to New York City, I took a side trip to Cambridge, Massachusetts, to take a meeting with Rounder's Marian Leighton Levy. We had known each other for years since my days at Stax and had been looking for something to do together. When she called I knew it was going to be something good. It turned out to be delicious! She wanted me to put together a project featuring Tish! We were at Hollywood Sound, now East-West Studios, in the big room, with David Hidalgo, singer and guitarist of Los Lobos, guesting on various stringed instruments. Tish's voice was strong and clear. Her performances, and the songs she wrote, were glorious. The project was coming together nicely.

The call came right after we got started, a little after eleven. Everyone knew Nan was pregnant with twins, and I rushed right out to the parking lot. Our next-door neighbor, JoAnn Dewitt, made everything possible. She took Olivia to her house and told me, "Go, just go! Don't worry about anything!" I squeezed Nan into the car, and we sped off to the hospital.

Fatherhood in my forties was a completely different prospect from that in my twenties. I was able to appreciate the miracle of life and to relish the moments with Nan and my family. At this age, I was aware of what a blessing it was to have children and to have a family, and I cherished every moment of it.

From the moment of conception, Nan was amazing at caring for the large household while carrying two children. She brought them to full term, both healthy, and never had help in the house. Then she gave two beautiful births, showing amazing physical strength and emotional will and stamina. I cannot express how happy I was to have those three souls separated in three different bodies on May 22, 1990. I had two car seats loaded in my Lincoln Mark IV for the joyous ride home.

With Nan safely ensconced at home with the twins and Olivia, I continued to work on the project with Tish.

The album went on to win Indie Folk Album of the Year by NAIRD in 1992.

SHERMAN OAKS, CA, Record 1 Studio—1992— ♪ 7

As the weeks wore on, I enjoyed being a family man, and my musical fortunes began to gradually improve.

"Booker T. don't know nuthin' about no gospel music" were the words coming from the mouth of Clarence Fountain, leader of the Five Blind Boys, over lunch in the dining room at the Sportsmen's Lodge on Ventura in North Hollywood. I was just joining the group of men for lunch. Clarence's lead singer, Jimmy Carter, in the room, and also blind, had no way of shushing the outspoken tenor voice of the group. Jimmy had always been more sensitive than Clarence, and even if he thought it was true, he would never have voiced it—especially in my presence.

In my defense, the first strains of music I ever heard were in the church, and my first public vocal performance was singing "In My Heart" for my Sunday school class at Mt. Olive in Memphis.

JAPAN—1992— ♪ 11

There were two Japanese artists that stood out in my life. The first time I visited Japan, a nice, generous man, Takuro Yoshida, the famous Japanese folk singer, filled my hotel room chock-full of gifts for me and my daughter when I produced an album for him. Another singer, Kiyoshiro Imawano, the Japanese "King of Rock," was the nicest, most generous man I ever met. Kiyoshiro, through kindness, bigheartedness, and openhandedness, outpaced even Takuro over the years. He made many special efforts to visit and bring gifts each time I came to Japan. One of my favorite times onstage was opening at Budokan in Tokyo with Kiyoshiro because of the long, enthusiastic reception from the audience.

By the time I was working with Kiyoshiro and traveling to Japan, things were good again. It's so easy to forget when times were hard, when work and money were scarce. When you're on the upswing, likewise, every day seems bright and sunny.

WEST HILLS, CA—1992— ♪ 2

With my marriage to Nan, my life began to glow and radiate with beauty and health. The most wonderful woman in the world, she takes such good care of my children, including the ones from previous marriages, as well as her three boys from her own previous marriage. Nan is a mother. It is her fullest expression of life to spend time in the presence of her children.

I implored Nan to be a stay-at-home mother, and she quit her job at Fred Sands Real Estate. Her mothering is the kind where our children flourished under her care. She read to the children—every night—for at least an hour. She made Halloween costumes. She took her children to the park or to the botanical gardens or the zoo. Nan taught her children to be kind and empathetic. She respected her children and understood they needed to be treated fairly. Most of all it was Nan's passion to be with her children. It was and always will be who she is—a mother.

"You're lucky to have me!" Nan tells me sometimes. You know what? She's right. I am lucky.

She creates a place for me to call home, and my life is full and happy because of her. She makes me mind my health, and she adds the color, variety, stability, and sense of belonging that I will always cherish.

Somehow, she manages to cook practically every day, do the dishes, read to the children, bathe them, and put them to bed. This is all after she has risen around seven or so, fed the kids, dressed them, and driven them to school. Many days she does volunteer work at both their schools, and she is room mother and has been soccer team mother to about twenty teams.

Nan has so much love in her heart. Her attitude keeps her looking young. Nan is not perfect, of course. I like to think that she's perfectly imperfect—like a Picasso painting.

If Nan gets angry, you don't want to be anywhere near. The very crust of the earth couldn't contain one of her sudden eruptions, which quell quickly. And that's if she feels you have misbehaved unintentionally. If she thinks you meant to hurt her, she's cold as ice at the North Pole.

Fortunately, Nan doesn't hold a grudge, and there is hope for reconciliation.

She and I connect in a myriad of areas. For someone who can't carry a tune, I think she has great taste in music. We love so many of the same songs. I listen carefully to her critiques of my work. And she doesn't pull any punches there. Nan's painfully honest, and I take advantage of that. I know she believes in me as an artist, and in our daily lives, Nan is a supporter and an active, positive force in my career.

Nan is an identical twin, and her twin's proper name is Janine, and Nan's is Nanine. Janine usually calls when something is wrong or when something is right, and sometimes just to say hi. She is unbelievably good to Nan.

Right now, back at home, I can hear that Nan's rolling the trash cans out to the curb. The kids are in the bath, I'm in my pj's relaxing, and you're going to tell me this is not heaven? I mean, my mother never took the trash out. That was my dad's job, or my job. Her brother Blane, and most of her siblings, complain that she spoils me.

Nan loves color and has definite opinions about their combinations, probably because she has a mother who is an artist. Sometimes, when I come out of the bedroom wearing a green shirt with a green T-shirt or something, she puts out her hand in the stop position, turns her head, and closes her eyes. "Stop, don't come any closer. I can't stand those colors together; they hurt my eyes!" I look down at my thoughtful selection, turn around, go back to the bedroom, and change clothes.

Now she can just say, "Oh, is that what you're wearing?" and I'm already halfway back upstairs before she can finish the sentence. I love being married to Nan. Now I know what it means to be in love. It means there is someone who is always on your mind.

Waking up with Nan in the morning is the best thing ever. She's the only person I know with such a huge capacity for happiness. I cannot be happier than when Nan is smiling, and when she directs it at me, it's like bright sunshine...I am in love. In the mornings, I just want to pick her up and twirl her around on my shoulders like a ballerina.

On a visit to Chicago, my brother, Maurice, said, "Booker, that girl is the best thing that ever happened to you, boy!" I knew the way I felt about Nan would last forever no matter what she did or didn't do.

TIBURON, CA—1992—♪ 11

I coughed, and the wheezing in my chest made an annoying noise like a chest of drawers being dragged across the floor. It died down, then happened again. There was no denying I had chronic chest congestion. Nan and I had an ongoing disagreement about my persistent cough—"It's because of the smog!" I insisted. "It's just a summer cold" was Nan's opinion. Then she had a bad dream about my health and declared it was time to move.

"I know just where I need to take you," I told her, and we left church and school friends and moved to Marin County, where I had visited with Narada and Carlos. With its lower population, fresh air, and beautiful topography, Marin bested the San Fernando Valley's smog and crowded freeways. In addition, there was a music community there that I felt part of.

Shortly after moving from Belvedere to Tiburon and into Sausalito's Plant Studios, I was blessed with the comely presence of Wendy Matthews of Australia to produce her *Witness Tree* album. The songs she brought into my life have provided me with a lasting strength.

WASHINGTON, DC—January 1993—♪ 3

As soon as we moved, we got word from Washington that President-Elect Clinton's inaugural ball committee had selected Booker T. & the MGs to play at the event. Nan's sister Janine saved the day for us by coming up from Claremont and moving in for four days to babysit our kids.

In Washington, intricate, elaborate security precautions had been put into place, and everything from checking into the hotel to driving up to the White House was steeped in red tape and individual identity checks and long waits. Anything but the "exciting adventure" our friends and neighbors at home were jealous of. The "ball" we played at was one of many, this one held at the huge Washington, DC, train station, a logistical and acoustical nightmare for its cavernous space and general inaccessibility. With binoculars, I could have been more certain that the president and first lady were actually dancing to our music. The rumor was Mr. Clinton was keener on jamming with the musicians on his tenor sax than attending the multiple balls.

The White House press agents arranged on-camera interviews with some of the musicians on the South Lawn of the White House with San Francisco's Vic Lee of KGO-TV.

The following day, after the performance, the agents hustled me and Steve Cropper into cars and dropped us off in a large grassy area on the National Mall at the interview location. When Vic asked about the inception of Booker T. & the MGs, Steve leaned into the mike, looked into the camera, and said, "If there had never been a Steve Cropper, there never would have been a Booker T."

A veteran reporter, Vic allowed the silence that followed Cropper's remark to create dead time—rarely done in the world of live television. It proved to be a potent omission. As the commentator's eyes drifted to mine, he let the camera once again settle on Cropper's smiling face. I could not summon words. My facial expression may have said something. I looked over at Steve. He was still grinning that satiated grin. After more uncomfortable, vacant, unfilled moments, the announcer turned to the camera: "Live from the White House in Washington, back to you, Fred."

A few months later, we returned to the White House to play with Lyle Lovett in a performance for the Clintons. On that visit, I smuggled in a book from Olivia's third-grade class, *Letters to the President,* and presented it to President Clinton, who was happy to receive it. "I never get stuff like this," he said. "They won't let it through security."

CHAPTER 17

I Believe in You

DUBLIN, IRELAND—2014— ♪ 12

At the door, at the sight of me, Sinead collapsed. Her three young children rushed over, concerned about their mother. When she saw my face, the time since we were on stage at Madison Square Garden condensed. She mumbled, "I let you down."

That day in Dublin, all she wanted me to do was accept her apology, and I did. We went inside to meet her kids and go to work.

Sinead led me to her workspace, a dining room with a large black upright piano. I sat down, pulled out my pocket four-track, and started to twiddle with a few notes on the piano. The children stayed in the front room and the bedroom, peeking in occasionally. Sinead lit a cigarette. I tried to hide my discomfort with the smoke. She walked over and opened the double doors, then I was cold.

As I twiddled, Sinead picked up a writing pad from the shelf, jotting down some words. She looked off into the distance. The

278

tears were starting to come back. She still hadn't sung a note, and out of the blue she told me how blacks hadn't been the only slaves; the Irish had been slaves too. Then she told me I had no idea of the injustices that had occurred in the churches in Dublin. The extent and the brashness of it all. I did have an idea, somewhat.

Sinead lit another cigarette and started to sing of places she had been. New York, Canada. A song was beginning to show its head between us. I turned the recorder on. Her voice was that of an angel. Pure, uncontrollable.

Then there was more talk of church institutions and their mistreatment of children.

NEW YORK, Madison Square Garden—1992— ♪ 3

Next to the door in the rehearsal room at MSG was a long utility table. A clipboard, tied to a string that was attached to a Magic Marker, held a list of Bob Dylan songs that were to be chosen from to perform on the show. Most had been scratched through, crossed out, or initialed by one of the performers, indicating they were taken for the show.

Eric Clapton walked into the rehearsal room.

He tried out a few of the remaining songs, looking for one that suited him. Nothing was working. In the seventies, I had conjured up an arrangement of "Don't Think Twice" at my Malibu ranch that Duck Dunn heard.

So Duck, who was there, said to Eric, "Booker has an arrangement for 'Don't Think Twice' you can use. Hey, Booker, why don't you do your version of 'Don't Think Twice' for Eric?"

I did, on the piano. Played and sang my arrangement of "Don't Think Twice" for which I changed the meter to 12/8 time. That gave the music and the lyrics a nice little lilt. That night, Eric performed it with much success, the audience appreciating the unexpected fresh new take on an old Dylan song.

The night before the show, which the MGs were slated to open, I stayed up until dawn learning the seven verses of "Gotta Serve Somebody."

I never thought it would come to pass that I would sing with the MGs. It was an arrangement I secretly wanted, but all three band members were very vocal about being against it. Steve often repeated, "No one in the band can sing well enough for us to record."

In the interim, when the band was broken up, I sang on a regular basis. It was only the MGs that didn't regard me as a singer. And now, suddenly, was the opportunity on a high-profile concert and TV show.

Later in the evening, the MC introduced Sinead O'Connor.

There were a few boos when she walked out.

Sinead stood motionless on the immense stage—alone but for me. Emitting a silent scream, intense to the degree of pain she suffered as a child, a phantom, a wraith speaking for every abused child, she paused to look over at me.

I mouthed, "Sing!"

Then I played the chords. She didn't. I didn't get it. At rehearsal, she sang Bob Dylan's "I Believe in You" to my piano, and people gasped at the tenderness of it.

More people started booing. The roar mushroomed into a cacophony of rebuke, reprimanding Sinead for ripping up a picture of the Pope on *Saturday Night Live* to protest the complete lack of response to numerous reports of sexual abuse at the hands of priests. I still didn't get it. I started the chords a third time.

The boos were deafening—I became more determined with each wave. Sinead stood frozen. However, she was completely composed. The consummate artist, Sinead needed complete silence to begin the song because her first notes were whispers. I was the one lacking in artistic grace. The clumsy one. I started the song a fourth time, and Kris Kristofferson mercifully stomped out from backstage and led Sinead away from the vice we had created for her. On one hand, I was a strong force, desperately wanting her to sing the song. I felt even if she started softly, the power of the music would have taken over. Opposing us loomed the brute power of mob mentality. Sinead could have just as well walked off the stage on her own, but she strongly wanted to please me. And thus, the arms of the vice closed in on her.

NEW YORK, Rock and Roll Hall of Fame—January 21, 1992— ♪ 7

My family finally got to experience the sandwiches at New York's Carnegie Deli. The kids weren't actually able to attend my induction to the Rock and Roll Hall of Fame. I was only allowed a couple of guests.

Brian was the first of our big boys to wolf down the delicious, enormous pastrami sandwich, then he looked at me, smiling, as I was just starting on my fourth bite. "'Bout ready?" I tell you, those sandwiches were a sight to behold. For years, my friend Rick at the deli made sure I never paid for one, but on this day, unfortunately, he wasn't there. Rick sent huge grocery sacks of Carnegie Deli pastrami sandwiches to the Lone Star Roadhouse on Fifty-Second Street on a regular basis. We were so spoiled.

After a trip to the Natural History Museum, which had something to intrigue each of the children, we hoofed back to the Waldorf Astoria, but not before stopping at every market on the way. Nan loaded the boys down with paper plates, napkins, baloney, peanut butter, bread, fruit, and any microwavable item. People stared when we walked through the lobby.

Our troupe, however, the inveterate hikers that we were, just kept on trucking through, even as a crew was filming *Scent of a Woman* in that same lobby.

When we got to our hotel room, Olivia said, "It's like we're camping, but we're not!" Everyone agreed and laughed. The Jones crew could survive anywhere, even in a posh New York hotel.

That night, Booker T. & the MGs were inducted into the Rock and Roll Hall of Fame. I just couldn't believe it. It seemed so soon into the establishment of the award, and I was so honored and surprised they thought we were worthy of such a prestigious honor. I was so thrilled I grabbed the trophy when they handed it to me. The All-Star Jam for "Green Onions" lured so many musicians and guitar players they tripped over each other. Steve Cropper, Duck Dunn, Lewis Steinberg, Neil Young, Keith Richards, the Edge, Johnny Cash, Dr. John, Little Richard, Aaron Neville, John Fogerty, and Carlos Santana. With such a big crowd on stage, I was lost in the moment and found myself absently watching the jam.

The Rock and Roll Hall of Fame trophy sits on the top shelf of my trophy case between the Memphis Music Hall of Fame and the University of Memphis Distinguished Achievement Awards, above the Grammy Awards. Not that the Grammys aren't close to my heart. But the most significant trophy I have is a very small one I got from the school bands of Memphis. A group of high school students pooled their nickels and pennies together and presented it to me one night at a football game at Melrose High Stadium on a return trip to Memphis after I had recorded "Green Onions." They got a convertible on the field and drove me around the stadium with two pretty girls sitting on the back while "Green Onions" played on the loudspeakers.

LOS ANGELES—1992— ♪ 3

At this point in my career, I had become a session player in Los Angeles, playing on records for numerous artists and bands. It was a great relief to me to survive the dry period of the mideighties and have the financial resources that regular session work provided. Without asking, most artists paid me a premium rate—double or more what other session players received. I was called on to produce first demos for up-and-coming artists and did so for Melissa Etheridge, Joss Stone, and others.

Dave Pirner called, and I went in the studio with him and his band to play on ten tracks for their album. Soul Asylum's *Grave Dancers Union*, including "Runaway Train," is one of my favorite albums of all time. The minute I sat down at the organ, Dave walked over to tell me what he wanted. This wasn't going to be the usual Hollywood session experience.

Why did the band want me to play on this song? Why did they want the sound of my organ? Given the lyric, I believe their offer to have me play was a call for help, encouragement, and strength by way of my Hammond sound in the music, and my physical presence in the studio, in the battle against hopelessness.

LOS ANGELES, CA 1971; EUROPE—1993— ♪ 1

After I moved to Malibu in the early seventies, I was driving up LaBrea Avenue and saw a man standing at the corner of Fountain. It was Ringo Starr. This was my chance. I pulled over, introduced myself, and asked if he would be available to play some sessions around town for me. The nerve I had. He was a Beatle. He graciously reached into his pocket, pulled out an old business card, and wrote down the name and number of Jim Keltner. "Call this guy." I thanked him, got back into the car, and drove to the studio. It was a great tip. I loved Ringo's playing. He was the type of drummer who played the song, not the beat.

However, it was Jim Keltner who turned out to be the godsend. He played on most of my productions from then on, with the exception of John Robinson. It was Keltner at the drum set on stage at Madison Square Garden when Neil Young decided we were his band of choice.

So in 1993, Neil Young took Steve, Duck, Jim, and me on his worldwide tour. A family man, I brought my wife and young children along, a decision that none of Neil's tour handlers were happy with. I wouldn't go otherwise, though. I was getting good at doing what I wished.

In the States, I rented my own bus. In Europe, however, because of logistics and costs, my family and I shared the common bus with Neil's band, including Cropper, Dunn, and Keltner. Nan and I shared a double room with our three kids at hotels. In Norway, when the sun came up at 3:00 a.m., Cicely flung open the drapes and shouted, "It's a good day! It's a good day!" Needless to say, the rest of the family hastily subdued her enthusiasm and insisted she get back in bed and go to sleep.

One day near the start of the tour, my three-year-old son Teddy donned a cape fashioned from an old receiving blanket and held together with a safety pin and generously anointed Neil with "magic."

"Now you have magic!" declared my young son, waving a drumstick that Keltner gave him in place of a wand. Neil was amused and took it in stride, until one day, unhappy with something Neil had done, or failed to do, Teddy took Neil's "magic" away. That night, after a less-than-perfect show in Paris, of all places, Neil prevailed on Teddy to restore the "magic." Teddy reluctantly complied, but not before Neil trashed the dressing room.

Neil is very passionate onstage. He doesn't phone it in; all of his performances really do have magic. He cares deeply about giving his all for his fans and for himself. Neil has studied the blues—the roots for his music—and often listens to Jimmy Reed after a show to unwind.

After the tour, Duck and I took Neil into a San Rafael studio and produced Neil's *Are You Passionate?* LP. The making of *Are You Passionate?* was a labor of love. The production location—San Rafael's the Site studios—provocative lyrics, and musical content of the songs all combined to make it a unique album.

Neil's music has always moved me. The irony of "Only Love Can Break Your Heart" sparked some soul-searching on my part, and I started looking for true love. "Southern Man" stands tall as a beacon illuminating hypocrisy. No other musician has incited or provoked me more. The tension between Neil and Stephen Stills has been palpable for a long time, as has the respect and admiration between them. The chemistry I observed during my time working with Crosby, Stills, Nash & Young remains an enigma in so many ways. David Crosby gave me the name Buddha, and the others started calling me that. Short for Booker, I guess.

Like good old books, Neil's best songs lurk in your subconscious rather than on the Top 40 charts. They visit when you least expect. There are just so many of them—"When You Dance," "Words," "Down by the River," "Don't Let It Bring You Down." There are some gems on *Are You Passionate?*: "Differently," "When I Hold You in My Arms," and "You're My Girl."

I loved David Crosby, Stephen Stills, and Graham Nash to their souls because they wrote "Wooden Ships," "Suite: Judy Blue Eyes," and "Carry On." Their debut album was in my bag when I left Memphis for California. They were a world unto their own. The addition of Neil Young added exponentially to create a universe. What holds a universe together? What held Crosby, Stills, Nash & Young together? Neil Young. They are the kings of rock. I got my

1972 Les Paul out of storage and started playing guitar again because of Stephen, David, and Neil.

Neil Young. You don't have to like him; you just have to love him.

NEW YORK—1994— ♪ 12

We were still living in the Canoga Park house when Steve Berkowitz, head of Columbia Records' Sony Legacy unit called.

"How'd you like to do a solo project for us, Booker?"

"I'd love to!"

"You got it, man!"

A few months went by. In the interim, we moved to Marin County, and I rented the back room at Sausalito's Plant Studio for the purposes of songwriting and record production. The back room at the Plant, though small, was fully equipped with a multitrack tape recorder and a twenty-four-channel console. Still no word from Berkowitz.

When my lease at the Plant was up, I rented an old two-story warehouse in San Rafael and set up my writing studio. I got a call from Berkowitz, just like it had been no time at all since we spoke.

"What if we got Cropper and Dunn involved in the project?"

"Well, that'd be great!"

"You're on, man."

Contracts were drawn up, money was advanced. Cropper came out and spent some time working with me in my San Rafael space, and we came up with a tune we called "Cruisin'."

I had done some work for Linda Ronstadt at a great studio up the hill called the Site, so I booked it. My little San Rafael space was little more than a songwriting room. Cropper and I wrote more tunes. Berkowitz called Steve Jordan to coproduce and play drums. These were the sessions that finally confirmed

Hollywood's "sex, drugs, and rock and roll" reputation for me. Most times, because everyone knew I didn't do coke, people wouldn't flaunt it too much around me. Same to a lesser extent with the booze. There was no dearth of tables full of cocaine and closets full of wine and booze in my memory, but I never witnessed a recording project to surpass this one in that category. Truth be told, the other sessions may have had the same degree or more of indulgence, just not as visible to me.

The album was called *That's the Way It Should Be*, and in 1994, "Cruisin" won the Grammy for Best Pop Instrumental Performance, our first Grammy.

LOS ANGELES—1997— ♪ 6

My beloved father passed while we were at the 1997 Grammy Awards in New York. Since 1992, I had spent countless hours at his bedside when doctors told me the end was near, but Dad came roaring back.

This time, when the phone rang, we were at the Hilton Midtown. Nan answered, and she didn't have to say a word. I was standing at the closet putting my coat away. We hadn't won the Grammy. Dad was gone.

At the memorial service in LA, I reached over and put my finger on a bulging vein on the back of my father's hand the way I used to as a very young boy. I always loved seeing the vein spring back up after I pressed it down. This time, the vein didn't spring back up. My father's hand was cold. He was lying in his casket. Touching his hand helped me realize the truth of the situation. I caressed it for another minute, then walked to the podium.

I started to sing. Impromptu. No one had arranged for music at his service, and that was a travesty. My father was music. He couldn't be put away without music at the service. "His eye is on the sparrow," I sang, "and I know...He watches...me." I felt my father's spirit give me the strength to continue the song. To remember the words I had not memorized. I had been so fortunate to know him. It had been a blessing to be his son. Happiness and sorrow mixed and swelled up in me. I could have exploded with either one.

We took his body to be laid next to my mother at Inglewood Park. I felt her spirit come to say hello. It was good to feel her again.

CANADA—2000— ♪ 1

Our ambitious plan was to take our new Dutch Star all the way cross country, park in Montreal, play the Montreal Jazz Festival with the MGs, and have a leisurely drive back home to Marin across Canada and along the US West Coast.

We made the mistake of entering Canada at the Detroit crossing, where Canadian agents stopped our family and separated parents from children for over four hours. The agents kept asking the kids if we were their parents. It would have been reasonable to ask the kids some questions at an international border, but not to let them see us from 2:30 p.m. to 6:30 p.m.? Nan and I waited, helpless, in another room. That was a misuse of international privilege, mean-spirited and cruel. I was beside myself, struggling to keep my temper. Looking for contraband, hoping to seize the expensive motorhome, the agents found none and reluctantly let us go on our way.

At Montreal, our reception was warm and enthusiastic, and the concertgoers were gracious and appreciative. Traveling across Canada proved to be a heartwarming experience. We encountered friendly people at every stop. The scenery was inspiring and fulfilling, with lake after lake. The only bummer was the entire Canadian Highway 1 was under construction, and by the time we got to Winnipeg, my new motorhome's chassis was rattling like a junk wagon. Still, it was turning out to be the trip of a lifetime.

We trudged happily along in our noisy RV, the Canadian Rockies off to our right. "I'd love to take a side trip to see Pine Lake," Nan said.

"You got it, baby."

It was a gorgeous day only the way that Canada can be, in the middle of July, year 2000. Around 11:00 a.m. we left Medicine Hat. I sat in the cockpit, rolling west. Around one o'clock, we turned north on Highway 2 to explore the Pine Lake area. After an hour, I noticed a storm on the eastern slope of the Canadian Rockies, a little southwest of us. Thirty minutes later the storm was still there on my left, and I mentioned it to Nan. I started to note my GPS positions to see if it was moving nearer. It was. After forty minutes, I told Nan we should divert.

I saw the sign for Highway 27. It led directly in the direction of the storm. I had maintained about sixty-five or seventy miles per hour, and the storm was moving at least that fast, because it was at the same location on my right.

Nan was dead set on spending the night at the lake at Green Acres. "It doesn't look like much to me," she said, regarding the storm.

We drove and argued another fifteen minutes before I said, "Honey, you've got to trust me on this one." I took my best chance and turned left onto Highway 27 and headed due west. If I drove the right speed, we should get behind the storm, then we could head south on Highway 2, provided the storm stayed its course. I wanted to see that storm in my passenger-side window, then in my rearview mirror, or not at all. My calculations and gamble worked, and we arrived safely at a little campground outside Calgary that had one vacant space.

Nan said she thought I had "overreacted" until she saw the paper next morning while checking out. The headline: "July 14—F3 tornado struck Green Acres Campground in Pine Lake, Alberta." Known as the Pine Lake tornado, it killed twelve people and caused over $13 million in damage. It was ranked as the fourth-deadliest tornado in Canadian history. RVs were destroyed at Green Acres Campground, where our reservations were, and that F3 twister only hit the campground and a trailer park.

LOS ANGELES—2000— ♪ 8

Lonnie has a fine mind and could easily have been an entrepreneur. The most likely business she'd go into would be something involving cars, her first love.

Daughter Lonnie and her husband, Tony, gave me three more good-looking grandkids—D'Laynie, Bella, and Charlotte! Lonnie is a wonderful mom and works full time outside the home. She has always been a hard worker.

LOS ANGELES—2018— ♪ 2

Even during times when I couldn't pay my bills, having my large family made me feel like I had all the trappings of wealth, each child such a unique treasure.

Our first child, Olivia, is a loving and attentive daughter, mother, and wife. She's smart and a hard worker who pays attention to details and the big picture.

Olivia remodeled her home, essentially acting as the general contractor for the project—a complete remodel while she was pregnant.

Livvy loves to laugh and is a talented mathematician.

A graceful and passionate dancer, she got into UCLA's dance program, which is very competitive. Not satisfied with just one major, she also doubled in Spanish. She is still very proficient in Spanish and speaks to her child in Spanish.

Olivia's not afraid to try new things, and she loves to travel. She has a fun giggle, and she's a dog lover.

Our daughter Cicely is a natural-born leader with an active native intelligence. In second grade, she predicted the next perfect square in an algebraic formula that she devised. Her older brother Michael said, "Maybe in high school, but certainly not in second grade! Call a math psychologist, quick!" She's a party planner with an eye for beauty in clothing and home decor. While in third grade, Cicely rewrote the play *Annie* to accommodate six other neighborhood kids and convinced her mother to cook for the parents and kids for the play's performance at our house. How she managed to corral five boys to give up their street hockey games for *Annie* rehearsals is still a mystery to me.

Cicely's generous with her time and maintains her friendships. She's funny too. She's very natural with young children and babies. Cicely is a sweetly sensitive person. She *loves* her twin brother, Ted.

Our son Ted wants everyone to get along. He appreciates calm and peace. Ted's an amazing soccer player—he worked very hard at this and accumulated thirty-seven scholarship offers when time came to go to college. It came down to two schools, and he chose Cal Berkeley because of the educational opportunities it provided.

Ted is a creative writer—his word choices and combinations are unusual and spot-on. He is a curious young man who loves to read. Teddy is very helpful with a project or day-to-day work. I won't go into the studio without him.

Like Olivia, Ted *loves* his *dog!* He enjoys his friends, likes to philosophize, and is a loving son. He *loves* his twin sister. Ted seeks out new environments and loves to travel. Teddy plays fantasy soccer and community soccer.

TIBURON, CA—1992–2011— ♪3

Nan and I made lifelong friends in the Bay community. Numerous people offered support and love, and we joined fun groups. Nan took up hiking with a great group of women and enjoyed the exercise and making new friends. We joined a couples' film group, and a book club sprang out of the original hiking group. Some of my buddies created a men's pool group.

Mary Crowley was one of the first people we met. She is a sailor and environmentalist. She is spearheading the cleanup of the ocean, gathering world leaders and sailors alike. Lisa and Michael Coffee became dear friends of ours. Lisa has always been there for Nan, even hosting an after-wedding brunch for our son Michael.

Nan became very involved in the kids' school and soccer games. As do most parents, we found ourselves shuttling the kids to dance, soccer, and so on. I started working on this book in the stands at some soccer games. Additionally, the older boys flew up from LA and spent many weekends with us. The family remained our center, and we relished the time together.

The kids all took piano lessons and eventually decided to stop. Nan and I proudly attended dance performances, piano recitals, football games, track meets, and soccer games. Our children worked hard at school and their outside activities; they were involved in community service in multiple organizations. We vigorously promoted higher education, and six of our children went on to get college and graduate degrees.

In my spare time, I took the ferry to San Francisco for Pro Tools courses at SF State and Pyramind music schools, as well as a screenwriting course at College of Marin.

LOS ANGELES, CA—2007—♪ 8

To my astonishment, Booker T. & the MGs were presented with the Lifetime Achievement Award by the Recording Academy, an award that recognizes a rich contribution of a band to a musical genre. That my peers thought our band was worthy of this recognition humbled me.

My children continue to amaze and humble me as well.

Matthew, my oldest stepson, has hiked the PCT and the CDT and is currently on the AT. In 2002, he received a BA from Berkeley in comparative literature. In 2006, he received a master of public policy degree from UCLA with an emphasis on natural resources management and policy. In 2013, Matthew received a master of environmental science degree from Yale University, specializing in hydrology and water resources science. Before taking off on his latest trek, Matthew was a consultant in an environmental firm. Nan says he's our runaway.

Brian received a BA from Claremont McKenna College in 2001 with a major in economics. In 2004, he earned a JD from Loyola Law School, Los Angeles. In college, Brian played both football and rugby. Brian is a phenomenal gardener and turned his yard into a natural succulent extravaganza. He also loves to cook and has prepared many wonderful meals for Nan and me in his home. If you need help with anything, Brian is there before you ask.

In 2002, Michael received a BA from Princeton University in politics. In 2008, he received a master of public health degree from Yale School of Public Health. Michael earned a doctor of science from the Harvard TH Chan School of Public Health in 2013 in social and behavioral sciences. He played football in college as well. Michael loves to cook and became a vegetarian early in his twenties. He is a messy cook—I mean, the kitchen is a whirlwind after he is done. But the plates of food are creative and nutritious.

In 2007, Olivia earned her BA from UCLA in Spanish and world arts and cultures. She also received a master of business administration from UCLA's Anderson School of Business.

Cicely got her BA from Princeton University in 2012 with a major in political economy. Cicely danced from grammar school through high school in a dance company in Marin. She was also a cheerleader for two years at Princeton. Cicely, always a self-starter, has been working in NYC since graduating. She also bought her first apartment and is finding all the joys and woes of home ownership.

Graciously, she has a bedroom set aside for us whenever we travel to NYC.

Theodore Jones received a BA from Berkeley in 2012, majoring in cultural anthropology. Ted played soccer in college and was team captain during his junior and senior years. Everyone thought Ted would play professional soccer, and he did too, until he picked up a guitar. Trading in one passion for another, Ted has dived into music, and his guitars line the walls of his apartment. People tell me they love seeing the two of us together on stage—how tight the musical connection is and how close we seem. My time with Ted on stage came as a big surprise and a huge blessing.

CHAPTER 18
Representin' Memphis

WASHINGTON, DC, the White House—February 21, 2012— ♪ *12*

B.B. asked me if I remembered Shinny Walker.

Of course I remembered Shinny. With the outline of his gun showing through his topcoat, he was the quintessential Beale Street music manager, sending young bluesmen into clubs or studios and onto buses for tours. Memphis musicians had to go through him to have a career during that era.

Then he asked me if I remembered Tuff Green. I played my first gigs on piano in Tuff's band, and B.B. made his first demo at Tuff's home studio.

He wanted to know if I remembered George Coleman and Phineas Newborn. "I was Phineas's paperboy, B.B. His house was the first on my route, and I was always late throwing my papers on days he was practicing."

"How about Ben Branch and Earl Forrest? Remember them?"

"I sure do."

"How's Floyd?"

"Which Floyd? Floyd Newman or Floyd Golden?"

"Floyd Golden. Him and Gwen, how are they doing?"

"They're fine, B.B. Thanks for asking."

Floyd Newman was a baritone sax player at the Flamingo in Memphis who was in B.B.'s band from time to time. Floyd Golden was my brother-in-law. He and B.B. were classmates at Manassas High School in Memphis.

The conversation was taking place on a makeshift stage in the East Room of the White House. B.B. was positioned across the stage from me, so it was an awkward interruption of the rehearsal for me to linger there talking to him about old times. In addition, his mike was live, so every word of our conversation was heard around the room.

Directly, I went back to my place at the Hammond B-3 across the stage. I was music director and band leader for *In Performance at the White House: Red, White and Blues,* a PBS special. The show was created to celebrate Black History Month and was hosted by Taraji P. Henson.

Besides B.B. King, featured performers included Jeff Beck, Gary Clark Jr., Shemekia Copeland, Buddy Guy, Trombone Shorty, Warren Haynes, Mick Jagger, Keb Mo, Susan Tedeschi, and Derek Trucks.

B.B. played the opening notes to "The Thrill Is Gone." Soon after, a man in a white shirt with rolled-up sleeves slipped in a side door and stood in back.

It was the president. Barack Obama.

This was music that came from the Mississippi Delta and that birthed rock and roll. That it was being played in the East Room under portraits of Thomas Jefferson wasn't lost on anyone. The political implications were huge, and that essence filled the air. It would be a historic concert.

President Obama told me he'd like to enter the room to "Green

Onions" instead of "Hail to the Chief." At the concert, I hit the "Green Onions" funky organ intro when he and the first lady appeared at the back of the room. They walked to the stage to the music shifting and bouncing like they might break out dancing. The first couple walked onstage dignity intact, but not before I got a little tradition-breaking wink and smile before he took the podium.

SAN FRANCISCO, Private Fund-Raiser—Spring 2012—♪ 3

My wife, Nan, a coach's daughter, is competitive. Some of President Obama's reelection team members told her the president's enthusiasm was waning. Probably due to the fact he had slipped a few points against challenger Mitt Romney. Nan was disturbed. She saw her opportunity at an election fund-raiser in San Francisco when she and I had a private photo with the president.

The occasion was at the expansive home of Robert Mailer Anderson and Nicola Miner, daughter of the late Robert Miner, founder of Oracle. I had been asked to provide music, along with Les Claypool and Charlie Musselwhite, for the $38,500-per-plate dinner.

Nan told the president of the United States, "Next November, you're going to kick butt."

Big grin from Mr. Obama, and he replied, "With your help." She was embarrassed after the fact when she realized what she had said.

I appreciated his warmth and relaxed demeanor. During the twenty-minute talk, a man of quick wit and human caring who was unafraid to speak to the very powerful on behalf of the less fortunate was revealed to me. I became respectful of his courage and humanity and his regard for generations to follow. The president underscored values that were close to my heart, and I was proud that our country elected a person willing to represent all of us, regardless of skin color or differences of beliefs and origins.

Clearly, a black man at his core, born of a white mother, Barack Obama identified himself as a humanitarian and a fighter, defiantly optimistic about uplifting this and future generations.

WASHINGTON, DC, the White House—April 9, 2013— ♪ 9

I returned to the White House after President Obama's reelection as music director and band leader for another PBS special, *In Performance at the White House: Memphis Soul.* Al Green, Ben Harper, Queen Latifah, Cyndi Lauper, Joshua Ledet, Sam Moore, Charlie Musselwhite, Mavis Staples, and Justin Timberlake were all on the show. I told the producer that President Barack Obama would prefer "Green Onions" for his entrance song instead of "Hail to the Chief." The producer was highly skeptical until the White House staff returned the answer—*Yes*, the president would like "Green Onions."

President Obama made the mistake of singing a few bars of "Let's Stay Together," revealing a smooth singing voice and sounding almost as good as Al Green. It's just from that point on, he was asked to sing anytime he stepped on the same stage as an R & B band.

Before the show, during the photo op in the reception room, the president included me, Nan, our three children—Olivia, Cicely, and Teddy—and Nan's twin sister, Janine, and her husband, David. Walking in, President Barack Obama pointed a finger at Nan and said, "I did what you said!" All smiles.

At the photo op, the first lady (a Princeton graduate) had a long conversation with Cicely about Princeton. Michelle broke the line to run after Cicely to wish her good luck. C. C. said to her mom, "Is this really happening?"

ATHENS, GA—2009— ♪ 1

Andy Kaulkin took us all over LA, driving aimlessly to listen to music in his car. It was an old Chevy that he should have traded in years ago. I never said anything because he truly loved driving that old car. A music aficionado, Andy played me all kinds of music, and we had vibrant discussions, becoming friends in the process. After a few of these sessions, he played something by the Drive-By Truckers, an awesome southern rock band. Something went off in my brain. Every new song I had written started with a guitar. Drive-By Truckers had three guitars.

In Austin, at South by Southwest, I jammed down on Sixth Street with Jason Isbell, and he also said something to me about the band. Shortly, I found myself in Athens, Georgia, at the Truckers' studio, eating homemade pies and other dishes the band's families brought to the studio. Patterson Hood told me I had been a household name in their family, that his dad, David, played our music all the time. "What? Your dad is David Hood?" People had mistaken David's bass lines for Duck Dunn bass lines more than once, especially the one on the Staple Singers' "I'll Take You There."

I signed with Andy's Anti-Records and prepared to record with the Drive-By Truckers. It took a while for us to find our groove. Then they gave themselves musically over to me. My melodies and my guitar parts came to life in their heads and their hands, and we became a musical family.

The result was *Potato Hole*, an instrumental rock album featuring heavy guitars and B-3 organ. My stepson Michael had turned me on to "the golden ratio," and I experimented with that form on the title track, "Potato Hole."

Booker T. Washington's "Up from Slavery" was the inspiration behind the music and the title. A potato hole was a hollow cavity concealed in the dirt floor of their quarters where slaves stowed food from unkind, parsimonious owners. Potatoes were the most common food hidden there. The song juxtaposes an eight-bar phrase against a thirteen-bar phrase—a perfect golden mean.

Anti-Records president Andy Kaulkin was hands-on during the final mixing in Los Angeles. It was my first album in a very long time, and come award season it won for Best Instrumental Album. Not bad.

The Grammy Award from the Recording Academy is the most prestigious music award in the world.

During the lead-up to the announcement, I tried to stay still in my chair. I really did want to win.

In the final moments, another category was added that wasn't listed, so I looked down at my program. I lost my place. I heard my name, and my wife screamed. I said to myself, "Just get up the steps to the stage." A lot of time went by, it seemed. I kissed my wife and turned as the award music played. Jimmy Jam, the face of the academy, handed me the Grammy and said, "Knock 'em dead." I had written down eleven names on a three-by-five index card but couldn't get it out of my tux coat pocket. I fumbled a little more, then muttered heartfelt thanks to my wife, my producer, and a few others, then they played the get-off-the-stage music, and I was behind the curtain, holding a Grammy. People were smiling, standing off, looking at me.

"What just happened?"

NEW YORK—2011— ♪3

In the studio, Lou Reed and Biz Markie were different as night and day. "Is there anyone in this whole f—ing building who knows the lyrics to this song?" Lou barked at me from the other side of the glass. For me it was an exercise in poise, patience, and tolerance. On the other hand, Biz came in with a huge entourage, a big smile on his face, laughing loud at everything, and in the best mood.

Up until the time I got to SFO, Andy Kaulkin was undecided about whether he wanted vocals on my next album. That is until the day of my departure to New York for the recording, when he thought vocals would be cool. I called my songwriter daughter, Olivia, from the airport and laid out my thoughts and the direction the four songs should take.

By the time I landed at JFK, she had words for my idea for "The Bronx" and had written lyrics to four songs. I called Lou from the hotel that night, read the words to him, and he said, "I'll be there."

Recording would begin in NYC at MSR Studios with the Roots and Questlove. Questlove, my coproducer, had a commitment to *The Tonight Show Starring Jimmy Fallon* and let nothing interfere with that. Sometimes he showed up as late as 4:00 p.m. for my recording sessions.

When it comes to making music, I'm more like a weed than a flower. It takes more than a late drummer to discourage me. Plus, Jimmy Fallon's a great music supporter and a great guy. I just *had* to have his drummer is all.

Questlove's steady drumming is inimitable and unmistakable. Captain Kirk Douglas (guitar) and Owen Biddle (bass) were both gale forces. Gabe Roth of the Dap-Kings was very smooth in the control room. Thanks to him, the record came out sounding great. The other New York guests were Matt Berninger and Sharon Jones. Matt and I established a lasting friendship, partly because, like me, he let Sharon tell him everything to sing and do in the studio. Sharon was the Otis Redding type. A force of artistry not to be denied.

Back in LA, Rob Schnapf and Andy Kaulkin put their hearts into the mix. Motown's Dennis Coffey lent his unmistakably soulful guitar. Yim Yames phoned in the album's most positive track, "Progress." The jewel of the week was Lauren Hill's "Everything Is Everything." Timelessness is embedded into her music. I wrote the autobiographical "Representin' Memphis" with Olivia. The album, *The Road from Memphis*, also won a Grammy for Best Instrumental Album!

Mojo magazine placed it at number forty-two on its Best Albums of 2011.

LOS ANGELES—2013— ♪ 12

In 2013, I returned to the Stax label. John Burk, the main instigator, had been wining and dining me at a famous Beverly Hills restaurant, often inviting my friend Bill Withers.

It was a reissue-based company, but the essence of the original Stax Records remained, even with the completely different location, staff, and management. The family atmosphere of the 1960s prevailed and transferred to the Beverly Hills office. When I walked in, people stopped their work and applauded, making me stop dead in my tracks and absorb the welcome.

I reached out to some of my favorite artists to play on this album, including Gary Clark Jr., Anthony Hamilton, Mayer Hawthorne, Luke James, Estelle, Sheila E., Poncho Sanchez, Kori Withers, Vintage Trouble, and my own son, Ted Jones. Olivia Jones, my daughter and manager, was superb at negotiating the guest artists' contributions.

A special moment happened when Ted and I played a song together, "Father-Son Blues." We Joneses have a family affair happening: Booker as the lead artist, Ted full-time guitar player, Olivia as manager, Nan as tour manager, and Cicely as social media director. Somehow, we all get along.

TOKYO, JAPAN—2012—♪ 6

On May 13, 2012, my good friend bass player Donald "Duck" Dunn passed away in Tokyo. He was in the company of Eddie Floyd and Steve Cropper. Luckily my daughter Cicely called me before I saw it splashed all over the news. Steve said he died in his sleep.

I am struck deeply by Duck's death. I had played many times with Duck at the Blue Note in Tokyo and witnessed how hard it was for Duck to do two shows a night. God is calling names in the music world. I can't imagine not being able to hear Duck laugh and curse.

"*Got daaamn!*" he would bark ten times a day, and cackle.

Everyone loved him. His intensity both on the bass and in life was incomparable. No one could ever replace him musically, replicate his sense of humor, fill his bass boots, or say "Got damn!" like he did.

LAKE TAHOE—2014—♪ 6

In West Hollywood, Nan said, "I'm just not happy here, Booker."

"Never mind, honey; I know just the place."

I took my mountain girl back to the mountains. We took the first house we saw in the Lake Tahoe area.

We had been in Tahoe less than a year when I got the worst call of my life.

Tragically, in 2014, my firstborn—Booker T. III—died suddenly of a heart attack. There was no warning, and I was left with no way to say goodbye, tell him I loved him one more time, or show my love. I was left with my memories and a big, empty space inside and outside.

My stepson Matthew gave me a wooden box with a hidden compartment. Inside I found his letter to me.

Letter to Booker

You are the best step dad
In the history of the universe
I love you
Thank you for always
being kind
to me and to my mother
I helped bury T
That was hard for me
Thank you for that honor
It is way harder for you than me
I miss my grandma
Thank you for all of your wisdom
I think at 38 I'll start
flossing regularly because of you.

Love,
Matthew

A few months later, Prince died. I picked up the phone to call T. Then I remembered. Somehow, I had forgotten my son was dead.

I couldn't just call him up. After all, my son T was working for Prince. He was Prince's main engineer.

There's a deep connection between parents who've lost children. It goes beyond words, something felt deep in your bones and heard in your voice. You may hear each other's screams even though no one is making an outward sound. You hold on tight to each other so neither of you fall. I held on tight to my brother-in-law Blane at his son Andrew's memorial service, and Blane looked at me. "Now I know how you feel."

Willie Nelson called to offer his condolences—he lost his son Billy fifteen years before.

After five years at the lake—several with record snowfall—Nan and I moved down the hill. Still close to Lake Tahoe but a lower elevation. Now we are able to make our frequent flights out of Reno, avoiding the treacherous Mt. Rose snow-covered pass in the winter.

LOS ANGELES—2019— ♪ 8

I have at last reached the point in my career where audiences demand my early work. Each show must include "Green Onions" and a couple of others from that era. Thankfully, I have a substantial repertoire, and I can always vary my set list.

For my part, playing live, particularly now with my son Ted, carries that thrilling sensation like it did when I first started in front of audiences in junior high. I never lost the feeling that it was a privilege to have people listen. Our audiences are so kind to me and always ask me to return. Some of my shows now feature the Stax Revue, and that's a treat with a ten-piece ensemble parading through the Stax catalog—Otis Redding, Sam & Dave, Wilson Pickett, Carla Thomas, Jean Knight, William Bell, Albert King, and, of course, Booker T. & the MGs.

The quartet I play with is fresh, experimental, and tight. Ted helps direct me to new gear, advances the shows, gets the stage ready, and gives support during the show. He's also my musical director, my guitar player, and my son. I could not have hoped for a more ideal situation.

Ted and I are working on a new joint project. I love hearing his perspective, his youthful angle. I get to touch and create music with the next generation.

I am eternally thankful.

Thank you. All of you.

LOS ANGELES—2019— ♪ 2

Good fortune continues to follow me with the new production of the National's Matt Berninger's debut solo album *Serpentine Fire*. He came to me wanting the magic I applied to Willie Nelson's *Stardust* album. There was an abundance of magic on the *Serpentine* project. Benefiting from the huge amount of work and effort put into the songwriting by multiple pairs of Matt's cohorts, the project is brimming with creative melodies and lyrical nuance.

Just before embarking on Matt's project, a bright shining light appeared and opened my heart. His name is Elliott Long, child of stepson Brian and his wife, Megan—an awesome, perfect grandson.

At three years old, he's already on the move and talks more than many adults.

Michael, another of my stepsons, with his wife, Elisabeth, gave birth to a bright, redheaded fireball named Elena. She has so many facial expressions that she might become an actress. She's my little granddaughter/starlet.

Olivia, my daughter, and her husband, Deshalen, are the proud parents of my most recent grandson, Dylan. "He's so curious," my daughter says and laughs. "He gets it from his father," she says, because her husband is also curious. Dylan is a heartbreaker with big dimples and a huge smile.

All my children who have become parents provide loving, day-to-day attention and care to the young ones, which is something the world needs. These next generations of people are going to be the ones that protect, defend, and enrich the future of humankind.

MUSICAL PHRASES

ACKNOWLEDGMENTS

Before this book was written, fans listened to and purchased my music and traveled to my concerts. For that, I want to express my deep gratitude.

This book was started at a hotel on the south side of Chicago, scribbled on the little notepad next to the bed. I was staying over between gigs and writing essays as practice for writing song lyrics. At home, I showed the essays to my wife, Nan, and she said, "Why don't you turn them into a book?"

Without Nan Jones, who envisioned this book before I did and suggested I write it, this book would not exist. She supported and encouraged me during the long process. Nan made early editing suggestions and encouraged me to weave in wider, more encompassing themes as well as focusing on and staying close to the truths of my own unique journey. From the beginning to the end and in the middle, it was Nan. Always Nan.

Acknowledgments

A book is not the product of one person alone; it takes a team to bring a book to life. My team is small and tight, and I want to acknowledge and thank the following:

My intuitive, ingenious, strong-willed manager-daughter, Olivia Jones, took my dream of a book and turned it into a reality. Olivia navigated the arduous process of finding the right home for my book. She curated the photos, which required making sensitive decisions. Olivia has always been my go-to person for finding the missing pieces and making the process seamless.

My agent, Sarah Lazin, fought for me and believed in me from the beginning. Sarah read my little gems (stories) and gave me the confidence to make a continuous narrative. She repeated many times that I had a story worth telling. Sarah matched me with a terrific editor and publishing house.

Phil Marino, my editor, came to the project with the enthusiasm and excitement I always hoped my editor would have. He pushed me to consider a new creative format and offered countless timely suggestions. Phil's positive approach gave me, a new author, the confidence to tackle the project. I am proud and happy to be published at Little, Brown. The team there included Reagan Arthur, Ira Boudah, Liz Gassman, Gregg Kulick, Molly Morrison, Katharine Myers, Erica Scavelli, Megan Schindele, Jennifer Tordy, Jayne Yaffe Kemp, and Craig Young.

I want to acknowledge and thank the following for their help:

My parents, Booker T. and Lurline Jones, who raised me with tenderness and love. Their nurturing gave me the foundation to grow into myself. From the beginning and here still, my beloved sister, Gwen, and brother, Maurice, root me to my origins. Thanks to all my children, who became my safety net and gave me leeway to disappear into my writing den during the long hours, days, and years devoted to this book.

Acknowledgments

Rob Bowman for being Stax's chronicler and greatest fan, critic, and friend.

Holly-George Warren for her early editing advice.

Alan Light, early editor, who asked the right questions to help me make my meanings clear.

Thanks to Michael Long for suggesting *Time Is Tight* for the title of the book and the use of song titles as chapter titles.

Thank you, Memphis, Tennessee—for the fertile soil for learning music, for the spirit of Memphis, and for spawning me and providing a home and a place to grow.

INDEX

Index

E

Eagles, 242–244

Earth, Wind, and Fire, 49

Easley, Frank, 45–46

East-West Studio, 271

Ebenezer Baptist Church, 39

Edge, 282

Edwards, Scottie, 245

Ellen DeGeneres Show, The, 110

Elliot, Ramblin' Jack, 2, 205

Ellis, Herb, 175

England, 132–133, 147

English, Paul, 233–234

Epic Records, 222, 250

Ertegun, Ahmet, 102, 115, 153, 177

Escovedo, Coke, 42

Estelle, 302

Etheridge, Melissa, 283

Ethridge, Chris, 86, 207, 217–218, 233–234

Ethridge, Necia, 217

Europe, 131–132, 145, 283–288

Evans, Bob, 224

Evergreen, 221–222

"Everything Is Everything," 302

F

"Fa-Fa-Fa-Fa-Fa (Sad Song)," 123

Fairmont hotel, 42

Fallon, Jimmy, 301

"Father-Son Blues," 302

Fields, Venetta, 195

Fillmore Ballroom, 97, 161

5/4 Ballroom, 115

Flamingo Room, 9, 36, 48, 52–53, 55–58, 72, 181

Floyd, Eddie, 6, 55, 119, 126–127, 131, 144, 151, 178–179, 193–194, 303

Flying, 214, 246

Fogerty, John, 282

"Fool in Love," 65

"Forever Young," 210

Forrest, Earl, 295

"For What It's Worth," 174

Fountain, Clarence (Five Blind Boys), 272

Four-Way Grill, 128, 143–144

Frampton, Peter, 253

France, 171–176

Franklin, Aretha, 44, 66, 252

Frayser (TN), 54–55

Fred Sands Real Estate, 270, 273

Freeman, Charlie, 106–108

Friesen, Gil, 214

Fritts, Donnie, 230

Frog, 52–53, 55–56

Frontiere, Dominic, 184

Frucht, Phil, 250

G

Garner, Bonnie, 235

Gary (IN), 117–118

Gaye, Marvin, 252

GDIs (God Damned Independents), 99

324

H

I

Index

M

N

Index

S

Sam & Dave, 6, 81, 121, 131, 305
Samudio, Sam (Sam the Sham and the Pharaohs), 180
Sanchez, Poncho, 302
Sands, Evie, 207
San Francisco (CA), 28–29, 42–44, 97–98, 220–221, 223
San Juan (Puerto Rico), 42
Santana, Carlos, 41–44, 251, 275, 282
Santana, Debbie, 251
Satellite Record Shop, 47
Satellite/Stax Records, 5, 9–10, 16–17, 42, 56–58, 63–65, 67, 74, 78–81, 98, 102–104, 107–108, 114, 118–120, 123, 127, 129, 135, 137–138, 142–145, 147–148, 157, 162–166, 178, 184–186, 189–190, 192–194, 206, 211, 213–214, 221, 226–227, 253, 302, 305
"Satisfaction," 119–120, 142
Satterfield, Laura, 196, 204, 221–222, 247, 249
Satterfield, Paul, 204–205
Satterfield, Paul, Jr., 196, 204, 221–222, 247, 249
Saturday Night Live, 280
Scent of a Woman, 282
Schick Center, 42
Schnapf, Rob, 302
Schon, Neal, 42
Security Pacific Bank, 250
Segovia, Andres, 179
"The Sermon," 36
Serpentine Fire, 306

"Shake," 141–142
Shandel, Bill, 219
Shangri-La, 207–208
Shann, Richard, 45–48
"She Came in Through the Bathroom Window," 198
Sheffield (England), 132–133
Sheila E., 302
Sherman Oaks (CA), 271–272
Shindig, 114–116, 168
Short, Dick, 75
Shrake, Bud, 257
Shreve, Michael, 42
Sides, Alan, 207, 269
Silver, Horace, 78
Silvera, Frank, 169
Simms, Carl, 107
Simon, Joe, 153
Sinatra, Frank, 130
Site studio, 285–286
"(Sittin' on) The Dock of the Bay," 149, 151
Skokian, 14
Slim, Peg-Leg, 205
Slim Jenkins' Joint, 143–144
"Slim Jenkins' Place," 142–143
"Slumpety Slump," 65
Smith, Emmitt, 26
Smith, Jimmie, 144
Smith, Jimmy, 36, 48, 129
Smokey Robinson and the Miracles, 92
Snow, Tom, 243
Sole, Annika, 134
"Somebody's Sleeping in My Bed," 119
"Somebody to Love," 140

T

ABOUT THE AUTHOR

Booker T. Jones is an American instrumentalist, songwriter, record producer, and arranger. Best known as the front man of the band Booker T. & the MGs, he has worked with countless award-winning artists of the twentieth and twenty-first centuries and has earned a Grammy Award for lifetime achievement. Along with the band, he was inducted into the Rock and Roll Hall of Fame in 1992. Jones continues to record and tour internationally, both as a solo artist and as head of Booker T.'s Stax Revue.